STUDIES IN IMPERIALISM

general editors John M. MacKenzie and Andrew S. Thompson

When the 'Studies in Imperialism' series was founded more than twenty-five years ago, emphasis was laid upon the conviction that 'imperialism as a cultural phenomenon had as significant an effect on the dominant as on the subordinate societies'. With more than ninety books published, this remains the prime concern of the series. Cross-disciplinary work has indeed appeared covering the full spectrum of cultural phenomena, as well as examining aspects of gender and sex, frontiers and law, science and the environment, language and literature, migration and patriotic societies, and much else. Moreover, the series has always wished to present comparative work on European and American imperialism, and particularly welcomes the submission of books in these areas. The fascination with imperialism, in all its aspects, shows no sign of abating, and this series will continue to lead the way in encouraging the widest possible range of studies in the field. 'Studies in Imperialism' is fully organic in its development, always seeking to be at the cutting edge, responding to the latest interests of scholars and the needs of this ever-expanding area of scholarship.

Garden cities and colonial planning

MANCHESTER
1824

Manchester University Press

Garden cities and colonial planning

TRANSNATIONALITY AND URBAN IDEAS IN AFRICA AND PALESTINE

Edited by

Liora Bigon and Yossi Katz

MANCHESTER UNIVERSITY PRESS

Published by Manchester University Press
Altrincham Street, Manchester M1 7JA, UK
www.manchesteruniversitypress.co.uk

British Library Cataloguing-in-Publication Data is available

Library of Congress Cataloging-in-Publication Data is available

ISBN 978 1 5261 0678 0 *paperback*

First published by Manchester University Press 2014

This edition first published 2017

The publisher has no responsibility for the persistence or accuracy of URLs for any external or third-party internet websites referred to in this book, and does not guarantee that any content on such websites is, or will remain, accurate or appropriate.

Printed by Lightning Source

CONTENTS

LIST OF FIGURES

LIST OF CONTRIBUTORS

Liora Bigon is an urban historian, a Research Fellow in European Studies at the Hebrew University of Jerusalem, Israel. She has contributed to numerous books and journals (*Journal of Historical Geography, Planning Perspectives, Urban History*) on the subject of indigenous and British and French colonial planning cultures in Africa. Her PhD in architecture – gained from the University of Manchester, and published as *A History of Urban Planning in Two West African Colonial Capitals: Residential Segregation in British Lagos and French Dakar (1850–1930)* (Lewiston, NY: Edwin Mellen Press, 2009) – compares metropolitan, colonial and indigenous planning aspects with regard to British Lagos and French Dakar.

Charlotte Jelidi is an architectural and urban historian. She is currently based at the Institut de recherche sur le Maghreb contemporain, Tunis, where she coordinates a research programme on 'evolution of the Maghrebian cities under colonial situation'. Since she gained her PhD in history from the University of Tours, on the creation of the *ville nouvelle* of Fes under the French Protectorate in Morocco, her teaching and publications have dealt with colonial urbanism and the history of modern architecture, and with conservation politics in Tunisia and Morocco.

Ruth Kark is a professor at the Hebrew University of Jerusalem. She has written and edited over twenty books and 200 articles on the history and historical geography of Palestine and Israel. Her research interests include the study of urban and rural settlement processes, the urban and architectural history of the Middle Eastern city, land use and land ownership in the Middle East and Palestine/Israel in the nineteenth and twentieth centuries, and the interaction of Western nations/civilisations with the Holy Land, including the impact of missionary societies on architecture there.

Yossi Katz is a full professor in geography at Bar-Ilan University, Israel. He holds the Chair for the Study of the History and Activities of the Jewish National Fund at his institution. He specialises in the modern history of the Land of Israel and the State of Israel, Zionism, the process of Jewish settlement in the Land of Israel and in Western Canada. He has published twenty-two books including *Partner to Partition: The Jewish Agency's Partition Plan in the Mandate Era* (1998), *Between Jerusalem and Hebron: Jewish Settlement in the Pre-State Period* (1999), *The Last Best West: Essays on the Historical Geography of the Canadian Prairies* (with J. L. Lehr, 1999), *The Religious Kibbutz Movement in the Land of Israel* (1999, 2003) and *Inside the Ark: The Hutterites in Canada and the United States* (with J. L. Lehr, 2012).

Makame Ali Muhajir is a Minerva Fellow at the United States Military Academy, West Point, New York. He gained his PhD in 2011 from the University of Kansas, and his research interests include dialogic planning approaches for Africa with specific emphasis on how planning works in the age of reform. Over most of the 1990s, he directed the Department of Surveys and Urban Planning in Zanzibar formed within the defunct Commission for Lands and Environment. He also managed the Sida-funded community-based rehabilitation programme in Stone Town in Zanzibar in 2001–05.

Garth Andrew Myers is Paul E. Raether Distinguished Professor of Urban International Studies at Trinity College, Hartford, Connecticut. He is director of the Urban Studies Program, as well as a member of the Department of International Studies and of the Centre for Urban and Global Studies at Trinity. He is the author of several books, including *African Cities: Alternative Visions of Urban Theory and Practice* (2011), *Disposable Cities: Garbage, Governance and Sustainable Development in Urban Africa* (2005), and *Verandahs of Power: Colonialism and Space in Urban Africa* (2003). Myers was previously Professor of Geography and African Studies and Director of the African Studies Centre at the University of Kansas, Lawrence, Kansas.

Alain Sinou is a full professor at the Université Paris 8. He began his career as a researcher at the IRD (Institut de recherche pour le développement) and studied West African urbanisation. He is a member of the 'Centre de recherches historiques' – a newly initiated research laboratory in his university, and in recent years he has been working on urban heritage processes, especially in West African societies. His publications include *Les Villes d'Afrique noire entre 1650 et 1960* (co-authored, 1989), *Porto-Novo ville d'Afrique noire* (1989), *Comptoirs et villes colonials du Sénégal, Saint-Louis, Gorée, Dakar* (1993) and *Ouidah, une ville africaine singulière* (1995).

Ines Sonder is an art historian and researcher of architecture in the Land of Israel at the Moses Mendelssohn Centre for European-Jewish Studies in Potsdam, Germany. She wrote her PhD on 'Garden Cities for Eretz Israel: Zionist Urban Visions from Theodor Herzl to Richard Kauffmann' (published by Georg Olms Verlag, New York, 2005, in German). She compiled a catalogue of buildings and projects planned by the female German-Israeli architect Lotte Cohn (Bauhaus Center, Tel Aviv, 2009) and published the first biography on her. She currently teaches the history of Jewish settlement, architecture and art in the Land of Israel at Potsdam University.

Miki Zaidman is a practising architect involved in urban planning as well as designing individual buildings. His academic interest lies in the area of the history of urban planning, with emphasis on the processes and concepts that shaped the current Israeli urban environment. Besides his degree in architecture and town planning from the Technion (Haifa), he has an MA and a PhD in historical geography from the Hebrew University of Jerusalem. His research attempts to delineate the Eretz-Israeli adaptation of the garden city and to define the 'Zionist urban pattern' from past to present.

SERIES EDITOR'S INTRODUCTION

The global circulation of ideas about municipal planning and reform within and beyond Europe's empires is an important strand of an unfolding story of urbanisation and its impact upon the making of the modern world. This volume explores concepts and cultures of urban planning through the prism of garden cities, a term first coined in 1898 by the visionary and idealist Ebenezer Howard (1850–1928). Concerned like many of his contemporaries with the overcrowded and unhealthy conditions of England's fast-growing cities, in 1899 Howard founded the Garden Cities Association (now known as the Town and Country Planning Association). The garden cities movement quickly became an international phenomenon, influencing urban design and planning in diverse parts of the globe. Reflecting a growing interest in transnational history, the editors of the volume bring together for the first time expertise across the British and French empires to explore how the garden cities concept was adapted to, or resisted in, a range of colonial urban environments. The dynamics of cultural translation point not only to the flexibility with which the Howardian model was interpreted in the colonies but the multi-faceted nature of that model itself. Ideas, moreover, rarely move in simple or linear fashion, and the contributors – who include urban, architectural and art historians, historical geographers, planning practitioners and a practising architect – skilfully chart the different routes via which British and French interwar town planning policies travelled as well as investigating the interests which they came to serve. As with all colonial development policies the tensions were palpable: between the desire to transform urban environments and the often meagre resources at developers' disposal; between development undertaken privately or in partnership and that firmly under the control of the state; between the competing desires and needs of white expatriate populations and those of colonised populations; and between the original notion of social harmony embedded in the garden city concept and the way that concept could be cynically appropriated (and distorted) by supporters of segregation in order to keep apart different racial or ethnic groups. The book is therefore a very valuable contribution to the wider theme of how urban geography and history can inform our understanding of colonial relations and situations, as well as a most welcome addition to the *Studies in Imperialism* series' growing number of comparative imperial histories.

Andrew Thompson
Professor of Modern History
Exeter
July 2013

PREFACE AND ACKNOWLEDGEMENTS

This book arose from a conversation between its editors about the transnational character of garden city concepts and their quite unexpected 'flows' in our respective areas of expertise, different historical circumstances and colonial situations. The marriage between Africa and Palestine based on colonial experiences and garden city ideas and practices became fascinating, intriguing and challenging the longer the conversation continued. We were also stimulated by the enthusiastic response of each contributor we approached, and we finally decided to initiate this volume – a pioneering work in exposing the extra-European history of European garden city planning, which also addresses areas outside the Western world. Moreover, as a book-length endeavour that focuses on colonial Africa and Palestine, it is unprecedented in the relevant historiography. In fact, it seems that in embracing comparative views and critical approaches concerning the territories chosen, we have not only challenged the more conventional, Eurocentric narrative relating to garden cities, but in many senses have created a subaltern research literature. Of course, illuminating transnational aspects through which planning ideas were transmitted, diffused and modified has meant the blurring of distinctions between this 'other' literature on garden cities and the more traditional academic canon on garden city developments in the Global North itself.

First and foremost, the editors would like to thank the contributors for their responsiveness, cooperation, hard word and patience. The very essence of this project consists of an international network of professionals; we have found the mediation between several disciplinary backgrounds a challenging task, including coordinating their various (academic) languages (French, English, Kiswahili, German and Hebrew).

We would also like to acknowledge those editors under whose aegis earlier versions of some chapters or parts of chapters were published in several of these languages. References are: Liora Bigon, '"Garden city" in the tropics? French Dakar in comparative perspective', *Journal of Historical Geography*, 38:1 (2012), 35–44; Ines Sonder, *Gartenstädte für Erez Israel: Zionistische Stadtplannungvisionen von Theodor Herzl bis Richard Kauffmann* (Hildesheim: Georg Olms Verlag, 2005); Yossi Katz, 'The extension of Ebenezer Howard's ideas on urbanization outside of the British Isles: the example of Palestine', *Geo-Journal*, 34 (1994), 467–73; and Miki Zaidman and Ruth Kark, 'The beginnings of Tel Aviv: the Ahuzat Bayit neighborhood as a "garden city"', *Zmanim*, 106 (spring 2009), 8–21 (special issue commemorating the hundredth anniversary of the founding of Tel Aviv, in Hebrew).

In addition, financial support from two organisations is gratefully acknowledged – the Society of Architectural Historians of Great Britain (the Dorothy Stroud Bursary for publication) and the Chair for the Study of the History and Activities of the Jewish National Fund (KKL), Bar-Ilan University, Israel. This money was mainly used for translations into English and English editing, for which our thanks are due mainly to Alan Clayman.

Our thanks are due to the generosity and hospitality of many people in each region studied, and to innumerable archivists and librarians located around the world: among others, the Institut français d'Architecture, Paris; Archives municipales de Fès, Morocco; Archives Nationales du Sénégal, Dakar; Rhodes House, Oxford; Archives du Mali, Bamako; Zanzibar National Archives; the Central Zionist Archives, Jerusalem; and Tel Aviv Municipal Archives.

Although not all of them are aware of this, and some might even challenge it, many people have contributed to the production of this collection, more or less directly. The editors, however, remain responsible for errors and omissions. We would like to record our special gratitude to Francesca Bondy, Zeynep Çelik, Louis Dioh, Papa Momar Diop, Felix Driver, Mohammed Fawez, Eran Feitelson, Dov Gavish, the Gutman Museum and family, Robert Home, Nechama Kanner, Alan Mabin, Tammy Soffer, Mottie Tamarkin, Viktor Yatyenko and Oren Yiftachel.

We are also indebted to the cheerful, critical encouragement made by the peer reviewers of Manchester University Press, and to the team effort of everyone at this Press.

Garden cities and colonial planning: transnationality and urban ideas in Africa and Palestine

Liora Bigon

The present collection is intended as a study of European planning histories beyond Europe. It focuses on garden city concepts and practices in their broadest sense, and on the processes by which these were transmitted, diffused and adapted in the imperial context in various colonial territories and situations. The socio-political, geographical and cultural implications of these processes will be analysed here by means of cases from the global South-East, namely French and British colonial territories in Africa as well as Ottoman and British Mandate Palestine. The focus on the extra-European planning history of Europe – particularly in Africa and Palestine in the context of the garden city – is unprecedented in research literature. The latter tends to concentrate on the global North-West. Moreover, as noted by the chartered town planner and planning historian Robert Home in his (still today) pioneering paper 'Town planning and garden cities in the British colonial empire 1910–1940', '[a]s planning history becomes more international in scope, an emerging theme is the transfer of imperial countries' planning systems to their colonial possessions ... This process of transfer has, however, received little attention from planning historians.'[1]

These inter- or rather trans-national aspects of the garden city require a study of frameworks and documentation that extends beyond national borders. The present collection is composed of chapters written by an international network of researchers. Their comparative views and critical approaches challenge the more conventional, Eurocentric narrative relating to garden cities. The tangled network of metropolitan–colonial relationships in the modern period enabled the conveyance of garden city features to dependent territories on a selective and uneven basis. All the contributors to this collection were thus asked to trace these processes of conveyance in their historical accounts. A guiding principle that runs through our collection is that the spread of garden city ideas into the selected colonial territories was not uni-directional, contrary to the 'traditional', reductive, centre–periphery analytical framework that characterises urban studies.[2] This spread of ideas – by nature an uncontrolled process – was, rather, diffuse, crossing complex and multiple frontiers, and, as we shall see, sometimes included quite unexpected 'flows'.

Ebenezer Howard coined the term 'garden city' in 1898, in his book *To-Morrow: A Peaceful Path to Real Reform* (slightly revised and re-titled *Garden Cities of To-Morrow* in 1902).[3] Since that time, Howard's concept, in all its diversity of both theory and practice, has spread through professional, academic and popular circles of urban planning, design and architecture. Although *Garden Cities of To-Morrow* has a modern-day sound, the contemporary sources of its theoretical inspiration and the planning evolution in England and the Western world have been amply discussed in planning literature. Our collection takes Howard's book and its related literature as a point of departure, in terms of a visionary programme of social and political reform for the gradual transformation of overpopulated British industrial towns into decentralised networks of self-sufficient 'social cities' or 'garden cities'. While Howard's original ideas, as well as later concepts and practices, gained their greatest momentum in Britain, they were quickly disseminated far and wide, particularly in the northern hemisphere. Whether in professional practice or theory, the term 'garden city' has been rediscovered, re-examined and reinterpreted many times over the years. However, as a result of its popularity, it is often loosely applied to a variety of other forms of urban planning and design.

In dealing with the implications of garden city models and varieties of applications for the planning histories of colonial Africa and Palestine, we embraced a flexible approach to defining and capturing garden city expressions. We sometimes use the term 'Howardian ideas', referring to Howard's original thought and its immediate variant applications in Britain, his mother country. This country is also, in the context of our collection, a *métropole*, that is, a colonising country. The term 'Howardian ideas' implies the inherent variance of these expressions, preparing the ground for the understanding of subsequent garden city models and overseas transmissions beyond the original geographic and conceptual sphere. It therefore indicates our multiple, comparative analysis in terms of both time and space. More generally, our flexible approach towards garden city notions means that a considerable freedom of interpretation was left to each contributing author, in accordance with the socio-politics, economics and culture of the urban location he or she studied. What this means is that garden city concepts are interpreted in multiple ways. Interpretations oscillate between the purely fictional (chapter 5) and the actual (chapter 6), and from a more strict comparison with Howardian ideas in order to delimit any colonial 'diversions' or 'distortions' from them (chapter 1) towards quite an associative relationship (chapter 3). They range from analogous or complementary to challenging and antithetical, referencing various aspects of garden city planning. Although there is some repetition, especially concerning the original Howardian aspects, we welcome this, since the aspects considered are both independent of and integral to each of the colonial urban sites or regions discussed, and the conclusions drawn are always contextualised.

While presenting the ways in which modern urban design has been aligned to power, we shall assess the relationship between colonialism and modern planning through the varieties of garden city. The transmission process has never been a uni-directional, clear and simple radiation of ideas from a European 'centre' to a Near Eastern or African 'periphery'. Our aim, accordingly, is to expand on the diffuse, dynamic and contested aspects of this process, including those involving indigenous agencies. We shall address questions such as who imported the planning models to the selected colonial urban areas, why certain models were selected rather than others at a given moment, how exactly these models were translated and for whom. Through such questions we hope to better understand the gap between metropolitan modernity and modernity as conceived for the colonies. By putting the 'periphery' at the 'centre' of the discussion, our aim is not to 'provincialise Europe'. It is rather to recognise the difference between metropolitan planning culture and its colonial counterpart through the common thread of the garden city.

In this respect, our expanding on the multilateral channels for the transmission of garden city ideas might be equivalent to the role played by sugar cane in Sidney Mintz's insightful work *Sweetness and Power*. By focusing on something that connects colonial 'centres' and colonial 'peripheries', but in a way that blurs any hierarchy between these hemispheres, Mintz manages to avoid the portrayal trap:

> Once one begins to wonder where the tropical products go, who uses them, for what, and how much they are prepared to pay for them – what they will forgo, and at what price, in order to have them – one is asking questions about the market. But then one is also asking questions about the metropolitan homeland, the center of power, not about the dependent colony, the object and target of power. And once one attempts to put consumption together with production, to fit colony to metropolis, there is a tendency for one or the other – the 'hub' or the 'other rim' – to slip out of focus ... While the relationships between colonies

and metropolis are in the most immediate sense entirely obvious, in another sense they are mystifying.[4]

In what follows, we hope to shed more light on the theoretical and conceptual frameworks that have guided this edited collection. We shall begin with some historiographic notes setting out the salient international and transnational threads in our discussion. We then continue with contextual remarks on the circulation of (colonial) urban planning policies and colonial segregationist policies. Our methodologies, chosen time span and presentation of chapters will be discussed against the background of these issues.

Garden cities and colonial urban planning: historiographies

The publications of Howard himself and some of his contemporaries (Raymond Unwin, Barry Parker, Patrick Geddes, Frederick Osborn, to name but a few) can certainly be regarded as primary sources. Their ideas did not emerge independently in terms of national metropolitan borders, that is, those of Britain, but were internationally flavoured from the start. The inter- as well as trans-nationality of their ideas came mainly from their sources of inspiration, whether direct or indirect. Among these sources are the writings of French socialist utopians (Charles Fourier, Saint-Simon), Austrian and German planning theoreticians (Camillo Sitte, Theodor Fritsch) and American reformists (Edward Bellamy). It can be concluded that these inspiring ideas and practices were geographically centred in Europe and North America. They mainly consisted of the experimental precedents of the model villages and towns built by industrialists in Europe during the second half of the nineteenth century, especially in Britain and France.

This was also the case regarding the second international aspect of the garden city movement, its members' origins and areas of influence and activity. From the Frenchman Georges Benoît-Lévy to the German brothers Jules and Heinrich Hart and the Canadian Louis de Soissons, the movement attracted considerable attention in Europe and America. By the First World War, garden city associations had been established in eleven countries, mostly European, and the International Garden Cities Association had been set up.[5] There were only a few exceptions to this Europe–America axis, such as the Russian Garden City Society, organised in 1913. And, as noted by the urban historian Stanley Buder, '[a]ccording to the British association, its London Office in 1912 received many inquiries from other nations (including Ottoman Palestine, the Dutch East Indies, and Japan) for information and assistance'.[6] Indeed, most English-language urban historians agree that by 1910 the garden city idea and movement had become a rich source of concepts. These concepts had been adopted, adapted, conceptualised and developed technically through the newly emerging international practice of town planning.[7] Yet it is surprising that in the literature of town planning, relatively little attention has been paid by scholars to these 'exceptions' in terms of geography and location, that is, to garden city developments and derivatives outside Britain, Europe or America.

A considerable number of books and book chapters on the history of the garden city movement and its concepts, including some biographies of Howard himself, naturally enough highlight the British experience.[8] Within Great Britain in particular, for several decades following the Second World War there was an even stronger impetus for publications related to 'green-belt' cities, 'new towns' and their actual and legislative developments.[9] Written by urban experts, mainly but not exclusively in English, some of these publications provided glimpses of relevant modern issues, such as the new urbanism, the sustainable city and community design.[10] Good as they are, the main disadvantage of these academic works with respect to our project is that they expand very little on these issues beyond the North-West. The narrow boundaries of the Western world in this literature tend to encompass only North America, Germany and France, and sometimes, in passing, Australia and Russia, in that order of preference. For the best characterisation of the works in question, both intellectually and geographically, we shall cite the words of Peter Hall. Exceptional in their synoptic perspective and professional force, these words are from the introduction to his book *Cities of Tomorrow*:

> This is supposed to be a global history, yet – given the all-too-evident confines of space and of the author's competence – it must fail in the endeavor. The resulting account is glaringly Anglo-Americocentric. That can be justified, or at least excused: as will soon be seen, so many of the key ideas of twentieth-century western planning were conceived and nurtured in a remarkably small and cosy club based in London and New York. But this emphasis means that the book deals all too shortly with other important planning traditions, in Spain and Latin America, in the Russian Empire and the Soviet Union, in China. Those must provide matter for other books by other hands.[11]

In this context, we would like to highlight an original contribution, pioneering in terms of its conception and theorisation: *The Garden City: Past, Present and Future*, edited by Stephen V. Ward. Though some twenty years old now, with a primary focus on the northern hemisphere, this collection was virtually the first to aim at a thorough analysis of international arenas. It discusses garden city planning in England, France, Nazi Germany, Australia, America and Japan, by experts in the field, all of them from Europe, North America and Japan. The book also traces the diversification of the garden city tradition in widely differing contexts: economic, institutional, cultural and aesthetic.[12]

Our project is in fact very much in the spirit of Ward's book, though ours, owing to its focus on early twentieth-century colonial situations, deals with Asia (Ottoman and British Mandate Palestine) and Africa. In fact, as far as we are aware, this edited collection is the only book-length project that considers overseas garden city developments in these geographic areas in the modern colonial period. The few exceptional works in English that cover the experience in Africa in this regard (mainly North and South) are in the form of articles or book chapters only.[13] In Israel, there is a growing interest in the garden city concepts embedded in the Zionist project, an interest that has yielded several book-length publications. Uninformed by a postcolonial perspective, quite a number of the latter are still only in Hebrew and have thus far gained only a limited regional influence.[14]

Garden city historiography as outlined above actually intersects with the historiography of colonial urban planning and architecture – a field to which our book directly corresponds. In this respect, its main contribution is twofold: first, it shifts scholastic attention away from the more researched urban history of Europeans in the North-West towards their less researched urban history in the South-East. Moreover, in the urban historiography of Europeans outside their countries of origin in the modern period, there is a clear preference for treating those colonies with a higher economic and political status. Thus, research on British India and Singapore, French Indo-China or Algeria (not to mention Australia, Canada and the US, and in many respects, South Africa), is much more abundant than research on sub-Saharan Africa. Secondly, apart from the indigenous languages within the geographical and intellectual scope of this book (referred to below), this collection brings together two normally disparate research traditions, the British and the French. Though closely related within the colonial project of these most powerful mid-nineteenth-century global powers, the extent to which the English-language research tradition ignores its French counterpart (and vice versa) is truly astonishing.

Until recently, according to Richard Drayton, many scholars exempted themselves from the tiring business of learning foreign names, places and languages, thanks to the idea that colonialism had expanded from the European core to the overseas periphery. Only now, he noted, a generation after the de-colonisation era, have we started to bind the histories of the former *métropoles* with those of their empires.[15] The connection between the domestic and the external histories of Europe – such as metropolitan industrialism and colonialism in the case of garden city ideas – involves the acknowledgement that Great Britain is, for instance, an outcome of imperial processes, exactly like its former colonies. That is, modern Europe was created by its extra-European history no less than it created it. The same line of thought was held by Jane Jacobs, who analysed colonial traces in the post-colonial city, and Felix Driver and David Gilbert, who edited a collection of historical essays on the subject of imperial influences in the European urban space.[16] Edward Said – who, in his geographical inquiry into historical experience, insisted on the idea that the earth is in effect one world and that cultures assume more 'foreign' elements than they consciously exclude – initiated this line of thought. 'Who in India or Algeria today', he asked, 'can confidently separate out British or French component of the past from present actualities?' – and vice versa.[17]

This geo-cultural understanding is not yet sufficiently reflected in recently published literature. This is especially true regarding the African continent in general and sub-Saharan Africa in particular. 'It is remarkable', said Janet Abu-Lughod in 1965, referring to the North African colonial urban experience, 'that so common a phenomenon has remained almost unstudied.'[18] A decade later, Robert Home acknowledged the lack of historical depth and the inapplicability of exclusively Western models to the understanding of colonial urbanism and planning policy. He therefore chose to embrace 'the historian's rather than the geographer's viewpoint' with reference to British Nigeria.[19] Paradoxically, as Alain Sinou pointed out in 1993, more works deal with the urban history and architecture of the Spanish in sixteenth- and seventeenth-century Latin America than with those of the French or the British in modern sub-Saharan Africa. In fact barely any studies, according to Sinou, deal with the latter history.[20] 'Historians have made only a limited impact on the interdisciplinary field of African urban studies', wrote John Parker in the introduction to his study dealing with the shaping of early colonial Accra by the Ga people.[21] Similar concluding remarks were made by the coordinators of one of the special issues of *Afrique et Histoire* that was dedicated in 2006 to African cities. Only in recent years, they say, have we proceeded towards a historical perspective regarding the city in Africa, a domain which was traditionally researched by geographers, sociologists and anthropologists.[22]

In addition, only a few researchers took into account the different research traditions, as Catherine Coquery-Vidrovitch commented in her comprehensive overview of the history of urbanisation and urban planning in Africa:

> Anglophone urban anthropology, so attentive to human social behaviour or feelings, has paid little attention to people's physical surroundings ... in the French literature a city is considered a place, defined by its location, its situation, and identified by its forms (urban morphology). Particular attention is given to relations between demographic trends, urban space and the built environment, but little attention is paid to social process.[23]

It can be argued that, in general, the English research tradition of the colonial urban sphere has dealt with 'history-in-the-city', the history of social movements and popular struggles around community issues, whereas its French counterpart has dealt with the 'history-of-the-city' itself.[24] It should be noted that exceptions to the general research trends described above do, of course, exist. However, 'it appears desirable to build a bridge between the two approaches', as Coquery-Vidrovitch remarked in 1991, 'and to combine their methods in order to grasp both the content and the container.'[25] This characterisation is surprisingly up to date. In the preface to the English edition (2005) of her study on the history of cities in sub-Saharan Africa, mostly focused on ancient cities, she mentions a project entitled *Africa's Urban Past* (2000). Based on a London conference that was conducted by David Anderson and Richard Rathbone, the latter project is broad and provides an overview of current research in political, economic and cultural urban history. However, 'rare exceptions aside', says Coquery-Vidrovitch, 'the authors overlook French-language publications despite the fact that this is one of the areas where French-speaking historians have done the most work'.[26] A similar recent example is *African Urban Spaces* (2005) edited by Steven Salm and Toyin Falola[27] – in most of its essays the city serves only as a background for research into social history, which is often frustratingly vague about the physical frame of things.

Yet, more generally speaking, it seems that the aforementioned bridge has indeed been built during the last two decades. While literature on the history of European planning outside Europe has gradually been growing, it is still rather meagre, and thus worth mentioning in detail.[28] Whether case-study specific or comparative, the works that deal with the British dependencies constitute a valuable contribution to the understanding of colonial planning cultures and architectural forms.[29] They refer to the main designers of the British colonial urban landscape, to the nature of their profession, and to ideologies that prevailed during periods from the very formation of a city until the post-colonial era. Conceiving these cities as laboratories for cross-cultural interaction, special attention is given in these works to conflicts involving the negotiation of power between those vested with formal power to control the city and those who lived in and used it. That is, the colonial urban sphere is dealt with in these works as a dynamic sphere, a sphere in which various interpretations and perspectives were constantly in dispute over health and disease, order and disorder, past and present, race and nation.

As to studies that deal with the French dependencies – conducted by a single scholar or as a collective initiative of architects, urbanists and historians – it may seem inappropriate to refer to them *en bloc*.[30] One can say, however, that they have considerably enhanced our under-standing of colonial architecture and urban forms by relating them to history, politics and culture. By expanding on the formation of French colonial spatial practices, as manifested both at home and overseas – from Algiers to Antananarivo, and from Riyadh to Hanoi – these works have opened new paths to the study of colonial planning cultures. The broad and interdisciplinary attitude towards the history of urban design – for instance, the use of ethnography in Çelik's *Urban Forms* – shows the dynamic nature of this discipline. These works exemplify how far colonial domination was from being homogeneous in its spatial and formal projects. These projects were characterised by great variety, and affected by metropolitan, colonial and local influences. They could be quite different from each other even within a single colony (as exemplified by Laurent Fourchard regarding colonial Upper Volta) and within one city (see Gwendolyn Wright on Casablanca, Saigon and Antananarivo, for instance).

Several edited works bring together collections of case studies, each of which deals with a city under one of the colonial powers (Britain, France, Italy, Japan).[31] Yet usually in these works the task of summa-rising the common, or diverse, themes of the individual chapters is left to the reader. This leaves open, among other things, the issue that this book partly tries to handle – a comparison between the various colonial powers, particularly the British and the French, regarding their urban planning concepts and practices in Africa and the Near East. Moreover, by shifting the research orientation from the afore-mentioned anglophone tendency towards the francophone one, we have aimed at adding another layer to the latter history-of-the-city model. Indeed, the motivation for this arose in the course of a dialogue with the literature described above.[32] Hence, though physical patterns always encapsulate an extra-physical reality, we shall pay considerable attention to the underlying explanations of urban form in particular historical circumstances. Our project is in many respects 'a discussion of some patterns and elements of urban form seen in a historical perspective' – emphasising 'patterns and elements of urban form'.[33] An emphasis on 'seen in a historical perspective' is also critical, as our project is engaged more with urban history than, for instance, with social or urban geography. Using Spiro Kostof's words:

> My difficulties with urban geographers have to do with aims and means. Much of their effort goes to generating theory, which brings with it an insistence on measurement, statistical samples, and reductive diagrams. A practical side of these preoccupations is the definition of type independent of particular historical circumstances.[34]

'Studying through' the 'transnational': from neoliberal to colonial policies of urban planning

Two main, interconnected themes repeatedly emerge from recent literature that discusses both theoretical and applied aspects of neoliberal urbanism. The first is variegation, multiplicity and transformative capacity as a striking feature inherent in current neoliberal spaces and policies. This serves as a potent foil for the orthodox thesis of globalisation, which argues for the latter's virtually unifying or hegemonic character while occupying end-of-history/death-of-geography narratives.

The second theme is the high importance that is assigned to national specificity, path-dependency and territoriality in understanding the spatial aspects of neoliberal processes.[35] 'It is important to recognize that cities are not merely localized arenas in which externally generated projects of neoliberal restructuring are imposed' say Jamie Peck, Nik Theodore and Neil Brenner.[36] In drawing our attention to the local 'embeddedness', scale-specific and uneven aspects of this global economic phenomenon, they have not ignored cultural aspects of neoliberal urbanism, unusual among economic geographers and comparative political economists. They also seek to explore 'distinctive national, regional and local contexts, defined by the legacies of inherited institutional frameworks, policy regimes, regulatory practices and political struggles'.[37] Pointing to the centrality of the issue of variegation as set against the conceptualisation of neoliberalism as a globalised-superordinate form, they call for a nuanced understanding of the incomplete, experimental and polymorphic character of neoliberal processes.[38]

Similar discontent with the meta-narrative of the literature concerning world/global cities, with its exclusive focus on particular cities as powerful nodes in the networked geographies of economic flows, is shared by other scholars.[39] Among them, Eugene McCann and Kevin Ward also elaborated on these two themes, though on a much less abstract level. Looking at the nature of urban policy mobility and thinking beyond the hierarchical classifications rooted in world/global cities theories, they developed the concept of urban 'assemblage'. This concept seems to encapsulate both the variegation and multiplicity theme, together with the tension between relationality ('global' flows) and territoriality ('local' impacts) now perceived as productive. Inspired inter alia by John Allen and Allan Cochrane's interpretation of cities as 'parts of elsewhere' that are constituted relationally and territorially, McCann and Ward encourage methodological openness in urban policy studies towards the multi-directional, the transnational and the multilateral; towards the unexpected and the non-linear; and towards mobility, fluidity and heterogeneity.[40]

McCann and Ward adopt an approach of 'study through' the sites for an understanding of the circulation of planning ideas, expertise and knowledge. In this way, they enable us to move beyond the anthropological conception of the 'field' as a single and relatively geographically bound place, towards a relational conception of space. Aside from the territorial, emphasis is again given to the study of 'situations', that is, the various relationships that exist beyond the physical, and the processes of creating webs, relationships and discourses between agencies, institutions and the players involved.[41] This perception of the relational situatedness of sites might balance critical geographical scholarship, as 'more analysis is needed on *how* – through what practices, where, when, and by whom – urban policies are produced in the global-relational context, are transferred and reproduced from place to place, and are negotiated politically in various locations'.[42]

Such an understanding reflects Home's comment at the beginning of this introduction as to the meagre attention that has been given in urban planning literature to the very processes of transfer of urban norms and forms in colonial contexts. It welcomes innovative and comparative research paths in urban studies that reveal power relationships and transnational networks. It also invites the exploration of the direct and indirect channels for the spread of ideas and practices, connecting cities in the global North-West and South-East in complex ways. The present collection is framed by this understanding – in fact, while leaving the definition of 'garden city' open for our contributors, they were solely asked to focus carefully on the 'how', that is, through what practices, where, when, why, what for and by whom garden city concepts and applications were transferred, adapted or diffused into the territory under discussion. The consequences of this mission have two dimensions, reflecting the conjunction of variegation on the one hand and relational situatedness on the other – both dimensions are inevitably rooted in our historical cases of urban policy circulations.

As to the variegation and multiplicity theme, garden city notions were interpreted here in a broad sense, as each chapter provides us with another view of its 'site', within its own context. To provide just a few examples, there is the move from prestigious housing estates for white and elite minorities in colonial North Africa to an equivalent for the traditional 'plateaux' in French West Africa; and from colonialist developments for certain indigenous residents in East Africa to the leading vision and form of urban settlement at the time in Palestine's Jewish sector. What can we learn from these multilateral 'garden city' varieties? The foremost issue is, of course, the transformative capacity of such global ideas, and their non-linear and always surprising paths. Another issue that comes to mind in the light of this variety is the understanding of urban planning as anything but a technical, rational, neutral and apolitical practice.

As to the theme of relational situatedness vis-à-vis global and local mobility, it is only through the contextualisation of garden city expressions that the meaning of their perceptual and actual variety can be grasped. Examination of the territorially embedded translations of garden city notions reveals dynamic environments, rich in their particular interests and visions on the cultural, economic and socio-political levels. 'Studying through' our chosen sites also means drawing away from what is referred to in anthropology as 'studying up' (researching those who are considered powerful, such as colonisers) and 'studying down' (researching those who are considered powerless, such as the colonised), while advocating 'tracing ways in which power creates webs and relations *between* actors, institutions and discourses across time and space'.[43] This not only turns our attention to the 'situational' quality in each 'field' or 'site', but also lets us conceptualise any site-related situation as transnational in character.

> We have not used the word 'transnationality' in the title of this collection in urban history because we wanted to dissolve the symbiotic relationship between history writing and the nation state, that is, to correct history's complicity in helping forge the nation state.[44] Nor have we used this word because 'a cottage industry of definitions quickly developed as the label became a must-wear'.[45] Rather, we advocate this notion because both urban planning and colonialism are inherently transnational phenomena, and because, if we are permitted to fully empathise with the idiosyncrasies of Akira Iriye and Pierre-Yves Saunier, the editors of *The Palgrave Dictionary of Transnational History from the Mid-19th Century to the Present Day*,

We are interested in links and flows, and want to track people, ideas, products, processes and patterns that operate over, across, through, beyond, above, under, or in-between polities and societies. Among the units that were thus crossed, consolidated or subverted in the modern age, first and foremost were the national ones, if only because our work addresses the moment, roughly from the middle of the 19th century until nowadays, when nations came to be seen and empowered as the main frames for the political, cultural, economic and social life of human beings.[46]

By expanding on the centrality of the nation in creating imperial geographies, politics and economics in the late nineteenth century, Saskia Sassen's philosophical account sees a turning point in this historical period, which extends until the interwar period. This period is characterised by the creation of a world-scale through the projection of national capitalism on to foreign geographic areas; by accelerated industrialisation in the mother country/*métropole*, a colonial modernisation that was distinct from metropolitan modernisation, and lack of development in the colonised territories; and by the multiplication of national imperialism and hence competition, all in the name of national aggrandisement and commercial gain. The various colonising efforts therefore took place within the context of the domestic and imperial expansion of national capitalism.[47] The transnational approach enables us to blur the expected hierarchies and to contribute towards the advancement of knowledge in our chosen, relatively neglected territories. This is especially true against this nation-centric background and together with our emphasis on the extra-European planning history of Europe. In this sense, transnationality can be conceived as a mobile and hybrid assemblage that 'unfolds in a shifting terrain of borrowings, appropriations and alliances'.[48]

In trying to trace the first usages of the 'transnational', its connotations and evolved meanings through recent decades, Pierre-Yves Saunier has managed to portray an etymological genealogy for this notion. From philology to transportation, thence to international law, international relations and economics, and (a-)political activism, its spread has included the social sciences and related disciplines, with an increased presence in history and geography.[49] A prominent appearance of the 'transnational' in the field of architecture and colonial urban planning, which also inspired the present volume, was in a recent proposal by the French architectural historian Mercedes Volait, which had the aim of producing 'a broader understanding of the worldwide spread of European architecture across empires during the nineteenth and twentieth centuries ... in a large range of geographic and linguistic contexts, both Western and non-Western environments'.[50] 'Transnationality' therefore means that colonial architecture's vectors, connections, semantics and materiality involve not only a bilateral colonial channel – such as British architecture in India or French architecture in Algeria – but also exemplify more complex, extra-colonial facets.[51]

In a similar manner, the transnational aspects of our project are threefold. First, there is the perceptual level of the dissemination of urban ideas, that is, of garden city conceptions and practices. Beyond the bilateral channels, which, in the cases we examine include the British in colonial Zanzibar or Mandate Palestine and the French in North or West Africa, there are also multilateral and transnational aspects. Garden city notions were diffused from Britain to France, and only then through the French channel to francophone Africa. Thus, the Howardian ideas realised in Britain, far from being uniform, were already 'diverted' or 'distorted' in mainland France, a situation further accelerated through the colonial dimension of French Africa. Similarly, colonial Zanzibar is treated in our collection not merely through its metropolitan, British connections, but within the framework of its post-colonial urban development. Reflections on the garden city in Zanzibar are thus presented vis-à-vis a current Finnish planning project. In addition, and maybe surprisingly, garden city ideas in early twentieth-century Palestine did not filter in through British town planners during the British Mandate. Rather, they were introduced through Zionist activists, mostly of German origin, during the Ottoman regime. Moreover, even the investigations of more 'traditional' bilateral channels between *métropole* and colony are more innovative than might be initially expected, especially considering the state of garden city historiography as outlined above.

A second transnational aspect inherent in the structure of our project is the assemblage of international scholars, each a professionally trained urban specialist in one or more relevant fields. These include an urban and architectural historian, an architect and urban planner/designer and a historical geographer, as well as experts in a particular colonial situation and geographical area. While the international scope of the contributors encompasses Tunisia, France, North America, Zanzibar, Germany and Israel, there is another transnational impulse at work in our collection. This derives from the fact that the scholars examining the cases of formerly colonised territories are not always from the formerly colonising countries themselves, though of course this does not necessarily imply complete objectivity.

A third aspect of transnationality is rooted in our methodology: this is the linguistic issue, as well as the character of fieldwork and archival research. We believe that our challenging and interdisciplinary approach, which combines planning history with area studies, is achieved through multi-site exploration and a proper re-reading of primary and secondary sources. From Dakar to Tel Aviv and from

Rabat to Zanzibar, we have been faced with the task of filling the gaps in a variety of sources divided between the ex-colonising nations and those of the ex-colonised. With only one native English-speaking scholar among our contributors (who, in contrast to many native English-speaking scholars, actually bothered to learn a new subaltern language, Kiswahili), the languages covered in our book range from French and English, to Swahili, German and Hebrew. Among archival collections consulted, in addition to various contemporary sources, are the Institut français d'Architecture, Paris; Archives municipales de Fès, Morocco; Archives Nationales du Sénégal, Dakar; Rhodes House, Oxford; Archives du Mali, Bamako; Zanzibar National Archives; the Central Zionist Archives, Jerusalem; and Tel Aviv Municipal Archives. Moreover, all the contributors have an intimate acquaintance with their area of urban studies, either by nationality or as a result of repeated visits.

The time span

Howard's ideas were quickly disseminated through transnational and international channels. In fact by the first decade of the twentieth century they had reached the colonial sphere, in one variation or another, directly or indirectly. Combined with modern colonial histories from the mid-nineteenth century till the 1960s (with some exceptions in the cases of colonial Morocco and Ottoman/Mandate Palestine), there is a particular focus in our collection on the interwar period. References to contiguous periods are occasionally made by the contributors as appropriate, be it to the pre-Howardian colonial formative years or to post-colonial times. The Second World War constituted a turning point in the British and French colonies in general, expressed both in terms of decolonisation programmes and political, administrative and economic reforms. These affected colonial urban planning policy, particularly after 1945. Yet in the early twentieth century and especially after the First World War, European imperialism was at its apogee, with Britain and France among the most active powers on the international scene. Palestine was inherited by Britain from the Ottomans; and in Africa, the 'heroic' or 'military' phase of the conquest of its vast hinterland was, on the whole, complete. Under the *pax colonia*, aimed at the establishment of internal political and administrative systems, economic gain was promoted.[52]

The physical environment in the interwar period, particularly in the main colonial urban centres, underwent considerable change in order to adjust to colonial exploitation. The basis of the infrastructure of the modern empire was laid down at this time. It was referred to in colonial planning literature in terms of 'development', 'betterment', 'efficiency' and the like, reflecting the apparent scientific and rational facets of the colonial enterprise. British and French town planning policies, intended for the benefit of the expatriates rather than that of the colonised populations, were most blatant in Africa. At this point, as we shall see, garden city concepts played an important role. At the same time, the limited economic resources at the disposal of the colonial authorities not only affected the implementation of colonial urban planning schemes, but were also very favourable to the interests of the indigenous populations. This was particularly true in sub-Saharan Africa and in the case of the Ottoman regime. Zionist activists, for instance, occasionally took advantage of this weakness, and here again garden city concepts played an unprecedented role in the establishment of a modern network of settlements within the Jewish sector.

What this meant was that colonialism was simultaneously exposing both its strengths and its weaknesses. On the one hand, it was characterised by extreme exertions of power on behalf of the colonial state. These led to the tempting idea, from the coloniser's point of view, of using garden city rhetoric in favour of the expatriate community alone – as exemplified by most of the cases in North and West Africa. On the other hand, colonialism was characterised by an unmistakable weakness of control on the part of that same state, which engendered *laissez-faire* in planning, sometimes used by colonised agencies for their own benefit. As noted by Timothy Mitchell, describing French colonial urban sites, these were far from being 'unambiguously expressive', nor were they an incarnation of 'a system of disciplinary power'.[53] And, as shown by Jennifer Robinson, 'a perfect system of control' was not achieved even through the planning practices in South Africa during the apartheid regime.[54]

Yet there were differences concerning the colonial project even within spheres of the same colonising power, and these emphasise the importance of a thorough comparative view and the sharing of specialist knowledge of the case studies concerned. While, for instance, French colonial Saigon, Tunis and Fez were all seen as examples of thoughtful and often imaginative planning, it was Lyautey's Rabat that became renowned as a colonial showcase in the interwar years. According to the historian Raymond Betts, there was a persistent lack of skilful urban specialists who actually lived in French West Africa, and there is a clear contrast between the exemplary case of Rabat and the 'miserable' outcomes in Dakar in matters of urban planning. This partially attests to the view that 'the French had not lost their architectural genius but seemed to have geographically restricted its exercise'.[55] What were the reasons therefore that one portion of the empire seemed to reflect urban development so well and others so poorly? A prominent reason for this was the formal political status of each territory in the colonial order of preferences.

Colonial contexts: garden cities and the planning of residential segregation

Proposing a model for colonial town planning activity under the British Empire, Robert Home portrayed the relations between the colonial status of a territory and its geographic location, the type of planning activity and the usual planning mechanism.[56] For instance, in places over which direct rule was exercised, usually the rapidly growing ports, severe housing and transportation problems were created. Reluctantly forced to address these newly created urban problems – in the words of Garth Myers, more than the British being 'there to help', they were 'here to help themselves'[57] – the colonial administration tended to act through improvement trusts. To Home's examples of Bombay, Calcutta, Madras, Lagos and Singapore, one can add British Zanzibar and even in many senses French Dakar, as discussed in this volume. Where colonial government followed an indirect rule or protectorate pattern, metropolitan town planning experts were normally recruited on a consultancy or contract basis to design new administrative headquarters, commercial centres, mining or railway towns.[58] From the megalomaniac project of New Delhi to the more modest Lusaka in Northern Rhodesia (present-day Zambia), it would not be over-fanciful to include here the French *villes nouvelles* in the Protectorate of Morocco, as well as their Saint Louis in Senegal or Bamako in French Sudan (Mali) – also discussed in this volume.

A third type of colonial urban governance involved the indigenous cities, which usually attracted little town planning activity and were administered through local or native authorities or foreign consultants. This was a result of general neglect (such as the Ottoman regime in our Palestine case until 1917);[59] of the paternalistic and preservationist tendencies which characterised British colonial policy (such as in Jerusalem from 1922, and other parts of Palestine); or of the fact that the colonial rulers tended to reserve modernist planning features exclusively for themselves. At the same time, under economic, orientalist or other considerations, they left urban conditions to deteriorate, as was the case for some time with the North African *casbahs*.

The fourth and final type of colonial urban governance provided by Home is white settler colonies, where planning was normally carried out through the private sector, and included company towns and garden cities. While his examples include Vanderbiji town, an upper-class garden suburb in Poona, and the most overt case of Pinelands, a garden suburb of Cape Town,[60] the present volume shows that garden cities were in fact associated with each mechanism of colonial town planning activity, and not only this fourth one. However, at this point a few words should be said about South Africa as a representative of white settler colonialism, for our collection deals with 'softer' colonial cases. This is with respect to the extent of friction between the colon-iser and the colonised and the consequent segregationist measures.[61] Such cases are also less discussed in the relevant literature.

In dividing up the history of town planning in South Africa into different periods in the light of governments' attempts to reshape society from 1900 to the present, Alan Mabin and Dan Smit describe aspects in the reformulation of planning at several political turning points. While during and after the First World War the long-standing garden city movement was flowering in Britain, the authors clearly show that in South Africa, reformist social aspects and the technical concerns of urban planning were separated from the start.[62] Not only did the movement in South Africa concentrate on the implementation of the 'technical' and 'practical' side, especially zoning, but this was achieved through planning discrete and self-contained, racially defined communities. In this way, British garden city notions were easily trans-lated into the idea of planning well-separated zones on a racial basis in the South African context. This was through the creation of coherent communities separated by green belts, careful planning of residential and employment locations, and appropriate transportation.[63]

Following a direct contact with Ebenezer Howard himself, a Garden City Association was launched in South Africa in the 1910s, together with the initiation of Pinelands in 1919. Considered as 'South Africa's first garden city', the plan of this white middle-class suburb on the outskirts of Cape Town was prepared by the British architect Albert Thompson, who worked with Raymond Unwin on the planning of Letchworth.[64] In spite of the almost direct channel of British influence here, the 'sanitation syndrome' was central in producing Pinelands' legislation. Yet a relationship between colonial-state racism and the biopolitical struggle was not only present in the perverse case of South Africa (even before the rise of the apartheid regime in 1948 and its subsequent compulsory segregation). The recruitment of pseudo-sanitary arguments for the establishment of racial urban segregation also existed, though not to the same degree, in other colonial situations in tropical, sub-Saharan Africa, in North Africa and beyond.[65]

[18]

What is particularly interesting in the South African case is that garden city models had been partly applied to all 'racial' and social groups from an early stage. Originally intended for the white middle class and white working class, garden city experiments included Indian and later African model housing.[66] Needless to say, Africans were institutionally excluded from the 'disappointingly narrow' profession of town planning there. This model housing was thus implemented in separate areas for each of these 'groups' on the urban peripheries or designated 'locations'.[67] Moreover, similar experiments in which indigenous populations were involved were made in other parts of English-speaking southern Africa.

There has been a great deal of scholarly attention given to the diffusion of garden city concepts in Lusaka. This had been enabled by the British colonial authorities' invitation in 1931 to S. D. Adshead, a professor of town planning at London University and an ardent disciple of Howard.[68] While it is clear that under the rubric of 'garden city' a quite anti-social zoning system enabled the colonial authorities to maintain strict control over the indigenous labourers in this new capital city, it was Garth Myers who elaborated on its model African compounds. The plans for the African areas in the new Lusaka – intended to exemplify a highly ordered city segmented by race, class and gender – seem to reveal the ironies in the colonial situation and its accompanying imagery, disconnected from the then urban realities and autochthonous practices.[69]

We can learn about another example of a 'garden city' project intended for Africans in the 1930s, this time near Bulawayo, Southern Rhodesia (modern Zimbabwe), from one of the established professional journals, *Town and Country Planning*. This journal constitutes an extraordinary source for presenting transnational planning aspects and networks of expertise. We are told that the project was designated for a specific stratum of the indigenous population and presented in terms of governmental concern for their living standards. However, in fact it was meant to further residential segregation. In order to avoid a barrack-like appearance, typical to the regional African 'townships', the residential units were not built in rigid, straight lines. Each unit – which contained a large open fireplace in spite of the warm climate – had a garden plot close to the nearby river, as 'the Rhodesian native is a keen agriculturalist and loves his bit of vegetable garden'.[70] Such projects were limited to the more skilled 'native' of Rhodesia, since it was considered 'wrong to force him to live in a "location" [designated for "raw natives"], but he may not live in the European quarter. Indeed, he could not afford to.' Under the guise of residential amelioration for a thin social stratum, this 'garden city' actually increased racial segregation, was carried out in a spirit of paternalism and social evolutionism, and was perceived as an 'experiment of transplanting African natives from huts to houses'.[71]

Why are these three examples of garden city plans for the indigenous populations in colonial southern Africa or in white settler states (excluding Lusaka) important to our collection? First, as recent research in colonial cultures of planning in white settler states shows, it was especially in these territories – being an extreme case of (internal) colonialism – that the management of race in the city had great symbolic and economic significance. Inherently violent and coercive, it was paramount to the success of the settler-colonial enterprise.[72] That is, the city was particularly viewed as a reflection of the state and as a metaphor for the territory. This is also explicit, though to a lesser extent, in Alain Sinou's chapter on French Sudan and in other chapters of this collection. Moreover, as recent research shows, 'modern planning is constituted within colonialism itself, and ... far from being merely an "export" of Britain, is the product of colonial relations'.[73] Being an ever-dynamic physical manifestation of colonial situations, where planning ideas and practices were circulated, spread, adapted or redesigned, colonial territories can be thus considered as 'laboratories of modernity' or 'experimental terrains'.[74]

A second issue that rises from these model garden city experiments, setting aside their paternalistic spirit, is that they were not intended exclusively for the white population. This is important since, from a reading of our first contributions dealing with French Africa, the reader might get the impression that expressions of *cité-jardin* within this context generally meant the creation of a green, attractive and prestigious environment by the colonial administration to house its employees. Indeed, Jelidi mentions a garden city plan for Morocco's indigenous population (chapter 1). Yet this impression changes in the fourth case of colonial Zanzibar discussed by Myers and Muhajir (chapter 4), where garden city notions were selectively enforced over parts of the local urban tapestry to reorient it towards imperial needs. Although white settler colonialism is not formally discussed in our collection,[75] explicit segregationist threads, of course, pass through all of it, as residential segregation on a racial basis is an inherent phenomenon in the modern colonial period. Very obvious in North and South Africa (and in certain parts of East Africa such as Kenya's White Highlands) due to historical and physical climatic factors that encouraged white settlement, it was noticeable even in West Africa.

In West Africa, considered for a long time as the 'white man's grave', the white presence was usually kept to a minimum and tended to concentrate in the main urban centres. In Ikoyi in colonial Lagos

(Nigeria), for example, the British authorities were preoccupied with the planting of tree-lined avenues, public parks and green playgrounds. This was also the case in Yaba, a mainland quarter off Lagos Island designated for civil servants, which was often referred to as a 'garden city'.[76] Ikoyi and Yaba were established when the local and expatriate communities had become, in the words of Lord Lugard about colonial Lagos, 'hopelessly intermixed'.[77] A parallel comment was made by a French official about 1900 Dakar on the eve of the establishment of the prestigious Plateau quarter, that 'too many indigenous habitations surround the European houses'.[78] This situation was due to a *laissez-faire* attitude in planning that characterised much of colonial urban Africa, yet could hardly be perceived in South Africa.

As to the case of Palestine in terms of segregation, the situation is much more intriguing. It is clear that during the late Ottoman period (until 1917) no segregationist measures were enforced within the urban sphere between the majority Arab population and its counterpart Jewish minority. At the same time, there were certainly restrictions over certain sectors regarding land use, with a precedence given to state land ownership and the religious *waqfs*. During this period and also during the following period of Mandate Palestine (until 1948), prominent separatist drives – regarding residential segregation, agricultural and industrial developments, etc. – were originated in the Jewish sector and especially in the growing Zionist community.

As is well exemplified in the three relevant chapters of Sonder, Katz and Bigon, and Zaidman and Kark (chapters 5–7), several personalities in the Zionist movement held views that were similar to Howard's in terms of social and communal urban regeneration. These were translated into the Jewish national vision in the Palestinian context. The Zionist activists showed a considerable interest in the garden city movement, and saw – in their imagination and in actual projects – the combination of the two movements as something that could enrich both. Today, from our post-Zionist perspective, there is a tendency to conceptualise the various forms of settlement in the Jewish sector as 'instruments' solely designed to serve the national Zionist project.[79] Yet, at least with regard to some of the reformist figures discussed, the attitude seemed to be more balanced: they felt great importance in establishing the ideal form of settlement. By applying the garden city model they tried to find the most 'efficient' settlement pattern for the Zionist enterprise in Palestine.

Apart from national pride, other motives were also involved, such as, in the case of early Tel Aviv, the sanitary argument. This was one of the explanations for the establishment of a separate, 'modern' suburb in contradistinction to the indigenous port city of Jaffa, with its

'Middle Eastern' tapestry and associated images in the eyes of the late nineteenth-century Jewish immigrants, mostly from Eastern Europe. Sanitary considerations were underlined in the regulations for the new quarter, including the installation of water and sewage systems, and keeping the streets clean and ventilated in terms of air circulation and sunlight penetration. However, here again the same question arises as with the previously mentioned colonial situations (assuming there was a sub-colonial reality created by the Jewish sector, within the formal Ottoman and British colonial frameworks): to what extent were the sanitary considerations grounded in contemporary reality? A quote from one of the novels of the renowned Israeli author Amos Oz might answer this question, referring to his grandmother:

> But the truth is that my grandmother died from an excess of hygiene, not a heart attack. Facts have a tendency to obscure the truth. It was cleanliness that killed her. Although the motto of her life in Jerusalem, 'The Levant is full of germs', may testify to an earlier, deeper truth than the demon of hygiene, a truth that was repressed and invisible. After all, Grandma Shlomit came from north-eastern Europe, where there were just as many germs as there were in Jerusalem, not to mention all sorts of other noxious things.[80]

Chapter outlines

This collection is divided into two parts according to geographic considerations, with a thematic rationale within each part. The first part is entitled 'Garden cities and colonial Africa', with the word 'and' implying a very flexible relationship between the concept and the areas covered, which include French North and West Africa, and British East Africa. The second part, 'Garden cities in colonial and mandate Palestine (Eretz Israel)', explores the various modes by which garden city concepts spread during the Ottoman and British periods.

How can we navigate through this series of studies, each of which examines in detail the relationship between garden city ideas and practices in a single colonial urban settlement (Dakar, Zanzibar, Tel Aviv), or reflects on several towns within a political sphere (Morocco, French Sudan and Senegal, Palestine)? While it seems unconventional to bring Africa and Palestine together, a closer look shows that apart from the actual geographical continuity between these South-Eastern spheres, there are many other common issues. Garden city visions and applications included various shared discourses, including ethno-racial (overt or hidden), sanitary and segregationist. The employment of garden city vocabulary was directly related to the imagery that accompanied such discourses. Social and cultural constructs against the 'hutting' phenomenon in Africa, or the 'Middle Eastern' city of Palestine, and the range of ambivalent images concerning vegetation in 'the tropics' ('lands of fevers and barbarity') or the Levant were all decisive in the domestication of a 'savage' or 'oriental' environment and the building of a civilised, modern urbanity opposed to that of the indigenous Other.

But the main reason for bringing Africa and Palestine together is their shared colonial past. At this point Georges Balandier's classic definition of the 'colonial situation' might assist us in its inherent inclusiveness, when translated from the socio-political realm to the spatial one. According to Balandier this 'situation' can be understood as the overall influence of the foreign regime on the local (African) societies, the expatriate communities and other involved groups, in most aspects of life – political, economic, social, religious, institutional and psychological – from individual everyday lives to the public level.[81] This understanding is flexible in respect of the agencies that shared this situation and were encapsulated by it, the national diversity of colonial regimes, and the variety of colonial experiences, levels of frictions and geographies (from 'white settler colonies' to 'colonies agricoles'). It can be also applied to the character of colonial urban planning. In addition, both political and geographic rationales guided us in the cases discussed: starting from the Middle East – French North Africa – we proceeded to sub-Saharan Africa through the same colonial power, that is, French West Africa. Then East Africa is discussed, through the British regime, and this connects us to the next part about Palestine through the same regime and the Islamic component (Swahili, Ottoman), and back to the Middle East.

In the first chapter of Part I, Charlotte Jelidi examines the conceptual symbolic usage made by different colonial agencies of the idea of the 'garden city' – or cité-jardin in its francophone variations – during the French Protectorate in Morocco. Tracing the genealogy of cité-jardin expressions and actual practices within the colonial urban framework of this territory, Jelidi points out the particular elements that were borrowed from the Howardian model and the British garden cities, and those that were rejected. In this process, designed to serve colonial ends per se, the French metropolitan channel of transmission could not be ignored. Moving from Morocco to sub-Saharan Africa, which was ranked lower in the French colonial order of preference, Dakar comes to the fore. Chapter 2 thus focuses on French Dakar, a chief colonising centre in West Africa, a federal capital which served as a model space. Expanding on differences and similarities in the conception and realisation of garden city schemes from late nineteenth-century Britain to early twentieth-century France in terms of cité-jardin, Liora Bigon shows that in interwar Dakar (Senegal), the practical and terminological usages of the *cité-jardin* served mainly to create a prestigious image for the designated residential quarters of administrative employees. As a result, unofficial class segregation within the expatriate society was created, as was unofficial racial segregation between the coloniser and the colonised populations.

Reaching beyond the regional background to the overall territory of French West Africa, Alain Sinou's chapter elaborates on the urban *plateaux* – the most privileged part of French colonial towns. Indeed, it is somewhat paradoxical to examine the urban space produced there, designated exclusively for Europeans, using a concept that was evolved for social housing by socialist politicians in France. If the question of producing social housing was not on the agenda, the natural environment in sub-Saharan Africa became the subject of many questions. Through an analysis of the creation of several urban areas reserved for 'whites' in French West Africa, and especially the government town of Koulouba in Bamako (present-day Mali), this chapter focuses on the role accorded to greenery there and how it came about. The extent of influence of the garden city concept is then assessed through the identification of the logic behind the spread of relevant urban models.

The final chapter of Part I, on Zanzibar, also constitutes a bridge to Part II, which deals with Palestine, with respect to one of the colonising frameworks involved, that is, British rule. It was the renowned British architect Henry Vaughan Lanchester who in 1923 wrote the first comprehensive town planning scheme for Zanzibar, the capital of the British Protectorate of Zanzibar. With Geddesian and garden city influences, Lanchester's plan has cast a shadow over planning policies there – a shadow which Garth Andrew Myers and Makame Ali Muhajir deal with in the light of contemporary planning in Zanzibar. They argue that there are significant similarities in land management and planning policies between Lanchester's ideas and those being implemented in present-day Zanzibar. This especially concerns planning associated with the ongoing Sustainable Management of Lands and Environment (SMOLE) programme. They also contend that, from Lanchester's time until the present, planning reforms have continued to be developed within a system that lacks the sort of communicative social dialogue that might allow for genuinely participatory, integrated planning.

We shall simply direct the attention of the reader here to several issues that recur in this part. These issues had immediate implications for the conception and realisation of the garden city idea, in spite of the presumed differences between each case. The paucity of economic resources of the colonial state and its clear order of preference was oriented towards exploitation of raw materials and agricultural products. This orientation, aside from contemporary racial prejudices, directed the limited investment in urban planning and residence allocation towards certain sectors, usually but not solely the expatriate population. Even where it engaged with indigenous patterns of settlement, colonial planning was exercised in an authoritative manner, using a range of arguments to achieve its Eurocentric ends. In this context the ends and interests of the colonial states were essentially anti-social, which clearly contradicts Howard's original agenda. As we shall see, segregation constituted a key component in using garden city rhetoric or planning models, normally but not necessarily in the form of prestigious quarters for privileged expatriates, supporting residential separation on a racial and/or ethnic basis.

Part II opens with an analysis of the role of garden city literary visions, none of which were realised, within the Zionist discourse. From this conceptual theme through an intermediate chapter that surveys the implementation of garden city schemes during the late Ottoman and the early British period, this part ends with a detailed examination of a particular case study: that of Tel Aviv. Thus in chapter 5 Ines Sonder discusses the most important German-Jewish literary writing on garden cities in Palestine in the early twentieth century. This is in light of the fact that the garden city idea was actually the most important town planning model adopted by Zionist planners and architects for the Jewish homeland in Palestine (Eretz Israel). Realised since the 1910s with the establishment of numerous Jewish garden suburbs on the outskirts of Palestinian towns and in new plans for urban expansion, this model was even applied to the layout of contemporary agricultural settlements. Sonder includes Theodore Herzl's vision of town planning and publications by Zionist planners and architects, among them Davis Trietsch, Wilhelm Stiassny and Alex Baerwald. Although never carried out, these visions reflected the beginning of modern Zionist town planning. With far-reaching social, political, economic and architectural implications, they were also partly influenced by well-known German architects and garden city planners. Moreover, this chapter reveals that town planning was not disregarded within the early Zionist movement, but was part of a comprehensive social concept in the building of a modern Jewish society in Palestine.

The aim of chapter 6 is to trace the reception of Howard's widely disseminated ideas in early twentieth-century Palestine and their influence on Ottoman-era urban development, particularly in Tel Aviv, Haifa, Tiberias and Jerusalem. Yossi Katz and Liora Bigon also offer some glimpses of garden city development during the British Mandate regime (1922–48), most notably in the 1920s and during the Second World War, not ignoring relevant developments within the contemporary Arab sector. This chapter draws heavily on primary sources and its contribution lies in the synoptic view it offers of various case studies by means of brief comparisons. In many respects it bridges the gap between the purely literary conceptualisations of the preceding chapter and the ensuing chapter, which presents the particular historical circumstances of the establishment of Tel Aviv as a garden city.

Zionist historiography, argue Miki Zaidman and Ruth Kark in chapter 7, has often referred to Ahuzat Bayit (the Jaffa neighbourhood from which Tel Aviv developed) as a unique phenomenon. Placing this 'unique phenomenon' within the context of universal ideas and trends, the authors link the early garden city variations in England (1904, 1906) and Ahuzat Bayit (1909), which they term a 'garden neighbourhood'. On the outskirts of Jaffa, this neighbourhood was established as a suburb with middle-class aspirations. These included class, ideological and ethnic segregation following the model of European middle-class suburbs and colonial models of separate residential areas for Europeans and the native population. However, local conditions and mechanisms for its establishment, in addition to concepts of the early Zionist movement which shared a similar ideological platform with the garden city movement, transformed Ahuzat Bayit into a unique local model for the development of suburban life in Palestine. This chapter therefore considers the contradictions between universal models and local conditions by explaining how application of the universal message of the garden city movement to the physical model of the building of Ahuzat Bayit created a guiding principle for all Jewish urban development in Palestine from 1909 until the end of British rule in 1948, and how this continues to exert its influence in current planning.

From a transnational perspective, the embracing of garden city ideas by the Zionist movement signifies two reciprocal 'flows'. The first 'flow' is from the national level to the global one. That is, the comprehensive adoption of British garden city models (channelled directly or indirectly) underlines Zionism's openness to the absorption of universal innovative directions, even though the latter are essentially disconnected from Hebraic history, or European (Ashkenazi) or Oriental (Sephardic) Jewish traditions. In this sense, Zionism, as a movement that originated within western European culture, brought the garden city ideas on to new terrain that could not be realised in Europe. This movement not only served as a host for urban innovations, but it also regarded itself as progressive, endowed with a universal message of improving the world.

The second transnational 'flow' is from the global to the national level: the use of a globally spread model for specific, site-related, national needs. In the process of the creation of a new Jewish national identity in Palestine there was a constant need to recruit new grand models, symbols and ideas. Garden city applications thus represented the building of an exemplary environment, both physically and morally. On the one hand, these applications – usually in the form of urban quarters – had a lot in common with Howardian notions in creating a strong sense of community, with public buildings at the centre of the settlement and involving relatively small residential plots. These aspects are very much different from those discussed in the colonial situations in the first part of this collection, which were clearly anti-social. On the other hand, we might perceive the garden city developments within the Jewish sector as a sub-colonial situation within the wider, formal colonial and Mandatory regime, in the sense that these developments were intended for the benefit of one sector only, generally disregarding the Arab indigenous sector. There is also something colonialist in the importation of garden city models and their accompanying imagery as a very deliberate and explicit contrast to the 'Middle Eastern city'. Nonetheless, these sub-colonial developments were not 'colonial' in the strict industrial-capitalist meaning, that is, an imperial occupation of an overseas territory for the economic benefit of a metropolitan country, involving the forced labour or military recruitment of the indigenous population.

Notes

1   Published in *Planning Perspectives*, 5 (1990), 23–37 (23).
2   A framework that was well defined and effectively challenged by Jennifer Robinson, who pointed to 'the geographical division of urban studies between urban theory, broadly focused on the West, and development studies, focused on places that were once called "third-world cities"'. Rather than being an innocent acknowledgement of difference, and 'apart from the value-laden historical meaning of these categorical ascriptions, the persistent alignment of a "theory"/"development" dualism with the "West"/"third world" division in urban studies, suggests otherwise'. Jennifer Robinson, 'Global and world cities: a view from off the map', *International Journal of Urban and Regional Research*, 26:3 (2002), 351–4 (351).
3   Ebenezer Howard, *Garden Cities of To-Morrow*, ed. Frederic J. Osborn, introductory essay by Lewis Mumford (London: Faber and Faber, 1970 [1902, 1946]). Originally titled *To-Morrow: A Peaceful Path to Real Reform* (London: Swan Sonnenschein, 1898).
4   Sidney W. Mintz, *Sweetness and Power: The Place of Sugar in Modern History* (New York: Penguin, 1985), p. xvii.
5   Stanley Buder, *Visionaries and Planners: The Garden City Movement and the Modern Community* (New York and Oxford: Oxford University Press, 1990), p. 134.
6   Buder, *Visionaries and Planners*, pp. 139, 140.
7   See, for instance, Stephen V. Ward, 'The garden city introduced', in Stephen V. Ward (ed.), *The Garden City: Past, Present and Future* (London: E & FN Spon, 1992), pp. 1–27 (2); Walter L. Creese, *The Search for the Environment: The Garden City Before and After* (Baltimore and London: Johns Hopkins University Press, 1992 [1966]), p. 1.

8 Some outstanding book-length publications in English, in chronological order, are Creese, *The Search for the Environment*; Buder, *Visionaries and Planners*; Peter Hall and Colin Ward, *Sociable Cities: The Legacy of Ebenezer Howard* (Chichester: John Wiley, 1998); Standish Meacham, *Regaining Paradise: Englishness and the Early Garden City Movement* (New Haven and London: Yale University Press, 1999); and Kermit C. Parsons and David Schuyler (eds), *From Garden City to Green City: The Legacy of Ebenezer Howard* (Baltimore and London: Johns Hopkins University Press, 2002). For Howard's biography, see Robert Beevers, *The Garden City Utopia: A Critical Biography of Ebenezer Howard* (London: Macmillan, 1988). Important book chapters in English feature in Gordon E. Cherry's publications, such as *Town Planning in Britain since 1900* (Oxford: Blackwell Publishers, 1996). See also relevant chapters in Kenneth Kolson, *Big Plans: The Allure and Folly of Urban Design* (Baltimore and London: Johns Hopkins University Press, 2001); Peter Hall, *Cities of Tomorrow: An Intellectual History of Urban Planning and Design in the Twentieth Century* (Oxford: Blackwell Publishers, 1996 [1988]). For a thorough survey of garden city historical developments within France, see Paul Rabinow, *French Modern: Norms and Forms of the Social Environment* (Cambridge, MA, and London: MIT Press, 1989).

9 A few book-length examples, in chronological order, are Frederick J. Osborn, *Green-Belt Cities: The British Contribution* (London: Faber and Faber, 1946); Ministry of Housing and Local Government, *The Green Belts* (London: Her Majesty's Stationery Office, 1962); Hazel Evans (ed.), *New Towns: The British Experience* (London: Charles Knight, 1972); College of Estate Management, *The Future of the Green Belt* (Occasional Papers in Estate Management, no. 5, 1974); Martin J. Elson, *Green Belts: Conflict Mediation in the Urban Fringe* (London: Heinemann, 1986); John Herington, *Beyond Green Belts: Managing Urban Growth in the 21th Century* (London: Jessica Kingsley, 1990).

10 See, for example, Hall and Ward, *Sociable Cities*; Parsons and Schuyler (eds), *From Garden City to Green City*.

11 Hall, *Cities of Tomorrow*, p. 6.

12 For a similar endeavour, currently in press, that covers the United States, England and western Europe until 1940 but also touches Russia, Brazil and Australia, see David Fishman, Jacob Tilove and Robert Stern, *Paradise Planned: The Garden Suburb and the Modern City* (New York: Monacelli Press, 2013).

13 For examples, see Garden Cities, *Fifty Years of Housing: The Story of Garden Cities, 1922–1972* (Pinelands: Garden Cities, 1972) – written in a colonialist manner; Marianne Guillet, 'Mythe et limits: garden city ou l'espace réinventé', *Egypte/Monde arabe*, 22 (1995), 123–42 (this publication is thematically rare even considering the literature in French); and John Collins, 'Lusaka: urban planning in a British colony, 1931–1964', in Gordon E. Cherry (ed.), *Shaping an Urban World* (London: Mansell, 1980), pp. 227–41. Titles such as 'Garden city in the sun', *Landscape Design*, 292 (2000), 45 (referring in this case to Nairobi's botanical garden) are, of course, only puns.

14 For instance, Miki Zaidman, 'Garden cities – the "Eretz-Israeli" version: Hebrew garden cities and suburbs in Palestine, 1900–1948' (PhD dissertation, the Hebrew University of Jerusalem, 2010) (in Hebrew). Ines Sonder wrote her PhD on 'Garden cities for Eretz Israel: Zionist urban visions from Theodor Herzl to Richard Kauffmann' (in German), which was published in 2005 as *Gartenstädte in Erez Israel. Zionistische Stadtplanungsvisionen von Theodor Herzl bis Richard Kauffmann* (Hildesheim and New York: Georg Olms Verlag). Zaidman and Sonder are both contributors to our collection. See also parts of Marina Epstein-Pliouchtch and Michael Levin, *Richard Kauffmann and the Zionist Project* (Tel Aviv: Hakibbutz Hameuhad, forthcoming) (in Hebrew), and Zvi Efrat, *The Israeli Project: Building and Architecture, 1948–1973*, 2 vols (Tel Aviv: Tel Aviv Museum of Art, 2004) (in Hebrew) – though the latter encyclopaedic source covers the post-independence period. An exceptional English booklet is Gilbert Herbert and Silvina Sosnovsky, *The Garden City as Paradigm: Planning on the Carmel, 1919–1923* (Haifa: Technion, 1986).

15 Richard Drayton, *Nature's Government* (New Haven, CT, and London: Yale University Press, 2000), pp. xiii–iv.
16 Jane Jacobs, *Edge of Empire: Post Colonialism and the City* (London and New York: Routledge, 1996); Felix Driver and David Gilbert (eds), *Imperial Cities: Landscape, Display and Identity* (Manchester: Manchester University Press, 1999).
17 Edward W. Said, *Culture and Imperialism* (New York: Knopf, 1993), p. 15.
18 Janet Abu-Lughod, 'Tale of two cities: the origins of modern Cairo', *Comparative Studies in Society and History*, 7:4 (1965), 429–57 (429).
19 Robert K. Home, 'The influence of colonial government upon urbanisation in Nigeria' (PhD dissertation, University of London, 1974), p. 15.
20 Alain Sinou, *Comptoirs et villes colonials du Sénégal: Saint-Louis, Gorée, Dakar* (Paris: Karthala, ORSTOM, 1993), p. 5.
21 John Parker, *Making the Town: Ga State and Society in Early Colonial Accra* (Oxford: James Currey, 2000), p. xix.
22 See Odile Goerg, 'Villes, circulations et expressions culturelles', *Afrique et histoire*, 5 (2006), 9–14 (9). See also Laurent Fourchard, 'Les Villes en Afrique, histoire et sciences sociales', *Afrique et histoire*, 5 (2006), 267–78 (267).
23 Catherine Coquery-Vidrovitch, 'The process of urbanization in Africa (from its origins to the beginning of independence)', *African Studies Review*, 34:1 (1991), 1–98 (18). Some typical anglophone examples are Pauline H. Baker, *Urbanization and Political Change: The Politics of Lagos 1917–1967* (Berkeley: University of California Press, 1974); Josef Gugler, *Urbanisation and Social Change in West Africa* (Cambridge: Cambridge University Press, 1978). Some typical francophone examples are Assane Seck, *Dakar: métropole ouest-africaine* (Dakar: IFAN, 1970); Jean Delcourt, *Naissance et croissance de Dakar* (Dakar: Clairafrique, 1960s).
24 This latter distinction is based on Paul Maylam, 'Explaining the apartheid city: 20 years of South African urban historiography', *Journal of Southern African Studies*, 21:1 (1995), 19–38 (20).
25 Coquery-Vidrovitch, 'The process', p. 19.
26 Cited from Catherine Coquery-Vidrovitch, *The History of African Cities South of the Sahara: From the Origins to Colonization*, trans. Mary Baker (Princeton, NJ: Markus Wiener Publishers, 2005), p. x. She referred to David Anderson and Richard Rathbone (eds), *Africa's Urban Past* (Oxford: James Currey, 2000).
27 Steven J. Salm and Toyin Falola (eds), *African Urban Spaces in Historical Perspective* (Rochester, VT: University of Rochester Press, 2005).
28 In this partial list only book-length studies are mentioned, in chronological order.
29 Anthony D. King, *Colonial Urban Development: Culture, Social Power and Environment* (Henley and Boston: Routledge and Kegan Paul, 1976); Anthony D. King, *The Bungalow: The Production of a Global Culture* (New York and Oxford: Oxford University Press, 1995 [1984]); Jacobs, *Edge of Empire*; Brenda Yeoh, *Contesting Space: Power and the Built Environment in Colonial Singapore* (Oxford: Oxford University Press, 1996); Robert Home, *Of Planting and Planning: The Making of British Colonial Cities* (London: E & FN Spon, 1997); Parker, *Making the Town*; Mark Crinson, *Modern Architecture and the End of Empire* (Aldershot: Ashgate, 2003); and Garth Andrew Myers, *Verandahs of Power: Colonialism and Space in Urban Africa* (New York: Syracuse University Press, 2003).
30 For instance, Rabinow, *French Modern*; David Prochaska, *Making Algeria French: Colonialism in Bône, 1870–1920* (Cambridge: Cambridge University Press, 1990); Gwendolyn Wright, *The Politics of Design of French Colonial Urbanism* (Chicago and London: University of Chicago Press, 1991); Maurice Culot and Jean-Marie Thiveaud (eds), *Architecture française outre mer* (Liège: Pierre Mardaga, 1992); Sinou, *Comptoirs et villes colonials*; Zeynep Çelik, *Urban Forms and Colonial Confrontations: Algiers under French Rule* (Berkeley and Los Angeles: University of California Press, 1997); Patricia Morton, *Hybrid Modernities: Architecture and Representation at the 1931 Colonial Exposition, Paris* (Cambridge, MA: MIT Press, 2000); Laurent Fourchard, *De la ville coloniale a la cour africaine: espaces, pouvoirs et sociétés a Ouagadougou et a Bobo-Dioulasso (Haute Volta)* (Paris: l'Harmattan,

2001); Institut national du patrimoine, *Architecture coloniale et patrimoine: l'expérience française* (Paris: Somogy, 2005); and Thomas Shaw, *Irony and Illusion in the Architecture of Imperial Dakar* (Lampeter: Edwin Mellen Press, 2006).

31   Nezar AlSayyad (ed.), *Forms of Dominance: On the Architecture and Urbanism of the Colonial Enterprise* (Aldershot: Avebury, 1992); Jacques Soulillou (ed.), *Rives colonials: architecture de Saint-Louis à Douala* (Paris: Parenthèses, ORSTOM, 1993); Catherine Coquery-Vidrovitch and Odile Goerg (eds), *La Ville européenne outre mers: un modèle conquérant?* (Paris: l'Harmattan, 1996); Joe Nasr and Mercedes Volait (eds), *Urbanism: Imported or Exported?* (Chichester: John Wiley, 2003); and Salm and Falola, *African Urban Spaces.*

32   The historiographic awareness and the initiative behind this book stem directly from Liora Bigon's PhD dissertation (University of Manchester), published as *A History of Urban Planning in Two West African Colonial Capitals: Residential Segregation in British Lagos and French Dakar (1850–1930)* (Lewiston, NY: Edwin Mellen Press, 2009).

33   Spiro Kostof, *The City Shaped: Urban Patterns and Meanings through History* (New York: Bullfinch Press, 2009 [1993]), p. 9.

34   Kostof, *The City Shaped*, p. 25.

35   Jamie Peck and Adam Tickell, 'Neoliberalizing space', *Antipode*, 34:3 (2002), 380–404; Jamie Peck and Nik Theodore, 'Variegated capitalism', *Progress in Human Geography*, 31:6 (2007), 731–72; Jamie Peck, Nik Theodore and Neil Brenner, 'Neoliberal urbanism: models, moments, mutations', *SAIS Review*, 29:1 (2009), 49–66; Neil Brenner, Jamie Peck and Nik Theodore, 'After neoliberalization?', *Globalizations*, 7:3 (2010), 327–45; Neil Brenner, Jamie Peck and Nik Theodore, 'Variegated neoliberalization: geographies, modalities, pathways', *Global Networks*, 10:2 (2010), 182–222.

36   Peck et al., 'Neoliberal urbanism', p. 65.

37   Quoted from Peck et al., 'Neoliberal urbanism', p. 50. See also Jamie Peck, 'Creative moments: working culture, through municipal socialism and neoliberal urbanism', in Eugene McCann and Kevin Ward (eds), *Mobile Urbanism: Cities and Policymaking in the Global Age* (Minneapolis: University of Minnesota Press, 2011), pp. 41–70.

38   Brenner et al., 'Variegated neoliberalization'.

39   For a broader discussion on such discontent, see for instance Jennifer Robinson, *Ordinary Cities: Between Modernity and Development* (London: Routledge, 2006).

40   John Allan and Allan Cochrane, 'Beyond the territorial fix: regional assemblages, politics and power', *Regional Studies*, 41 (2007), 1161–75 (1171); Eugene McCann and Kevin Ward, 'Introduction. Urban assemblages: territories, relations, practices, and power', in McCann and Ward (eds), *Mobile Urbanism*, pp. xiii–xxv; Eugene McCann, 'Veritable inventions: cities, policies, and assemblage', *Area*, 43:2 (2011), 143–7.

41   Eugene McCann and Kevin Ward, 'Relationality/territoriality: toward a conceptualization of cities in the world', *Geoforum*, 41 (2010), 175–84; Eugene McCann and Kevin Ward, 'Assembling urbanism: following policies and "studying through" the sites and situations of policy-making', *Environment and Planning A*, 44:1 (2012), 42–51. See also Jennifer Robinson, 'Cities in a world of cities: the comparative gesture', *International Journal of Urban and Regional Research*, 35 (2011), 1–23; Allan and Cochrane, 'Beyond the territorial fix'.

42   McCann and Ward, 'Relationality/territoriality', p. 176.

43   Quoted from Janine Wedel, Cris Shore, Gregory Feldman and Stacy Lathrop, 'Toward an anthropology of public policy', *Annals of the American Academy of Political and Social Science*, 600 (2005), 30–51 (40). Based on Cris Shore and Susan Wright, 'Policy: a new field of anthropology', in Cris Shore and Susan Wright (eds), *Anthropology of Policy: Critical Perspectives on Governance and Power* (London: Routledge, 1997), pp. 3–39 (p. 14). Directly inspired by McCann and Ward, 'Assembling urbanism', p. 47.

44   'The question historians are now asking is: has history as handmaiden to the nation state distorted or limited our understanding of the past? And if so, can a transnational approach help develop new and more adequate forms of historical writing?' Ann Curthoys and Marilyn Lake, 'Introduction', in Curthoys and Lake

(eds), *Connected Worlds: History in Transnational Perspective* (Canberra: E Press, 2005), pp. 5–20 (p. 5).

45 Pierre-Yves Saunier, 'Transnational', in Akira Iriye and Pierre-Yves Saunier (eds), *The Palgrave Dictionary of Transnational History from the Mid-19th Century to the Present Day* (Basingstoke: Macmillan, 2009), pp. 1047–55 (p. 1054).

46 Akira Iriye and Pierre-Yves Saunier, 'Introduction: the professor and the madman', in Iriye and Saunier (eds), *The Palgrave Dictionary of Transnational History*, pp. xvii–x (p. xviii).

47 Saskia Sassen, *Territory, Authority, Rights: From Medieval to Global Assemblages* (Princeton, NJ: Princeton University Press, 2006), pp. 132–40.

48 Inspired by Roy's definition of 'neoliberalism' – Ananya Roy, 'Conclusion, postcolonial urbanism: speed, hysteria, mass dreams', in Ananya Roy and Aihwa Ong (eds), *Wordling Cities: Asian Experiments and the Art of Being Global* (Chichester: Blackwell, 2011), pp. 307–35 (311). And also Ananya Roy and Nezar AlSayyad, 'Prologue/dialogue, urban informality: crossing borders', in Roy and AlSayyad (eds), *Urban Informality: Transnational Perspectives from the Middle East, Latin America, and South Asia* (Lanham, MD: Lexington Books, 2004), pp. 1–6.

49 Saunier, 'Transnational', pp. 1047–55.

50 Mercedes Volait, 'European Architecture beyond Europe: Sharing Research Knowledge on Dissemination Processes, Historical Data and Material Legacy (19th–20th centuries)', proposal for a new COST Action supported by the European Council for Research and Innovation (Brussels: European Cooperation in Science and Technology, 2009).

51 Volait, 'European Architecture beyond Europe', p. 3.

52 Raymond F. Betts, *Uncertain Dimensions: Western Overseas Empires in the Twentieth Century* (London: Oxford University Press, 1985), Introduction.

53 Timothy Mitchell, *Colonising Egypt* (Berkeley: University of California Press, 1988), pp. 161, 177–9.

54 Jennifer Robinson, 'A perfect system of control? State power and "native locations" in South Africa', *Environment and Planning*, 8:2 (1990), 135–62. See also David Simon, 'South African cities in the 1980s: the political economy of urban change', *African Urban Studies*, 21 (1985), 81–94. As Simon notes, 'this perverse exercise in social engineering never succeeded entirely' (p. 82).

55 Raymond F. Betts, 'Imperial designs: French colonial architecture and urban planning in sub-Saharan Africa', in J. G. Wesley (ed.), *Double Impact* (London: Greenwood Press, 1985), pp. 191–207 (pp. 192, 194–5).

56 Home, 'Town planning and garden cities'.

57 Myers, *Verandahs of Power*, p. 67.

58 Home, 'Town planning and garden cities', p. 25.

59 The conventional research states that the Ottomans made no contribution to urban planning in the Syrian provinces (Lebanon, Syria, Palestine and Transjordan) and that it was the British who introduced it to Palestine. See, for example, Ruth Kark, *Jerusalem: Planning and By-Laws (1855–1930)* (Jerusalem: Magnes Press, 1991), pp. 58–9. However, recent research argues that spatial planning was a local priority to late Ottoman rule there. See Salim Tamari, 'Confessionalism and public space in Ottoman and colonial Jerusalem', in Diane E. Davis and Nora Libertun de Duran (eds), *Cities and Sovereignty: Identity Politics in Urban Spaces* (Bloomington: Indiana University Press, 2011), pp. 59–82.

60 Home, 'Town planning and garden cities', p. 25.

61 As to the case of French Morocco, discussed here by Jelidi in chapter 1, its colonial situation was not so harsh or extreme by comparison with French Algeria, regarded for instance as *France d'outre mer*. As to the complicated case of Palestine, though there are scholarly arguments for an internal 'white settler' 'colonialism of refugees' or a 'colonial present' – see for instance, the writing of Oren Yiftachel or Sofia Shwayri – these are less relevant for the time span discussed in this volume, as until 1948 the colonial framework was clearly Ottoman and then British.

62 Alan Mabin and Dan Smit, 'Reconstructing South Africa's cities? The making of

urban planning 1900–2000', *Planning Perspectives*, 12 (1997), 193–223 (p. 196).

63 Alan Mabin, 'Comprehensive segregation: the origins of the Group Areas Act and its planning apparatuses', *Journal of Southern African Studies*, 18:2 (1992), 405–29 (p. 415). See also Mabin's '"Doom at one stroke of the pen": planning and Group Areas, 1935–1955', paper presented at the History Workshop of the University of the Witwatersrand, Johannesburg, 6–10 February 1990, pp. 1–36.

64 Mabin and Smit, 'Reconstructing South Africa's cities?', p. 198; Home, 'Town planning and garden cities', pp. 28–31.

65 The celebrated notion of 'sanitation syndrome' with reference to colonial biopolitical struggles was firstly coined by Maynard Swanson in 'The sanitation syndrome: bubonic plague and urban native policy in the Cape Colony, 1900–1909', *Journal of American History*, 18 (1977), 387–410. We borrowed the term 'biopolitical struggle' from Sharad Chari, 'State racism and biopolitical struggle: the evasive commons in twentieth-century Durban, South Africa', *Radical History Review*, 108 (2010), 73–90. Chari borrowed it from Foucault, but elaborated into the colonial context, an aspect missed by Foucault. For its expressions in sub-Saharan Africa with relation to residential segregation, see Philip Curtin, 'Medical knowledge and urban planning in tropical Africa', *American Historical Review*, 90:3 (1985), 594–613; Bigon, *A History of Urban Planning*. For similar expressions beyond Africa (e.g. India), see King, *Colonial Urban Development*.

66 Garden Cities, *Fifty Years of Housing*.

67 Mabin and Smit, 'Reconstructing South Africa's cities?', pp. 198–9, 202.

68 Carole Rakodi, 'Colonial urban planning in Northern Rhodesia and its legacy', *Third World Planning Review*, 8 (1986), 193–218; Collins, 'Lusaka', in Cherry (ed.), *Shaping an Urban World*, pp. 227–41; Home, 'Town planning and garden cities'.

69 Myers, *Verandahs of Power*, pp. 55–75.

70 J. W. P. Logan, 'Garden cities for Africa', *Town and Country Planning*, 4:13 (1935), 26–8.

71 Logan, 'Garden cities for Africa', p. 27.

72 Penelope Edmonds, *Urbanizing Frontiers: Indigenous Peoples and Settlers in Nineteenth-Century Pacific Rim Cities* (Vancouver: University of British Columbia Press, 2010), p. 239.

73 Libby Porter, *Unlearning the Colonial Cultures of Planning* (Farnham: Ashgate, 2010), p. 3.

74 Porter, *Unlearning the Colonial Cultures*, p. 43; Ann Laura Stoler, *Race and the Education of Desire: Foucault's History of Sexuality and the Colonial Order of Things* (Durham, NC: Duke University Press, 1995), p. 15; Rabinow, *French Modern*, pp. 288–91; Wright, *The Politics of Design*, pp. 1–2.

75 See note 61.

76 National Archives of Nigeria, Ibadan (NAI), Com. Col. I, 356, vol. 1, European reservation, Ikoyi, 1927–29; and NAI, CSO 26, 11032, Additional recreation ground for Lagos African community, 1938.

77 Quoted from F. D. Lugard, *Lugard and the Amalgamation of Nigeria: A Documentary Record*, compiled and introduced by A. H. M. Kirk-Greene (London: Frank Cass, 1968), p. 90.

78 Claude Faure, *Histoire de la presqu'île du Cap Vert et des origines de Dakar* (Paris: Larose, 1914), p. 164 (our translation).

79 See, for instance, Mark Levine, 'Globalization, architecture, and town planning in a colonial city: the case of Jaffa and Tel Aviv', *Journal of World History*, 18:2 (2007), 171–98; Oren Yiftachel, 'From Sharon to Sharon: spatial planning and separation regime in Israel/Palestine', *Hagar*, 10:1 (2010), 73–107.

80 Amos Oz, *A Tale of Love and Darkness*, trans. Nicholas de Lange (London: Vintage Books, 2004), p. 32.

81 Georges Balandier, 'The colonial situation: a theoretical approach', in Immanuel Wallerstein (ed.), *Social Change: The Colonial Situation* (New York: John Wiley, 1966), p. 45.

PART ONE

Garden cities and colonial Africa

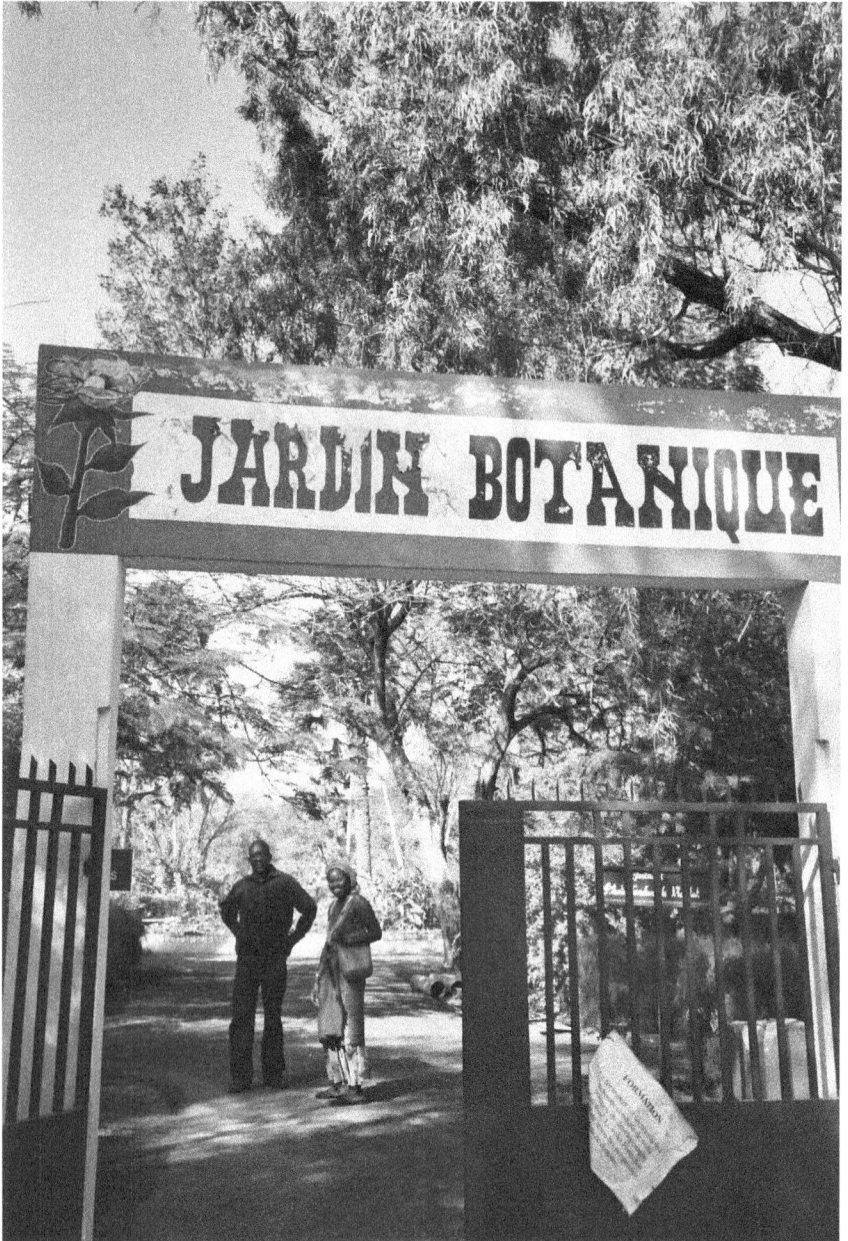

Hann Botanical Gardens, Dakar, Senegal. A combination of experimental gardens and a forestry park during colonial times, used, among other things, for the growing of imported and local species of trees for Dakar's avenues.

CHAPTER ONE

Symbolic usage of the 'garden city' concept during the French Protectorate in Morocco: from the Howardian model to garden housing estates[†]

Charlotte Jelidi

The expression *cité-jardin* ('garden city') was widely used[1] by colonial architects, urban planners, political leaders and property developers as well as by visitors and writers in Morocco during the French Protectorate (1912–56). The expression appeared at first in official circles, where it referred to most plans of *villes nouvelles*. These were established in French overseas territories during the colonial period, especially in Indo-China, Madagascar and North Africa, alongside indigenous 'traditional' towns. These *villes nouvelles* were designed primarily for the expatriate population, and the latest advances in modern urban planning were systematically applied. Indigenous cities not only remained virtually untouched by colonial planning schemes, but also experienced a process of preservation in an Orientalist spirit.[2]

In Morocco, the *villes nouvelles* were established under the aegis of the first Resident-General, Louis-Hubert Lyautey (1854–1934). From his rich military background in Indo-China and Madagascar, Lyautey developed strong pragmatist views concerning colonised populations, views that were crystallised in the urban strategy he promoted. Within this urban framework, the term *cité-jardin* had been used contemporarily to denote certain residential quarters within the *villes nouvelles* of Casablanca, Rabat, Fez or Marrakech. These residential quarters were situated on verdant terrain and consisted generally of one- or two-level homes built along curved streets. The street outline was designed to give a picturesque character to these areas, a quality which was often sought for by designers. Sometimes the expression *cité-jardin* was used to denote an entire *ville nouvelle*.

While inspired by English garden city ideas of the early twentieth century, the French colonial urban planners distanced themselves from the model defined by Ebenezer Howard, thus contributing to what can be regarded as an actual semantic divergence. This chapter aims to trace the means through which the notion of the garden city was transmitted – and above all distorted – from England to Morocco, through France, and more particularly through its Musée Social. Placing the burgeoning field of town planning at the top of its priorities list, the latter institution served as a live platform for the meeting of professionals of varied backgrounds – from social scientists to political reformers. Next, we shall examine how the *cités-jardins* were constructed in the course of the Protectorate, in terms of both the perceptual and the formal, actual plan. We will point out elements that the architects of the Protectorate chose to borrow from the Howardian model and the British garden cities, namely, the spatial relations within the built-up residential area, or the 'zoning' system; the special attention paid to landscape considerations in suburban planning; the preoccupation with the urban picturesque; and the use of abundant vegetation within the framework of planning.

Garden cities, the Protectorate's urban planners and the Musée Social

The concept of the garden city, which inspired the architects and urban planners who designed Morocco's *villes nouvelles* during the first years of the French Protectorate, emerged in the late nineteenth century. At that time, many English industrialists, paternalists and philanthropists laid out, usually on a higher tract of land by the side of their factories, cottages for their employees. These were aimed at providing more pleasant living conditions. Port Sunlight, established in 1895 by a soap manufacturer near Liverpool, and Bournville, near Birmingham, built by a chocolate factory owner,[3] were the precursors of the garden city as theorised by Ebenezer Howard in 1898. His ideal city – extending over 2,400 hectares with a capacity for 30,000 inhabitants – was an autonomous town that provided for all its inhabitants' needs: cultural facilities, sports installations, leisure areas, public parks etc. Howard's proposition was to create self-sufficient towns with low-level construction erected along circular, tree-lined boulevards. According to Howard, the garden city must be encircled by a vast cordon of agricultural land so as to ensure its total isolation and protection from possible suburban expansion and other peripheral land uses.

Starting in 1903, Howard set out to apply his urban principles, and these were realised in Letchworth garden city, about 60 km north of London.[4] Letchworth's plans were drawn up by the architect and urban planner Richard Barry Parker (1867–1947) and the engineer-planner Raymond Unwin (1863–1940). They were both inspired by the Howardian model[5] and were also deeply influenced by Camillo Sitte and his sense for the picturesque, preached in his 1902 work *Der städtebau nach seinen Künsterischen Grünsätzen.*[6] The latter suggested the theory that the informal principles of urban composition applied during the Middle Ages called for further exploration. Sitte's theories had Austrian, German and Finnish influences and spread in Britain just as the garden city idea was being conceived; they also intersected with the thirst for environmental beauty that reached its peak there in the 1890s.

Devoid of architectural details in matters of style and form, Howard's written works and the application of his ideas advocated architectural diversity and enabled architectural freedom. His general ideas, as well as the opportunity to embrace a particular aesthetic framework on the regional level, enjoyed immense success in Europe and the United States. Sitte's doctrine was introduced and made popular in France by Georges Benoit-Lévy (1880–1971),[7] a young journalist and a jurist who visited England in 1903, and was appointed by the Musée Social to study the garden city.[8] The results of Benoit-Lévy's work were published upon his return to France in professional journals, and later in a book published in 1904.[9]

Under the auspices of the French Garden Cities Association (l'Association Française des Cités-Jardins), founded by Benoit-Lévy in 1903, the development of a new urban model was promoted, a hygienic industrial town, or 'at least a model quarter', as he proposed for 'the part of the 200 hectares ... that are left available ... towards the northern and western fringe of Paris' municipal area'.[10] He did not focus on constructing self-sufficient towns, but rather on creating healthy and well-equipped suburban quarters for labourers, in the vicinity of the industries where they worked. This deviation from the original garden city notion steadily became more and more noticeable. From the first decade of the twentieth century, the term *cité-jardin* began to be employed by public authorities, urban planners and entrepreneurs in France. Distanced from Howard's doctrine, the term was used to denote new urban quarters, often devoid of factories but where vegetation was present.

The *cités-jardins* that flourished in Morocco under the French Protectorate showed exemplary evidence of the semantic misappropriation of the original idea. In Morocco, this misappropriation was not only a prerogative of property developers in their desire to make their housing projects more tempting and sellable by associating them with seductive vocabulary. In fact, the colonial administration, in its concern to offer an attractive image of the *villes nouvelles* that were newly founded under its initiative, used the term *cité-jardin* regularly as well.

Jean-Claude Nicolas Forestier (1861–1930), followed by Henri Prost (1874–1959), were among the chief urban designers and planners of Morocco's *villes nouvelles* who introduced the notion of *cité-jardin*. Their inspiration largely came from contemporary metropolitan debates concerning the birth of town planning as a scientific discipline. A landscape gardener and the head of the Department of Public Promenades and Plantations (Service des Promenades et des Plantations) of the city of Paris for twenty-six years, Forestier had been summoned to Morocco on the recommendation of the General Secretary of the Protectorate, Paul Tirard. He was the first professional to work on the *villes nouvelles* project, appointed by the Minister of Foreign Affairs to study 'areas available for the planning and establishment of – inside and around the more prominent towns of Morocco, from the present time and in provision for future urban development – public promenades (*promenades*) and public gardens'.[11]

Upon completing this mission, Forestier had managed to convince Henri Prost to create development plans for Morocco's *villes nouvelles*, advised by Georges Risler, the president of the section of urban and rural hygiene of the Musée Social. A professional expert, a French-registered architect (DPLG) and a receiver of the Grand Prix de Rome (1902),[12] Prost was renowned for winning the 1910 competition for the extension of Antwerp. Arriving in Casablanca in May 1914 to take up a three-month appointment, Prost was in charge of the study of plans for the *villes nouvelles* that Lyautey so desired to build. He stayed in Morocco until 1922, where he became the head of the Special Department of Architecture (service Spécial d'Architecture) and also the head of the Department of Town Planning (service des Plans de Villes).

Although each had undergone different training and experienced a different professional path, Forestier and Prost had very profound affinities. In 1911 they contributed towards the creation of the French Society of Architect-Town Planners (la Société Française des Architectes-Urbanistes, or SFAU), which was renamed in 1919 as the French Society of Town Planners (Société Française des Urbanistes, or SFU). Its objective was the establishment of a registry of documentary records, offering a framework for discussions for professionals in urban planning as well as creating an international network of specialists.

Above all, Forestier and Prost were both active members in the section of urban and rural hygiene of the Musée Social. Established in 1889, and finally inaugurated in May 1894, the Musée Social was at the time a documentation centre and a place for discussion on such diverse themes as work and industry, agriculture, teaching and health. The section on urban and rural hygiene of the Musée Social which treated relative, dialectic questions in urban planning was established in January 1908 for 'the amelioration of the material and moral conditions of the workers'.[13] In France, as well as in its overseas colonial territories, members of this section promoted the requirement, for French settlements of more than 10,000 inhabitants, of establishing a development plan. This plan, also called the PAEE, was aimed at beautification (*embellissement*) and extension. It was institutionalised by the Cornudet Law, passed in 1919,[14] whose formulation the Musée Social pioneered.[15]

The members of the Musée debated the most relevant contemporary questions within the urban planning profession, most notably the issue of *cités-jardins*. During the meeting of 10 July 1909, the members recognised the need for documenting and learning more about garden cities abroad, especially in Europe.[16] In the following year, Georges Risler wrote a memorandum on the open spaces in large French cities and on the *cités-jardins*.[17] The concept was thus debated. Still, the Howardian model was not imported in the strict sense; rather, it was adapted to the metropolitan environment. The *cités-jardins* planned in France consisted generally of simple residential lots composed of housing units for the local authorities, inserted within an abundant natural environment and dotted with numerous amenities (e.g., school, infirmary and commercial centre as well as recreation facilities).

This was notably attested in the realisations of *cités-jardins* in the period between the two world wars, initiated by the Office for Inexpensive Housing of the Seine Department (L'Office Public des Habitations à Bon Marché du Département de la Seine). The municipal area of this department, established in the 1790s, encompassed Paris and its immediate suburbs, while the office was created on 23 December 1912, with the backing of Henri Sellier (1883–1943). A socialist revolutionary, a pragmatist and an influential figure in the contemporary realisation of *cités-jardins à la française*, Sellier strove, through the application of sanitary considerations in planning, for the regeneration of the urban fabric and the amelioration of the housing conditions of underprivileged populations.[18]

Therefore, upon its arrival in Morocco, this model had already undergone many alterations. In the same manner, the term *cité-jardin* was sometimes used in Morocco in a general way, to describe a *ville nouvelle* in its totality. As we shall see below, in practice urban planners regarded the *cités-jardins* as housing schemes, borrowing some notions from the metropolitan models and readapting them to the new context that was coming into being in colonial Morocco.

Zoning and the Moroccan cité-jardin

Thanks to methodical processes in the burgeoning field of modern planning, the French colonial authorities in Morocco afforded their *villes nouvelles* the best possible conditions of public health, aesthetics and amenities. They hoped thereby to spare their towns the problems of air pollution and slums – problems that were well recognised in the great metropolitan centres of Europe as early as the mid-nineteenth century. Notably, the basis of such planning was the zoning system. While most members of the Musée Social between 1907 and 1912[19] seemed sceptical of this principle, Forestier, and later Prost, pioneers in rational urbanism, recommended its use.

Forestier and Prost proposed functional and morphologically well-designed zoning plans, all the while bearing in mind the important role of sanitary considerations in the planning of the future city alongside the quality of the urban landscape – that is, public health considerations went side by side with aesthetic ones. The *villes nouvelles* created under the Protectorate were all subject to this zoning system, based on the rational organisation of activities – a zone for residence and/or commerce, an industrial quarter, a recreation zone, the cantonment or military *casernes*, in addition to an administrative quarter in the most important towns. Furthermore, there was a spatial partition according to volumetric units, such as in a sector of villas or a sector of apartment buildings. Each of these zones was subject to different legislation, in this case a list of specifications (*cahier des charges*) adapted to the architectural typology reserved for the sector. The sectors dedicated to villas were generally those that carried the title *cité-jardin* on the designs proposed by Henri Prost. For Fez, for instance, he presented the basic principles of zoning for the *villes nouvelles* around 1915.[20] In the first plan applied by Prost in Fez, two sectors were designed for the expatriate population: the first consisted of villas and was named *cité-jardin*; the second, at once a residential and commercial quarter, was made up of apartment buildings.

The villa quarters were always planned so as to be situated at the margins of the *ville nouvelle*, that is, between the city centre and the countryside, as can be observed in Marrakech, Meknes and Fez. In the coastal cities, the villa quarters were situated between the city centre and the ocean. This is especially noticeable in the cases of Rabat and Casablanca. The aim was to offer a framework of agreeable landscapes for future buyers, as shown below. This formal arrangement also sought to respect the physical distance of these *cités-jardins* from sectors reserved for potentially dangerous industries and other pollutants, as prescribed by Forestier and Prost.

In the midst of the villa lots called *cités-jardins*, the municipal authorities of the Protectorate devised another type of zoning, which concerned individuals, on the basis of social or socio-economic status. In fact, the sectors were generally divided into many parts, each one regrouping lots of different sizes and intended for a particular social group. The villa sector of Fez's *ville nouvelle* was thus divided by the Avenue de General Maurial. The zone labelled 'north', very close to the medina,[21] was allocated for the building of spacious villas for the upper class, mostly expatriates. The zone labelled 'south', on the other side of the Avenue, concentrated the villas built for the less privileged social class among the French. This social zoning was extended farther to the south, with the creation of a villa quarter on the Sefrou Road, destined for low-cost housing.

The social utopia of Howard – who gave his most renowned work the subtitle *A Peaceful Path to Real Reform* – and that of the English industrial paternalists who enthusiastically defended this model were not realised either in Fez or in the other Moroccan *villes nouvelles*. In practice, it was only partially realised in Britain itself, although the social question had become inherently problematic in the colonial setting. For the colonial authorities and their modern planning agendas, the term 'public' normally denoted strata within the expatriate population, whereas the indigenous population seemed virtually non-existent.

The establishment of Casablanca's new medina quarter might be considered as a rare example in which colonial planning involving *cités-jardins* was intended for the indigenous population and where colonial authorities showed a certain degree of consideration, albeit paternalistic and limited, toward indigenous residential needs. Albert Laprade, on the occasion of the inauguration of the new medina of Casablanca in 1916, placed the social dimension and the notion of *cité-jardin* side by side for the first time. Laprade (1883–1978), the architect of the Résidence Général of France in Rabat, joined Prost, Lyautey's town planner, in the construction of this new quarter. In fact, Laprade claimed that the new medina project 'consists of creating, out of all parts [of the site] behind the Sultan's palace, an immense indigenous *cité-jardin*, the Habous, an admired social project whose realisation was made possible thanks to monies from charitable foundations. A built-up area that is scrupulously Arab, charming and hygienically managed' (fig. 1.1).[22] This imagery became associated with the new medina and was embraced by observers, who saw an opportunity to present a positive vision of the French colonial project in Morocco. Similarly, the French writer Louis Thomas affirmed that Casablanca's new *cité-jardin* would be 'a model [offered] to [indigenous] voyagers

[41]

279   CASABLANCA — Nouvelle Ville Indigène - Quartier des Habous
(Cadet et Brion, arch. S. A. D. G.)

Figure 1.1 Casablanca's new indigenous quarter (medina). Architects: Laprade, Cadet and Brion.

from far-away settlements, cadis, and pashas of other towns [to imitate]'.[23]

In most cases, however, the Moroccan *cités-jardins* were actually housing estates composed of villas intended mainly for expatriates and were simply areas within the *villes nouvelles*.[24] They were far from being autonomous cities and had limited public amenities. They were normally only supplied with schools, places of worship – such as Catholic, Protestant and Orthodox churches, or synagogues – and, more sporadically, parks. These *cités-jardins* were therefore quite distant from the Howardian model, though a few features were emulated: the sense of the 'picturesque' and the idea of abundant greenery.

From garden city to garden housing development: the green area as a common point?

Lush vegetation was undoubtedly the feature of the English garden city that enjoyed the greatest success among the French colonial authorities in Morocco. Following the example of Ebenezer Howard, who affirmed 'the town and the country *must be married*, and out of this joyful union a new hope will spring forth, a new life, a new civilisation',[25] Resident-General Lyautey attributed a sanitary and thus social role to the *cités-jardins*. Moreover, Lyautey assigned such

[42]

importance to garden city ideals in the establishment of the French Residency in Rabat that he invited a landscape artist, rather than a town planner, to lay out the project – Jean-Claude Nicolas Forestier, who was also involved in the first study of land allocation for Morocco's *villes nouvelles*.

Forestier was mostly influenced by the American landscape architect Frederick Law Olmsted[26] and his Parkway model, in addition to the English garden city idea. In his work on large cities and park systems, published in 1906,[27] Forestier stressed the complementary nature of the park network and the organisation of transportation routes. In the following years, Forestier developed these ideas further and, as shown by Bénédicte Leclerc and Salvador Tarragò i Cid,[28] he insisted on the need to elaborate the park system and the city plan simultaneously.[29] Forestier pointed out a host of aesthetic, sanitary and social advantages of green areas, which, according to him, the industrial cities could not ignore. In the years after his experience in Morocco, he wrote that 'the garden ... has a beneficial social role; it must be replicated all over, an addition as necessary to the factory unit as to the castle ... the increasing activity and the temperature of the cities could not be felt but in the garden of relaxation'.[30] Conscious of economic necessities and limitations, he added that 'the cities ... could not consist of vast gardens, but of built-up areas where the city-like appearance must sometimes be concealed'.[31]

Henri Prost, who took over the planning of the *villes nouvelles* after Forestier, shared this vision and imposed – in any place where such settlements were maintained by the administrative services – the creation of parks, planted walkways or tree-lined boulevards.[32] In the villa sectors of the *villes nouvelles*, he prescribed the planting of vegetation in areas surrounding residential units. In general, these quarters were planned within green zones dominated by olive or palm trees and gardens. Property owners in these villa quarters were required, by law, to preserve the trees that decorated the plots of their residents. Destruction of a tree was permitted only in instances where it constituted a danger to the population, in which case the owners were obliged to replant a tree in another place in their garden. For instance, the expatriate residents of the grounds of the prestigious Aïn Khèmis villa quarter of Fez were required to plant at least four trees for each 100 sq m of non-built surface. Immediate compliance was necessary since the permit to move into the residence was not granted by the colonial authorities unless this condition had been satisfied (fig. 1.2).[33]

Marcel Zaborski, a landscape architect and the technical head of the Public Walks and Plantations Department of Morocco,[34] emphasised the difficulties of combining pragmatism and the urban policy of planting and replanting. According to him, 'the concern for artistic decoration is often overlooked in the concern for practical facilities. Of this permanent conflict between the planted and the built-up, and within this unequal battle between the planted ground [*pot de terre*] and the iron pot [*pot de fer*], it is the latter that is destined to get the preference.' Moreover, as Zaborski continued with regard to Rabat: 'but if a friendly voice is raised each time a plant is destroyed ... the *cité-jardin* of Rabat, threatened by the stone city of Rabat, might not be so irremediably condemned'.[35]

It was the omnipresence of vegetation, which was sometimes at risk as noted by Zaborski, that led some commentators to say that the Moroccan *villes nouvelles*, and not simply the reserved villa quarters, were *cités-jardins* by themselves. Maurice de Périgny, for instance, described the town of Fez as 'a large and beautiful city, a real *cité-jardin* like the sociologists had dreamt of, where the houses are elevated and naturally situated among the greenery, in its need for open air and free life'.[36] Similarly, regarding Rabat, Louis Villème affirmed: 'the Europeans could not resist the attractiveness of the *cité-jardin* created around the Residency, situated on a hill which dominates the Bou-Regreg Valley'.[37] This point of view was shared by another French commentator, Jean Eyquem, who claimed: 'In the Rabat of tomorrow, the *cité-jardin* will remain one of the principal touristic, intellectual and artistic centres.'[38]

Figure 1.2 Fez, Mohamed V Avenue and Clémenceau Square. The villa sector and its curved streets are shown at the right margin.

In spite of these assertions, however, the *villes nouvelles* were not garden cities, even though they emulated some of the characteristics of the latter. Chief among these characteristics was the abundance of vegetation, as we have seen, or rather attention to the picturesque, as favoured in Britain especially by Raymond Unwin and Barry Parker.

The picturesque: another point in common between English garden cities and Morocco's cités-jardins

The French colonial urban planners wished to confer a picturesque character on those housing schemes called *cités-jardins*, reflecting the principles previously laid out by garden city advocates in Britain and reported in France by Georges Benoit-Lévy. In fact, the list of specifications that legally regulated construction in the villa quarters was reminiscent of the recommendations made by the founders of Hampstead garden city.[39] According to that list, as was explained by Benoit-Lévy, 'special care should be taken not to place the houses in uniform lines but in a picturesque way, both from the viewpoint of the place that they occupy in space as well as from the architectural point of view'.[40]

In Morocco, the picturesque quality that was sought by the urban planners and designers was generated, first of all, through the curves laid out in the road system. In fact, not one road in Moroccan *cités-jardins* followed a straight line. The straight line was banished. The streets, zigzagging around the curves of the different ground levels over which they were built, strove to be as irregular as possible. They were thus distinct from the road systems of other quarters.

As well as this irregular street layout, the picturesque quality so desired in *cités-jardins* was achieved by the variety of architectural designs in these sectors. As mentioned above, Howard was preoccupied with the general plan of the garden city and with the socio-economic dimensions of the idea, so that the issue of architectural details was left open to any kind of interpretation. In effect, the question in the Moroccan *cité-jardin* quarters was not at all one of creating architectural unity of the kind that could be seen in the commercial areas of the city centre, in certain sectors reserved for expatriates and local elites – these were apartment buildings *à la* Beaux-Arts.[41] Nor was it about developing unified blocks of flats for the indigenous urban population like those duplicated in the new Moroccan quarters. Here, in the *cité-jardin* sectors, the motto was variety, a variety that constituted the essence of the picturesque – a quality which urban planners, architects and public authorities never ceased to wish for.

Conclusion

Under the French Protectorate of Morocco, the Howardian model underwent considerable distortion. Admittedly, garden city notions – transmitted through the filter of metropolitan France – constituted a source of influence for the colonial architects and urban planners in charge of the plans for the *ville nouvelle*. Certain principles were transplanted to these plans, such as rationalism; a separation between industrial and residential zones; the use of nature in the creation of green belts, parks and green zones allocated for sports and recreation; tree-lined avenues; low urban density; and picturesque settings. Yet the differences, in comparison to the garden city as it was conceived by Ebenezer Howard, were evident.

First, the *cité-jardin* in Morocco was not a satellite-city, but simply an area of the town itself. Secondly, the social dimension continued, to a certain extent, to play a role in Britain, even if its application was somewhat problematic in many cases. This dimension was felt either as a source of inspiration, open to a variety of realisations, or at least as an element that was 'in the air', even if not concretely applied. Yet in the case of Morocco, the social dimension was virtually non-existent, particularly with regard to the indigenous population. In the colonial situation, the communitarian idea that underlined the project of Ebenezer Howard was disregarded.[42]

The *cités-jardins* of Marrakech or Casablanca were inhabited, most often, by the expatriate commercial elites, and rarely by labourers or low-ranking functionaries. In other words, the social divisions within the expatriate society were further intensified, rather than being resolved by the *cités-jardins* quarters. The latter were in fact of a segregationist nature that contributed to social division within the colonial society, not to mention the further divisions between the colonial society and the colonised groups. The garden city model had some influence, but the use of its terminology was aimed, above all, at creating an exclusive imagery in order to attract potential purchasers to the estate, preferably from the higher classes. Moreover, it was intended to provide a positive urban image for the whole *ville nouvelle*, a desire that was fully supported by the colonial authorities.

The use of the notion of the *cité-jardin* in the French colonial context, divergent as it was from the original garden city idea, was not an exclusively Moroccan phenomenon.[43] It is interesting to note, for instance, that in Algiers this divergence took a very similar form. The legislation that accompanied the Danger Plan, drawn up in 1930, 'permitted the realisation of the principles of the garden city, as the French urban planners conceived it at the time, with curved paths in accordance with the site's physical texture, public gardens that bordered with collective facilities, tree-planted crossroads and landscaped squares'.[44]

Notes

† Translated from the French by Liora Bigon. Originally titled: 'L'Usage Symbolique du concept de cité-jardin durant le Protectorat Français au Maroc: du modèle howardien au lotissement-jardin'.

1   To avoid confusion we have used the term *cité-jardin* for the relevant urban metropolitan developments in France and for their overseas applications within the French-speaking colonial world. The term 'garden city' is used here in reference to Howard's original idea and its accompanying urban developments in contemporary England. (Editors)

2   For more on the planning politics of the *villes nouvelles*, especially in the French colonial North Africa context, and on Lyautey, see the Introduction. In this chapter, the original French term is not translated into 'new towns' in order to prevent confusion regarding the garden city literature in English. In this latter context, the term 'new towns' refers to post Second World War developments initiated in Britain with the 1946 New Town Act, when the central government intervened more directly to achieve planned decentralisation of the main urban centres. (Editors)

3   Henri Nitot, *Les Cités Jardins: etude sur le mouvement des cités jardins* (Paris: Presses Universitaires de France, 1924), pp. 12ff.

4   In 1919 Howard renewed this experience in the creation of Welwyn, after the plans of Louis de Soissons.

5   See Raymond Unwin, *Town Planning in Practice: An Introduction to the Art of Designing Cities and Suburbs* (London: T. Fischer Unwin, 1909). Originally translated into French in 1922 under the title *Plan des villes*, it has been newly translated as Étude *pratique des plans de villes, introduction à l'art de dessiner les plans d'aménagement et d'extension* (Marseille: Parenthèses, 2012).

6   Camillo Sitte, *L'Art de bâtir les villes* (Genève-Paris: Atar H. Laurens, 1902).

7   See the PhD dissertation by Mayalène Guelton published as *De la cité jardin à la cité linéaire. Georges Benoit-Lévy: Parcours d'un propagandiste idéaliste, 1903–1939* (Versailles: LADRHAUS, 2008).

8   Christian Topalov describes the role of Georges Benoit-Lévy in the importation and development of the garden city idea. See Christian Topalov, 'Les "Réformateurs" et les réseaux: enjeux d'un objet de recherché', in Christian Topalov (ed.), *Laboratoire du nouveau siècle: la nébuleuse réformatrice et ses réseaux en France, 1880–1914*, Civilisations et Sociétés, 98 (Paris: EHESS, 1999), pp. 21–9.

9   Georges Benoit-Lévy published many articles in the *Bulletin de la Société des HBM* and in the *Mémoires et documents* of the Musée Social. See Topalov, 'Les "Réformateurs"', p. 22. Benoit-Lévy's book was *La Cité-Jardin*, which was published in Paris in 1904 and edited by Henri Jouve. He also published *Cités-Jardins d'Amérique*, edited by Jouve and published in Paris a year later.

10   Georges Benoit Lévy, 'Rapport présenté au nom de l'association des cités jardins en France au VIIème congrès international des habitations à bon marché', in *Actes du VIIème congrès international des habitations à bon marché tenu à Liège, du 7 au 10 août 1905* (Liège: M. Thone, 1906), pp. 3–14. Benoit-Lévy had been the general secretary of the French Garden Cities Association, and had also been in charge of studies on *cités-jardins* at the Musée Social and at the Ministry of Commerce.

11   Jean-Claude Nicolas Forestier, 'Rapport des réserves à constituer au-dedans et aux abords des villes capitales du Maroc. Remarques sur les jardins arabes et l'utilité qu'il y aurait à en conserver les principaux caractères' (1913), in Bénédicte Leclerc and Salvador Tarragò (eds), *Grandes Villes et système de parcs: France, Maroc, Argentine* (Paris: Norma édition, 1997), p. 162.

12   The prestigious Grand Prix de Rome was awarded annually to selected outstanding students from the Ecole des Beaux-Arts. Financed by the French government, they

spent four years in Rome, with visits to other parts of Italy and Greece. Enjoying a professional career upon their return to France, they were considered the best designers who worked within the classical tradition.

13 Annie Fourcault, *La Ville Divisée: les ségrégations urbaines en question. France XVIIIème–XXème siècles* (Grâne: Créaphis, 1996), p. 165.

14 *Journal Officiel*, 15 March 1919, p. 2726.

15 On these questions, see especially Raoul de Clermont, *Histoire de la législation et de la réglementation des plans d'aménagement* (Rennes: Association générale des Hygiènistes et des Techniciens municipaux, 1922).

16 This was the case during the meeting of the Musée of 10 July 1909, when official 'demand for documentation concerning garden cities abroad' was made. See *Annales du musée social*, 1909, cited in Carole Tucoulet, 'Section d'hygiène urbaine et rurale du Musée social, inventaire des travaux (1908–1939)', *Vie Sociale*, 3–4 (1999), 201–42 – a special issue titled *Le Social et l'urbain autour de l'année 1928*.

17 Georges Risler, 'Les Espaces libres dans les grandes villes et les cités jardins', *Musée social, mémoires et documents*, 11 (1910), 349–72.

18 Especially in the suburban areas of Gennevilliers, Arcueil, Surènes, Drancy, Champigny-sur-Marne and Stains. For more about Sellier, see Roger-Henri Guerrand and Christine Moissinac, *Henri Sellier, urbaniste et réformateur social* (Paris: La Découverte, 2005).

19 See Viviane Claude, 'Une solution pratique aux problèmes urbains au début du XXe siècle: le zonage', *Annales des Ponts et Chaussées*, 93 (2000), 23–9 (special issue on zoning).

20 Institut français d'Architecture, Paris, Fonds Henri Prost, 343 AA, Carton HP DES. 21/3.1, cote provisoire, Henri Prost, Plan de la ville nouvelle de Fès (probablement 1915), au 1/5000, crayon et aquarelle, 485 × 600.

21 The medina (*médina* or *médine* in French, based on the Arabic name for 'a town') usually refers to the medieval indigenous urban nucleus, sometimes also called the 'casbah' (for a differentiation between these notions in Morocco, see Janet Abu-Lughod, *Rabat: Urban Apartheid in Morocco* [Princeton, NJ: Princeton University Press, 1980], pp. 63–7). The French colonisers tended to use the term 'medina' for any indigenous urban quarter, old as well as new, locally planned or planned by the colonial authorities. (Editors)

22 Albert Laprade is cited by Pierre Jean-Luc, *Casablanca et la France, XIX–XXe siècles* (Casablanca: La croisée des chemins, 2002), p. 91. Within the framework of Islamic property legislation, Laprade probably referred to the public *Habous* (*Waqf*), which cover publicly owned establishments and works of public interest which yield profits for this institution's administration, such as health or religious education. (Editors)

23 Louis Thomas, *Le Maroc de 1917* (Paris: Payot, 1917), p. 155.

24 Nevertheless, during the congress on urbanism in the colonies and in tropical countries of 1931, the town planners recommended 'that the creation of satellite cities would be pre-planned, separated by screens of greenery'. Cited in Henri Prost, 'Rapport général', in Jean Royer (ed.), *Urbanisme aux colonies et dans les pays tropicaux, Communications et rapports du Congrès international de l'urbanisme aux colonies et dans les pays de latitude intertropicale* (La Charité sur Loire: Delayance Éditions, 1932), p. 22.

25 Ebenezer Howard, *Villes-Jardins de demain* [*Garden Cities of Tomorrow*] (Tienstin: Tienstin Press, 1902). Cited in Françoise Choay, *L'Urbanisme, utopies et réalités. Une anthologie* (Paris: Editions du Seuil, 1965), p. 279 (Howard's emphasis).

26 Frederick Law Olmsted, an American autodidact who exercised many different functions before launching his career of landscape artist, was the designer of numerous gardens and parks, particularly New York's Central Park (in collaboration with the architect Calvert Vaux), and Montreal's Mont-Royal Park. His writings are widespread in France where he published numerous articles. See especially Frederick Law Olmsted, 'Town planning', *Construction*, 5 (1912), 54–6.

27 Jean-Claude Nicolas Forestier, *Grandes Villes et systèmes de parcs* (Paris: Hachette, 1906).

THE 'GARDEN CITY' CONCEPT

28 Bénédicte Leclerc and Salvador Tarragò i Cid, 'La Mission de Jean Claude Nicolas Forestier au Maroc', in Bénédicte Leclerc and Salvador Tarragò i Cid (eds), *Jean Claude Nicolas Forestier, 1861–1930: du jardin au paysage urbain* (Paris: Picard éditeur, 1994), pp. 154–5.
29 'The two studies, that of the "reserves" of open spaces and public gardens, and that of the town plan itself, lie intimately together and must be established simultaneously, in parallel and coordinated.' Jean-Claude Nicolas Forestier, 'Rapport des réserves à constituer au-dedans et aux abords des villes capitales du Maroc: remarques sur les jardins arabes et l'utilité qu'il y aurait à en conserver les principaux caractères', in Leclerc and Tarragò i Cid (eds), *Forestier*, p. 215.
30 Jean-Claude Nicolas Forestier, *Jardins: carnets de plans et de dessins* (Paris: Picard éditeur, 1994 [1920]), n.p.
31 Forestier, *Jardins*, n.p.
32 A posteriori, Henri Prost explained his vision regarding the administrative quarters: 'not enormous constructions, but, as far as possible, pavilions merging in greenness, comfortably linked together by galleries or pergolas'. Henri Prost, 'Le Développement de l'urbanisme dans le Protectorat du Maroc, de 1914 à 1923', in Royer (ed.), *Urbanisme aux colonies*, p. 67.
33 Archives municipales de Fès, Salle des autorisations de bâtir, Dossier N.r., Art. 18 du cahier des charges pour parvenir à l'attribution avec promesse conditionnelle de vente de lots de terrains constituant le secteur nord du quartier des villas de la ville nouvelle de Fès, adjudication du 29 mars 1929.
34 Marcel Zaborski was appointed president of Rabat's section of the Protectorate's Society of Horticulture and Acclimatisation (Société d'Horticulture et d'Acclimatation du Protectorat). He therefore collaborated with Jean-Claude Nicolas Forestier.
35 On Marcel Zaborski's assertions in this context, see A. Meunissier, 'Rabat, cité-jardin', *Revue Horticole* (Paris: Société nationale d'horticulture française, 1936), p. 410. Notice Zaborski's word play between aesthetic (*pot de terre*) and pragmatic (*pot de fer*) attitudes.
36 Le comte Maurice de Périgny, *Au Maroc, Fès la capitale du Nord* (Paris: P. Roger, 1922 [1917]), p.72.
37 Louis Villème, 'L'Évolution de la vie citadine au Maroc', *Cahiers de l'Afrique et de l'Asie*, 1 (*L'Évolution Sociale du Maroc*) (1951), 87.
38 Jean Eyquem, *Les Ports de la zone française du Maroc: leur rôle économique* (Alger: Ancienne Imprimerie V. Heintz, 1933), p. 332.
39 The plans for this garden city, built from 1905, were carried out by Barry Parker and Raymond Unwin.
40 Cited by Benoit-Lévy in his 'Rapport présenté au nom de l'association des cités jardins en France', pp. 3–14.
41 These were designed in 1924 for the towns of Casablanca, Kenitra, Fès, Marrakech, Mazagan, Meknès, Rabat and Safi by the head of the Department of Public Instruction, the Beaux-Arts and Antiquities (le directeur général de l'instruction publique, des Beaux-Arts et Antiquités).
42 In the ideal city of Ebenezer Howard, the grounds were communal and belonged to the municipality in order to prevent speculation.
43 See particularly Catherine Coquery-Vidrovitch, 'A propos de la cité-jardin dans les colonies: l'Afrique noire', in Catherine Coquery-Vidrovitch and Odile Goerg (eds), *La Ville Européenne outre mers: un modèle conquérant? XVᵉ–XXᵉ siècles* (Paris: l'Harmattan, 1996), pp. 105–23; Mercedes Volait and Minnaert Jean-Baptiste, 'Héliopolis, création et assimilation d'une ville européenne en Egypte au XXe siècle', in Denise Turrel (ed.), *Villes rattachées, villes reconfigurées XVIᵉ–XXᵉ siècles* (Tours: Presses Universitaires François-Rabelais, MSH: Perspectives historiques, 2003), pp. 335–55.
44 Zohra Hakimi, 'Le Développement de "l'urbanisme de plan" à Alger', in Hélène Vacher (ed.), *Villes coloniales aux XIX–XXe siècles: d'un sujet d'action à un objet d'histoire, Algérie, Maroc, Libye et Iran* (Paris: Maisonneuve, Larose, 2005), p. 74.

CHAPTER TWO

From metropolitan to colonial planning: Dakar between garden city and *cité-jardin*

Liora Bigon

'Are the outlines of great concepts likely to lose their clarity when they become generally accepted?' This question is raised by Walter Creese, the late prominent architectural historian from the University of Illinois, in the preface to his 1966 textbook on the evolution of the garden city idea in England.[1] 'The garden city ideal', he continues, 'which was so immediately applicable, has been especially plagued by the constant semantic confusion in the literature describing the model villages, garden villages, garden suburbs, garden cities, and new towns as they appeared.' This is followed by an outstanding observation, touching on geographical areas otherwise untreated in the book: 'If a person has been accustomed to regard the garden city as a reaction against the highly industrialized and urbanized environment of the Western nations', asserts Creese, 'it comes as a further surprise to discover the terms "garden city" and "new town" turning up frequently in the housing pamphlets of the so-called underdeveloped countries to signify the increasing prestige of their industrial advance.' What comes next only adds to the confusion: 'When we move out of the realm of practical application toward the germ of the idea itself, the likelihood of distortion is nearly as great.'

Written more than forty-five years ago, Creese's description of the semantic and practical confusions of the garden city idea is particularly applicable to the history of colonial Dakar. Such confusions are inevitable, as they are in any intra- and especially internationally transferred ideology, taking into account the original British garden city developments, their transformation in France, and their further transformation in French West Africa. Yet the point here is definitely not to show that the realisation of Ebenezer Howard's garden city model – the normal, the original, the desirable – in colonial Dakar was pathological, artificial or simply misconceived. In other words, it would be erroneous to perceive Dakar's *cité-jardin* merely as a distorted design reference to its prior metropolitan models in Britain and France.

The aim of this chapter is to show that within the colonial context, and against the background of contemporary French metropolitan and colonial urban cultures, *cité-jardin* terminological and practical usages benefited the interests of the colonial administration in Dakar. The colonial administration used this model selectively, distorted it and adapted it to its needs in order to create a prestigious image of the quarters designated for its employees, to enforce unofficial class segregation within the expatriate society, and to foster informal racial segregation between white and indigenous residential sectors. Beyond the official discourse, the popular views of contemporary commentators concerning *cités-jardins* in French West Africa only strengthen the image sought by the colonial administration. *Cités-jardins*, and especially the greenness of their associated imagery, symbolised – in the colonial bourgeoisie context up until the interwar period – a civilising force, the domestication of a savage environment.

Garden city versus cité-jardin: *metropolitan variations*

As implied above, the responses of Western countries to the town planning problems that faced their expanding urban centres in an industrial age were grounded in history and socio-political circumstances, that is, they constituted an essentially cultural reaction. Here we would like to branch off from our first relevant geographical station in the diffusion of the garden city idea, that is, from Britain to France, to discuss briefly the deviations and differences that accompanied the transmission process. Thus we lay the ground for our next geographical station and the further divergence of the idea of the *cité-jardin*, this time from metropolitan France to its colonial territories overseas, with a focus on Dakar.

Unlike other early nineteenth-century planners of ideal societies, sometimes referred to as 'utopian socialists',[2] Ebenezer Howard proposed a garden city that did not remain a theoretical vision. It became – through his renowned work *Garden Cities of To-Morrow* (1902) – a practical contribution to contemporary urban planning.[3] As actual experiments, his ideas, in one version or another, spread quickly through Britain. Almost as quickly they influenced other European countries and the US as well. After the translation of his book into French at the beginning of the twentieth century, and the visits of French reformers to the first experiments in England, especially Letchworth, Howard's model became well known in France. The Association Française des Cités-Jardins was founded in 1904, led by Georges Benoît-Lévy, eventually its secretary and president, who fostered the garden city discourse in France in numerous publications. Other French reformers became internationally active, such as Henri Sellier, who joined the International Garden Cities and Town Planning Federation.[4]

In nineteenth-century France, according to the urban historian Gordon Cherry, industrialisation and urban revolution were far less prominent than in Britain, and urban problems were largely underestimated. Georges-Eugène Haussmann was preoccupied with improving street communications at the expense of housing, and it was only after the First World War that town planning became a national concern. Whereas Britain had 'drifted into town planning', Cherry concludes, 'France was simply reluctant'.[5] Focusing on the emergence of the national factor in planning the Paris region during the interwar period, Annie Fourcaut investigated suburban developments and the usage of *cité-jardin* rhetoric versus the previous anti-model of speculative, voluntarily emerging *lotissements* (parcelling). The latter, perceived as exaggerated private initiative and a morphological disaster, became a symbol of urban failure. But in the national efforts post-1920 to rationalise this suburban growth through *villes nouvelles* (new towns) and *cités-jardins*, 'the issue of the balance between habitation and employment was not resolved, neither was the transportation problem. The purpose was not really the creation of new towns, but rather the decongestion of Paris.'[6]

The expansionist urban growth in France had since the late nineteenth century followed a high-density pattern, using the Parisian apartment house (*immeuble de rapport*). In *cité-jardin* experiments in suburban areas, as noticed by the urban historian Jean Pierre Gaudin, there was a clear preference for apartment buildings, generally supported by the municipal authorities of greater Paris, especially in the interwar period.[7] This issue is of particular interest because, while Howard's vision was full of technical details and calculations, his famous ideal diagrams did not include any particular architectural designs. In spite of the resulting freedom in matters of style, nostalgic images of the countryside and other thriving vernacular traditions were noticeable in Britain, such as the cottage as a model housing unit. Detached or semi-detached, the cottage was designated for labourers or middle-class families and even had a small garden plot. Its neighbourhood was shaped in accordance with the apparently informal stylistic influence of domestic medieval forms and the theories of Camillo Sitte. This preference is manifest, inter alia, in the first realisation of Howard's ideas in 1903 by Barry Parker and Raymond Unwin in Letchworth.[8]

There also seems to have been no British equivalent to the garden city rhetoric of socialist urban discourse in France before the First

World War – 'sociological socialism' as it was labelled by Paul Rabinow; nor were there any private bodies similar to the Musée Social, which directed the modern national campaign for planning in France.[9] Founded in 1894 to bring together reformers from diverse professional, political and ideological backgrounds and to combat problems in all facets of social welfare, virtually every piece of socio-environmental legislation proposed in France between 1895 and 1920 was examined by the Musée. Nevertheless, in spite of this socialist discourse, there were fewer links between the garden city idea and statutory planning in France than in Britain.

Garden city and cité-jardin: *planning for class differences*

In what follows, we will stress the similarities rather than the differences between Britain and France concerning the emergence of the garden city model in theory and practice. Unusual though this may be for urban planning historiography, it will shed light on the common ground between the two metropolitan models that is particularly relevant to our discussion: planning for class differences. In the next geographical station, with the transition of the *cité-jardin* model from France to colonial West Africa, such planning became further accelerated and crystallised.

Despite the spirit of cooperative socialism that characterised Howard's vision and his famous sketches, he actually planned for class differences. The garden city was presented as a usable alternative to the contemporary overgrowth of urban industrial centres, which included mass migration from the countryside, the deterioration of sanitary conditions, slums, extreme poverty and crime. Each garden city – also called a 'social city' by Howard[10] – had to be planned in a rural area, restricted in space and population, and built on communal land, designed and developed to serve public interests. An admixture of earlier ideas lay at the heart of Howard's garden city concept: the bringing together of diverse elements to create a single unified, simple, practical and successful scheme.

One previous idea that inspired Howard's 'unique combination of proposals',[11] as he called it, consisted of 'colonisation' theories, meaning, in our context, an organised migratory movement of population in order to settle either in overseas territories or within the *métropole*.[12] Howard quotes the economist Edward Gibbon Wakefield with regard to the colonisation of Australia and New Zealand, believing, like Wakefield, that many colonisation schemes erred in representing only one class of the parent society, usually the most helpless and unfit. He quotes, 'The ancients, on the contrary, sent out *a* representation of the parent State – colonists from all ranks ... [The new colony] consisted of a general contribution of all members from all classes, and so became, on its first settlement, a mature state, with all the component parts of that which sent it forth.'[13] Howard's garden city was not meant to offer an ameliorated framework for the existing socio-economic system as its first priority; nor was it intended to foster environmental change; rather, it offered a social change out of which a new civilisation with new hope might emerge. Yet Howard's use of the above quotation implies that the kind of social reform he envisaged did not really challenge the prevailing social order and hierarchy in England, but rather acted within them, and even served them.[14]

Under such rhetoric the moral degradation of the poor tended to be linked to urban space. This idea had been prevalent in Victorian Britain since the mid-nineteenth century, and no less so in contemporary France.[15] It was a period in which knowledge about appalling urban conditions in the main industrial centres had spread through public and official circles, with the understanding that something had to be done to ameliorate the situation. 'Liquor consumption in large towns might fall if town populations possessed public parks and zoos, museums and theatres', wrote the renowned planner Edwin Chadwick in the early 1830s.[16] This rhetoric of social or cultural paternalism (that is, various patronising expressions directed by the higher socio-economic classes towards the lower classes within the European metropolis – which would develop into racial paternalism under colonial conditions) was crystallised by Howard in his garden city vision. Yet it had already crystallised in the general culture that influenced Howard's thought, and since he was neither an intellectual nor a systematic reader, it was difficult for him to acknowledge this. His was a vision and general culture of 'Englishness'.

The social historian Standish Meacham has examined the way in which the ideas and ideals that shaped the early garden city movement in England were embedded, especially before the First World War, in a vision of Englishness. The green and pleasant heaven that this vision represented was to be based on selective elements drawn from a mythic past, in order to replace an ugly and unhealthy urban hell and its accompanying fears of class struggle and expanding democracy. Meacham suggests that the early garden city movement should be examined in the light of these fears, as political parties and reformers within it established an exclusive hierarchy entitled to define what was and was not English, thus preserving their role as the dominant arbiters.[17] The latter reformist elite, though frequently disowning the paternalist label, argued that the cities and suburbs they were creating contained wealthy and poor alike, albeit spatial opportunities for their coming together were not provided. Howard was thus not alone in planning for class differences. In the establishment of the first garden city of Letchworth, Unwin understood that the provision of cheap cottages for labourers with a certain standard of comfort and design would only be suited to the income of skilled, and not unskilled, labourers.[18] In Welwyn – which never aimed at social experimentalism but was in fact a garden suburb, like most of the 'garden city' realisations in Britain – class division was also noticeable: working class to the east of the mainline railway, middle class to the west.

Similar to Britain's reformist elite, members of the Musée Social, in their search for solutions to social problems, had certain urban visions, idealistic principles and a faith in science. In spite of the socialist celebration into which ideas of *cité-jardin* were pushed in France, the Musée never questioned a commitment to the values of private property. This earned its members credibility among the more conservative elite and official circles. In France, as in Britain, there were hardly any references to Howard's radical communal land solutions, nor to his 'social city' as an independent unit. This fact, among other things, contributed towards the actual realisation of Howard's ideas as one form or another of *banlieues-jardins* (garden suburbs).

Here again, by the turn of the century, bourgeois metropolitan discourse on the 'otherness' of the urban poor – their vices, immorality, appalling sanitary conditions – had gradually been replaced by a more official and professional discourse. It was also believed that urban planning was a symbol of a new social order, an instrument for a whole new way of life.[19] Benoît-Lévy, with several other promoters, wished to bring a garden to each worker, with plots grouped near apartment dwellings and aimed at protecting traditional family values. It was typically paternalistic to expect the garden to stimulate welfare (with self-production of vegetables) and moral values, because the labourer would spend more time in the garden than in less morally uplifting leisure activities. Moreover, and similar to early British developments by the interwar period, the *cité-jardin* reference was in use to legitimate functional zoning within French town planning. That is, it enabled the justification of housing segregation for the purpose of hygienic and social improvement.[20]

Under colonial circumstances, the cultural paternalism of the home country turned to racial paternalism. Spatial class differences allowed for within the expatriate society were supported and consolidated by the colonial administration, side by side with segregationist moves on a racial basis among the colonisers and the colonised. Residential segregation, based either on race or social class – in colonial Africa, both British and French, as well as in other colonial territories such as

British India or French Indo-China – has received appropriate attention in the scholarly literature.[21] Yet what is innovative in this study is the examination of the particular role of garden city/*cité-jardin* ideas within segregationist colonial planning. Another contribution is on the historiographic level: while most of the literature on the history of garden city ideas is focused on Britain and the Western world, the diffusion of these notions beyond the West has hardly been studied. Moreover, sub-Saharan Africa is rarely treated in this regard, as most research in colonial urban planning tends to focus on territories given a higher priority by their respective *métropoles*.

Dakar's Plateau: colonialism and residential segregation

The strategic position of Dakar, the westernmost point in West Africa and thus a port of call on the way from Europe to South America or South Africa, was acknowledged by the French following the Crimean War and the later 'scramble' for Africa. Before 1857 the official French occupation of the peninsula of Cap-Vert over which Dakar extends consisted of several Lebu (Lébou) villages, numbering about 10,000 residents in all. Hoping it would one day become the capital of the French colonial empire in West Africa, the first town plan for a city-to-be was drawn up in 1862. It was an orthogonal plan in which a port, administrative headquarters and military and commercial facilities were marked. This area, known as 'Dakar-ville' or 'Dakar-propre', became the very heart of the city and grew considerably following the initiation of the Senegal–Niger railway line in 1885 and the designation of Dakar as the capital of the AOF (*Afrique Occidentale Française*) Federation in 1902.[22]

In the early twentieth century, the colonial administration of Dakar pursued two residential schemes. The first extended north-west of Dakar-ville and involved the African, mainly Lebu, population. This was a rigorous, controversial and dramatic segregationist move, imposed after the 1914 outbreak of bubonic plague and the prohibition of temporary building materials in the city centre. It consisted of forcing Dakar's indigenous inhabitants to resettle in the newly created outlying quarter of the Médina, where even the most basic infrastructure was not provided for a decade. The second scheme, inaugurated by the colonial administration from the mid-1900s, was the creation of a new urban quarter designated to house its employees. It was established on the high plateau at the tip of the peninsula, south of Dakar-ville, and became known as the Plateau (fig. 2.1).[23]

The orthogonal grid of Dakar-ville was typical of contemporary plantation schemes, and in the Médina's grid the function of surveillance

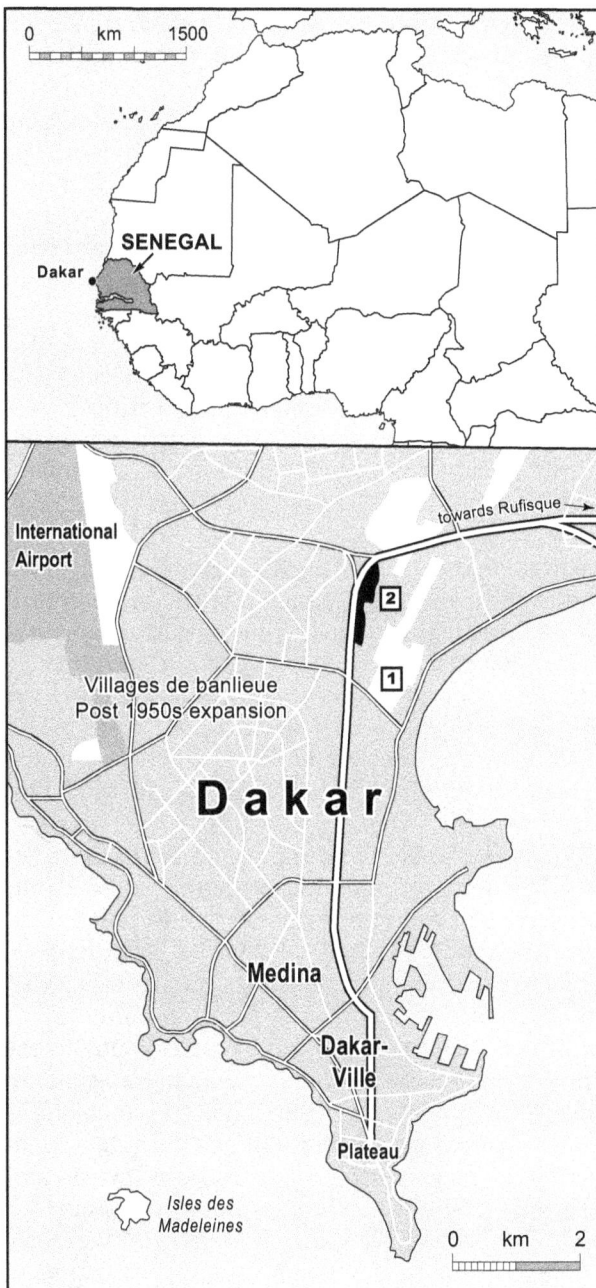

Figure 2.1 Dakar's quarters by the 1950s. 1) Forestry Park of Hann (Hann Botanical Gardens); 2) Hann Garden City (Cité-jardin de Hann).

over the African population was a chief consideration.[24] The Plateau, by contrast, was arranged according to an elaborate plan, which put several roundabouts in star-like intersections of four, five, or six wide avenues. It was realised under the ambitious Governor General of the AOF, Ernest Roume (1902–07), and through the cooperation of the Public Works Department with military engineers.[25] The concentric and harmonious arrangement of the Plateau's *ronds-points* had many metropolitan precedents. Though perfect examples are rare in France, one full *rond-point* is the Place de l'Étoile in Paris, with its twelve outstretching streets.[26] Another source of inspiration here was French Beaux-Arts aristocratic planning, like the gardens of Versailles, where pathways in geometric forms were intersected with *ronds-points* occupied by statues or fountains. Reflecting French colonial pretensions in this part of the world is the main *rond-point* in Dakar's Plateau, a simplified six-street version named Rond-Point de l'Étoile (today's Place Soweto) (fig. 2.1). It was a space representative of the colonising power.

As the capital of the AOF, the main function of the layout and design of Dakar-ville and the Plateau was the Westernisation of the city through the adoption of French colonial urban norms and forms. Dakar was intended to fulfil an international role rather than a local one, West African rather than Senegalese. It was accordingly regarded by the colonial authorities as a model space for West Africa in general, to which some Parisian planning elements could be imported. The white residential area of the Plateau in particular constituted a model space within the larger space of Dakar as a whole. It was meant not only to impress the Africans, who, according to Eurocentric and paternalistic views, would learn to imitate European modes of habitation, but also to 'pacify' critics at home, especially those who denounced the enterprise, by emphasising the visual aspects of colonialism.[27]

But while these urban amenities were directed towards the privileged white quarters, Dakar's indigenous population hardly benefited from them at all. In contrast to the Médina quarter – not to mention the African suburban expansion beyond it, which was generally ignored by the colonial authorities – the streets in the Plateau and Dakar-ville were the first to be paved and lit, and supplied with tree-lined footpaths, running water and sewage systems. Trade in permanent building materials imported from the metropolis was also promoted there. Emil Lengyel, a visitor to Dakar's Plateau in the early 1940s, wrote that if one 'closed his eyes and forgot the heat, which was of course impossible, he could imagine himself at a corner of a Parisian suburb'.[28] Lengyel's subsequent description of this white residential area as the 'Paris of the tropics' reminds us of its North African equivalents, the *villes nouvelles*. His portrayal shows that the term 'town planning' in the colonial situation involved the expatriate quarters almost exclusively. After the initial destruction of the indigenous living areas in most of the colonial cities, following the first, military phase of colonisation, the indigenous quarters were generally left untouched as 'traditional', 'authentically preserved' entities.[29]

This system of 'dual cities' was promoted by the French in North and sub-Saharan Africa, though French officials never imposed overt racial restrictions in residential matters. It was indeed highly discriminatory, yet does not deserve the term urban 'apartheid' given by Janet Abu-Lughod regarding Rabat, in order to 'rethink' French policies in Morocco's Protectorate[30] – a usage that is rather sensationalist. We shall favour the term 'residential segregation', bearing in mind the planning for class differences by the French authorities that was applied within the expatriate society as well. French West Africa, however, never experienced a permanent or massive presence of white settlers, mainly because of the tropical climate. Administrative fears with respect to the role played there by *petits blancs* – particularly their ability to undermine the bourgeois foundations of Empire – were never considerable in comparison to North Africa. Segregationist moves supported by Dakar's authorities within the white community were relatively soft, differentiating mainly between the private sector (Dakar-ville) and its own functionaries (Plateau). Putting aside residences designated for the military sector, we shall now turn to examine the role played by notions of *cité-jardin* in the spatiality of the colonial dominance equation.

Dakar's Plateau: between garden quarter and beau quartier

The focus of our attention is Dakar's Plateau quarter. This is so because almost every *cité-jardin* reference in colonial times relates to this quarter. By the 1930s the 'garden city' rhetoric, which was also fashionable in contemporary Europe, was extremely common in French-speaking cities in sub-Saharan Africa. The term *cité-jardin* was normally used by the French colonial administration with reference to its expatriate residential quarters, and in this regard Dakar's Plateau was not exceptional. It is clear, however, that more than any resemblance to Howardian notions, the *cité-jardin* in this context meant wide tree-lined streets, villas with verandahs and gardens, and an abundance of vegetation in general, predominantly for decoration.

Vegetation, and especially large trees like the baobab or kapok, have played a key role in the configuration of the Lebu and Wolof settlements from at least the thirteenth century to the present day.

Aside from purely aesthetic needs, vegetation fulfilled spiritual, didactic, pragmatic and recreational needs as well.[31] And within the colonial urban sphere, in Senegal as throughout sub-Saharan Africa, a self-sufficient supply of vegetables and fruit for the indigenous residents was an inseparable feature. Vegetable gardens, millet stores, fruit trees such as mango, guava and papaya – these village-like local urban practices are reminiscent of the kitchen gardens that were so popular among the French expatriates in Dakar. The expatriates were not keen to acknowledge these similarities and tended to emphasise the 'cultural differences' on which the colonial situation was based.[32] However, these indigenous green neighbourhoods or localities were rarely referred to or conceived of by Africans or Europeans as cités-jardins – a notion that is essentially occidental and expressive of essentially occidental imagery and pretensions.

Thus, wherever possible, the French ideal for housing expatriates in sub-Saharan colonies was a private residential unit with a garden, facing a straight street lined with trees. The spacious, green appearance of these quarters has been very much preserved to this day (figs 2.2, 2.3). The characteristic look was also noticed by several historians who dealt with the main French colonial urban centres,[33] and it was also pointed out by several contemporary colonial professionals. Some of those reports were published in 1932 by the International Conference of Urbanism in the Colonies and Tropical Countries, following the 1931 Colonial Exposition in Paris.[34] From Algeria to Madagascar and from Senegal to Congo Brazzaville, throughout the French dependencies, the expatriate residential form in these reports was most often labelled cité-jardin. The white residential area in Antananarivo (Madagascar) was described there as a 'satellite garden-suburb';[35] in Thiès (east of Dakar) it was described as 'a real garden city';[36] in Elisabethville (Belgian Congo) as 'a large garden city whose greenery creates its charm';[37] and even in Beira (Portuguese Mozambique) the white area was characterised as a desirable 'garden city'.[38] As stated above, one should not look here for a direct application of the British garden cities ideal, but rather understand the appellation as a successful inclusion of vegetation within the white residential quarters.

Archival evidence that refers to Dakar as a cité-jardin supports this argument: we find the notion mentioned in the context of planting the park of Hann, or the maintenance of the villa gardens of the colonial administration on the Plateau, both in the early 1920s.[39] There is another reference, from the late 1950s, to the establishment of a new residential neighbourhood by the administration to house its employees. A part of the post-Second World War impetus of urban development in the AOF, this neighbourhood was placed north of

Figure 2.2 Villa from the 1930s on Dakar's Plateau.

Dakar-ville, in the triangle created by the main road to Thiès and the Forestry Park of Hann (now Hann Botanical Gardens) (fig. 2.1).[40] The administrative villas were built on garden plots, arranged around squares and other areas reserved for small 'parks', and bore the title 'Hann Garden City' (Cité-jardin de Hann). This title was derived from the association with, and physical proximity to, Hann Forestry Park and other large plots nearby that were allocated to agriculture. Hann was the name of one of the Lebu villages which was there on the eve of the colonial occupation of the peninsula and which, following the realisation of the plan of Dakar-ville, was transferred farther inland. There was also an important source of ground water to be utilised for colonial Dakar, and, already by the early 1870s, an agronomic station had been created there designated, among other things, to supply trees for the main roadways of Dakar.[41]

The eventual materialisation of the ideal of green space within Dakar's Plateau resulted in the resemblance of this quarter to an urban park dotted with regularly arranged villas. Like the later Hann Garden City, Dakar's Plateau was not a garden city per se, in the sense of being an autonomous unit, nor was it really a garden suburb of Dakar-ville. While Dakar-ville operated as an administrative, commercial and strategic centre, it could hardly be regarded as an industrial core. This is because the colonial situation in Africa did not include any form of industrial revolution. Apart from a few white settlers' colonies, most of the colonies were reservoirs of raw materials and then markets for manufactured goods. Because industrialisation was necessarily reserved for Europe, expressions of the 'garden city' in Africa were by no means a reaction to highly industrialised urban environments. In the absence of a real industrial core, the Plateau should be perceived as an extension of Dakar-ville rather than its suburb. Moreover, Dakar-ville also served residential functions, mainly for white merchants from the private sector, known as *privés*. The latter seem to have been neither attracted to the Plateau for economic and social reasons, nor welcomed there by the colonial authorities. Those Lebu who survived the several transfer schemes also resided in Dakar-ville, alongside Lebanese immigrants who were gradually attracted to this commercially vibrant area, close to the seaport.

The particular zoning system that was applied to Dakar's Plateau, along with its land allocation and transportation arteries, was feasible thanks to the monopoly that the colonial authorities had on land ownership. By introducing a new land code, all previous land-property obstacles that originated in local, Islamic or pre-Islamic Lebu custom were removed.[42] The Plateau's land nationalisation or municipalisation was thus part of the colonial situation and far removed from any socialist dimension. In this, the *cité-jardin* of the Plateau was somewhat similar to other projects in contemporary

Figure 2.3 French postcard showing a street in Dakar-ville, 1910s.

France (and Britain), which lacked Howardian notions of communal land ownership, for country-specific cultural and political reasons. Socialist aspects contradicted the colonial situation, which was inherently anti-social. In France (and Britain), plans for *cités-jardins* were intended to upgrade the living conditions of the working class, or at least were perceived as such. Yet *cités-jardins* were never planned for the Dakarois subjects – the only sector of the colonial city that could be considered working class. Even the Office des Habitations Economiques, established by Governor General Jules Carde in 1926 in order to offer monetary assistance to Dakarois wishing to build permanent houses, had completed only twenty residential units by 1945. These were the sole initiatives for tens of thousands of Africans, in contrast to the hundreds of villas erected for French officials and largely supported by the administration.[43]

The metropolitan worker was therefore replaced by the expatriate employee, whom the colonial authorities strove to serve first. Accordingly, there still seems to be some similarity between the ways in which the *cité-jardin* model was used by its promoters in Dakar and its promoters in France. In both contexts there were paternalistic goals: in France, better morals and traditional family values through self-production of vegetables; and in Dakar, hygienic and social improvements for expatriates through the tempting living conditions of the tropics, expansive villas surrounded by gardens. Both sectors were in fact segregated: from the more wealthy urban population at home or from the African urban poor in the colonies. And, as in metropolitan *cité-jardin* applications, the Plateau's establishment was accompanied by a paternalism that verged on social engineering.

The administration presumed high moral standards among its intended residents, and was determined to change the conventional image of the colonial officer: no longer was he to be an adventurous bachelor, but rather a family man, living in a spacious villa with a private garden. By permitting the arrival of French women and children to Dakar's Plateau, especially from the 1930s, the administration hoped that its employees 'would attend churches instead of whorehouses, in which they constantly visit', and that interracial sex would be reduced.[44] Indeed, colonial social and spatial practices challenged traditional notions of French colour blindness and national identity. Sexual arrangements and affective intimate attachments played a critical role in creating colonial categories and distinguishing the ruler from the ruled. In the colonial situation, social and spatial classifications – distinctions among the colonisers and between them and the colonised – constituted a potent political act rather than a cultural one.[45]

In addition, Dakar's Plateau can be related to Haussmannian Paris no less than to the model of the *cité-jardin*. Its *ronds-points*, wide boulevards and avenues, and the diagonal street layout were reminiscent of the Grand Manner-like planning of the Beaux-Arts. The latter was inspired by aristocratic planning much more than by the 'organic' winding English street in Unwin's garden city plans; and the association of the Plateau of Dakar with green spaces had much in common with French upper-bourgeois culture and nineteenth-century Paris. This gave the Plateau a prestigious and exclusive image much sought by the colonial administration, originating in the discursive relationships between nature and bourgeois culture in contemporary urban France. It was not without good reason that a commentator in the early twentieth century called the newly established Plateau *la ville bourgeoise* (the bourgeois town).[46]

The spacious villas with gardens on the Plateau – domestic servants also had their own residential areas there – closely resembled the British bungalow-compound complex and its cultivated garden. These physical expressions, together with the admiration for aspects of the natural world, were common among the colonial elite and had an affinity to the way of living of Europe's upper classes. Continental mid-nineteenth-century expressions such as the 'colonisation of the countryside by urban bourgeoisie', *maison de campagne* (a country house), 'fresh air', 'horticulture', 'taking a walk', photography and 'landscape' drawing – such expressions signified an essentially urban perception of nature as an object of consumption. Inseparable from the emerging global economy, they also became associated with a certain socio-economic status.[47]

Thus, the metropolitan model of the *beaux quartiers* attracted the expatriates. If they were compelled to live for some time in the tropics, they aspired to live on the Plateau in the manner of the upper classes at home. In an effort to establish an attractive residential environment for its functionaries, the colonial administration could not furnish the Plateau with Paris-style apartment houses – these were connected with suburban *cité-jardin* developments for lower classes. The abundance of vegetal elements within certain parts of the urban sphere was associated, by contrast, with metropolitan elite culture, together with other notions such as pleasure, aesthetics and leisure time activities. It was a conscious and selective borrowing, intended to serve colonial needs by creating a prestigious image and to attract wealthy expatriates and entrepreneurs.

Anthony King outlined a basic typology for this situation, calling the metropolitan community the 'first culture', the indigenous community the 'second culture', and the colonial community the 'third culture'.

According to King the 'third culture' constituted an exceptional phenomenon, and the socio-physical forms that were produced by it were not simple duplications of metropolitan ones, but exceptional as well.[48] In the case of the British 'third culture' in India and the French 'third culture' in Senegal, certain metropolitan elements – always borrowed from the elite culture – were imported by the colonial communities. These elements, among which 'nature' played a key role, were modified in order to accommodate colonial interests.

The contrast between the *beaux quartiers* of mid-nineteenth-century Paris and its *quartiers populaires* was, however, of a different nature than that between its parallels in early twentieth-century Dakar. Beyond the *ville officielle* of the privileged expatriate quarters, planning legislation was less rigid, enabling the development of the *ville réelle* with a spatial organisation that did not correspond to colonial norms. While some Lebu land rights were preserved in the city centre, Dakar, the regional administrative capital and the focal point of commercial activity, attracted an extensive migration of Africans from all over the AOF. Its population doubled between 1926 and 1936, and slums and squatter settlements (to be partly dealt with only after the Second World War) were constantly growing around Dakar's periphery,[49] creating a scarcity of water, housing and general infrastructure.

Contemporary descriptions and photographs imply that most of the green spaces in early twentieth-century Dakar were connected to the above-mentioned aspects of bourgeois culture – pleasure, aesthetics and leisure. These green spaces, spread out within the administrative area of Dakar-ville and the Plateau, can be classified in five main categories: 1) 'Official' gardens, designed in the French formal tradition, such as those of Dakar's City Hall (Hôtel de Ville) (fig. 2.4) or the Palais du Gouverneur Général of the AOF, now Palais Présidentiel. This consisted of a garden of the *cour d'honneur* at the front and a garden with three terraces at the back, bordering on the sea. There is a decorative 'French garden', a central motif, on each side of the building, supervised by the Horticultural Service.[50] 2) Public gardens and parks, for example those of Place Prôtet at the very heart of the colonial city, with a pavilion in the middle for playing music (now Place de l'Indépendance, though without the pavilion) (fig. 2.5); or those of Jardin de Hann (the aforementioned Forestry Park of Hann, now Hann Botanical Gardens). Indeed, the function of the latter was not only recreational, but also included economic botany and a reservoir for the growing of imported and local species of trees.[51] 3) Tree-lined boulevards and avenues (fig. 2.3). Trees for this purpose were usually taken care of by the departments of agriculture, plantation and hygiene, which also chose

Figure 2.4 The gardens of Dakar's City Hall (Hôtel de Ville).

the species, the imported acacia and mimosa and the native mango and banana.[52] Apart from their aesthetic value, their resemblance to the urban arteries at 'home' and their provision of shade in the tropical climate, trees were considered most important for the sanitation of Cap-Vert. The sanitary function was through swamp reclamation and other anti-malarial countermeasures, and the prevention of erosion on the sandy peninsula. 4) A promenade along the eastern shore of the Plateau, namely the *corniche*, in which beautification (*embellissement*) was of great importance. (5) Decorative gardens belonging to European households, mainly on the Plateau (*jardins d'agrément*) and to a lesser degree in Dakar-ville.

Vegetation has a purely practical benefit, particularly in tropical environments. Plants, either imported or locally found, block out solar radiation, shade the house and reduce room temperature. It was also common among the French expatriates in Dakar, as well as in their other sub-Saharan settlements, to have a kitchen garden (*jardin potager*) as a further source of vegetables.[53] The French kitchen garden drew the attention of British neighbours, especially against the background of colonial rivalry and competition for national prestige. 'The French have a much more lively sense of the importance of kitchen gardens to the public health than the British have', wrote Lord Lugard in 1916, when he was Governor General of Northern and Southern Nigeria.

Figure 2.5 Public garden of the Place de l'Indépendance, Dakar.

Recommending kitchen gardens for Europeans in dry, Sahelian Kaduna, he explained, 'at every station in the French territory across our Northern border, the officer has, as one of his routine duties, to run an irrigated kitchen garden'.[54]

These practical aspects, cherished in colonial culture, were not regarded as more important than the recreational value that was ascribed to green spaces. Such values sometimes gained new symbolic meanings overseas. The garden even bore a certain 'civilising' significance when it was imported to 'savage' sub-Saharan Africa. Among the French in the AOF, for instance, the popular imagery of green surroundings in terms of 'conquest of the desert' was prominent. In 1935 a commentator on the first Sudanese congress on the modern city described Bamako (in modern Mali) in terms that represent the imposition of a complete *mise-en-valeur*, that is, a 'development' in the most colonialist spirit: 'In the heart of West Africa, Bamako appears ... emerging from the uncultured savannah with its electric lamps, the noises of gramophones, its wide streets, its cars, its flowery terraces, full of women in bright clothes.'[55] The flowery terraces of Bamako that 'conquered' the savannah are mentioned here together with other symbols of European civilisation and French modernity. The literally illuminating effect of some of these elements is noticeable – the lamps, the wide streets, the bright clothes. In addition, the local surrounding is flavoured by an orientalist attitude to the Sudanese (Malian) women, whose presence, like flowers, was not considered too intimidating by the colonising power.

Another description by a French visitor to Dakar's Plateau and its *corniche* in the late 1930s reflects similar aspects, which became popularised, that is, a preoccupation with the Plateau's modern appearance, its bright elements, the presence of local women and luxuriant vegetation. The vegetation, clearly decorative, is portrayed with almost mystic sensuality: 'Through avenues with bright houses, white villas with roses in gardens of splendid vegetation, where the hibiscus dominates, especially those that blaze with flowers of intensive red, I continued my walk towards the coastal road.' This road, the description continues, 'can compete with the most beautiful promenades set in front of the sea. Bougainvillea also enliven the wide shady avenues, where, among Europeans, black women pass by.'[56] Bougainvillea and tree-shaded areas can also be found in many other contemporary descriptions of the Plateau of Dakar,[57] which leads one to assume again that, more than being a proper *cité-jardin* or *banlieue-jardin*, the Plateau constituted a green quarter designated for a certain urban sector. If this neighbourhood was occasionally referred to as *cité-jardin* – both by the colonial administration and by contemporary commentators – it was due mainly to the greenness of the metaphor.

Conclusion

Recent research in colonial urban planning – usually concentrating on colonies of high metropolitan status such as India, Singapore, North Africa and Indo-China – shows the key role played by residential segregation, based on race or class differences. This chapter's main contribution is its examination of the role of garden city/*cité-jardin* notions within segregationist colonial planning in sub-Saharan Africa, with a focus on French Dakar. Thus it also expands the more 'traditional' garden city historiography beyond Britain, Europe and the Western, mostly Anglophone, hemisphere.

Along with metropolitan garden city developments, especially in Britain and then in France, the chapter points to common and diverse themes in the transformation, diffusion and realisation of ideas of the *cité-jardin* in French West Africa. It dilates on the peculiarities of the colonial situation in general and on the special features of Dakar as a regional capital city, both spatially and within the French colonial imaginary. Expressions of *cité-jardin* within this context well served Dakar's colonial administration in creating an attractive, prestigious and exclusive environment to house its employees, and in creating class segregation within the expatriate society by the interwar period. In this way, metropolitan features, such as planning for class differences, social paternalism on the part of statutory urban frameworks, and the formation of urban ideology, elite culture and its recreational activities, were accelerated and further crystallised against the colonial background. Moreover, popular views that referred to the green appearance of Dakar's Plateau and named it the 'Paris of the tropics' or *la ville bourgeoise* only contributed to fostering the desired official image sought for this neighbourhood.

Needless to say, racial segregation between the colonisers and the colonised, always informal in French sub-Saharan Africa, was also fostered in Dakar through the administration's reference to the *cité-jardin*. The modern, well-equipped, *pittoresque*, white residential areas within Dakar's ceremonious space only celebrated the colonial power. While the Africans were perhaps expected to imitate these residences, they never experienced similar planning developments. The 'dual cities' policy only put them in the waiting room of modern planning, and of being an integral part of the 'civilised' urban sphere. The 'garden city' idea in colonial Africa was promoted by narrow-minded urbanists and Eurocentric social scientists, asserted Coquery-

Vidrovitch; and, by promoting residential segregation, it only sharpened the gap between the expatriate bourgeoisie and the indigenous population.[58] This is true, but it also might be illuminating to regard the concept of the *cité-jardin* as it was implemented in French West Africa not just as a capricious experimental realisation of indirect British planning ideas on colonial terrain. We might also consider the inherent flexibility of this notion as another important development in the history of the garden city, even though it was selfish with regard to the indigenous population in colonial times, and, as opposed to the Howardian concept, essentially anti-social/ist.

Notes

1   Walter L. Creese, *The Search for Environment, The Garden City: Before and After* (New Haven, CT, and London: Yale University Press, 1966). All Creese's citations in this paragraph are taken from the first page of this source.

2   For example Robert Owen, Charles Fourier and Saint-Simon; see Martin Buber, *Paths in Utopia* (Boston: Beacon Press, 1960), p. 6. See also Peter Batchelor, 'The origin of the garden city concept of urban form', *Journal of the Society of Architectural Historians*, 28:3 (1969), 184–200.

3   Ebenezer Howard, *Garden Cities of To-Morrow*, ed. Frederic J. Osborn, introductory essay by Lewis Mumford (London: Faber and Faber, 1970 [1902, 1946]). Originally titled *To-Morrow: A Peaceful Path to Real Reform* (1898). Apart from Howard's book itself, there is an exceptionally high amount of secondary literature on his ideas. The immediate international diffusion of Howard's ideas, however, often involved their loose application to a variety of other forms of urban planning and design.

4   A. Sutcliffe, 'Le Contexte urbanistique de l'oeuvre de Sellier: la transcription du modèle anglais de la cité-jardin', in Katherine Burlen (ed.), *La Banlieue-oasis, Henri Sellier et les cités-jardins (1900–1940)* (Saint-Denis: Presses Universitaires de Vincennes, 1987), pp. 67–79.

5   Gordon E. Cherry, *Town Planning in Britain since 1900* (Oxford: Blackwell, 1996), pp. 32–3.

6   Annie Fourcaut, 'Débats et réalisations de l'entre-deux-guerres ou le lotissement comme anti-modèle', in Danièle Voldman (ed.), *Les Origines des villes nouvelles de la région parisienne, 1919–1969*, Cahiers de l'Institut d'histoire du temps présent, 17 (Paris: l'Institut d'histoire du temps présent, 1990), pp. 11–22 (pp. 19–20).

7   Jean Pierre Gaudin, 'The French garden city', in Stephen V. Ward (ed.), *The Garden City: Past, Present and Future* (London: E & FN Spon, 1992), pp. 52–68 (pp. 52, 58–9).

8   Kenneth Kolson, *Big Plans: The Allure and Folly of Urban Design* (Baltimore and London: Johns Hopkins University Press, 2001), pp. 100–3.

9   Paul Rabinow, *French Modern: Norms and Forms of the Social Environment* (Cambridge, MA: MIT Press, 1989), pp. 260–76. For more about the Musée Social, see Janet R. Home, *A Social Laboratory for Modern France: The Musée Social and the Rise of the Welfare State* (Durham, NC: Duke University Press, 2002).

10   Howard, *Garden Cities*, p. 138.

11   Howard, *Garden Cities*, p. 118.

12   Notice that the meaning of 'colonisation' as used in the text does not correspond with its meaning *à la française*. In French (colonial historiography) it refers to the various stages of the development of French colonial settlements in the sense of *mise en valeur* (development), for example, the construction of railways, ports, buildings etc. These physical aspects were usually discussed in heroic tones. See, for more, David Prochaska, *Making Algeria French: Colonialism in Bône, 1870–1920* (Cambridge: Cambridge University Press, 1990), p. 1. Of course, 'coloni-

sation' should be differentiated from 'colonialism' – which both in English and French refers to the practice of domination, involving the subjugation of one people to another. This could be done, especially in several regions in Africa, without the presence of massive movements of settlers and also did not essentially involve 'development'.

13   Quoted in Howard, *Garden Cities*, pp. 119–20 (Howard's italics). As remarked by the editor of this 1970 edition, Frederic J. Osborn, Howard was mistaken in attributing this passage to Wakefield. Wakefield indeed quotes it in his *Art of Colonization* (1849), yet it is borrowed from Dr Hind's *Thoughts on Secondary Punishment* (1832). It is, however, in line with Wakefield's favouring of an overseas colonisation by more representative migrant groups.

14   Howard's reference to the contemporary economist Alfred Marshall only reinforces such a view; see Howard, *Garden Cities*, pp. 121–2.

15   Susanna Barrows, '"Parliaments of the people": the political culture of cafés in the early Third Republic', in Susanna Barrows and Robin Room (eds), *Drinking: Behaviour and Belief in Modern History* (Berkeley: University of California Press, 1991), pp. 87–97.

16   For Edwin Chadwick's quote, see John A. Roebuck's 1833 *Report from the Select Committee on Public Walks*, in George F. Chadwick (ed.), *The Park and the Town* (New York: Architectural Press, 1966), p. 51.

17   Standish Meacham, *Regaining Paradise: Englishness and the Early Garden City Movement* (New Haven, CT, and London: Yale University Press, 1999), pp. 1–5, 7.

18   Creese, *The Search*, p. 204.

19   Nicholas Green, *The Spectacle of Nature: Landscape and Bourgeois Culture in Nineteenth Century France* (Manchester: Manchester University Press, 1990), pp. 41–5, 66; Rabinow, *French Modern*, pp. 274–5.

20   Gaudin, 'French garden city', pp. 55, 57, 61, 63.

21   On India, see Anthony D. King, *Colonial Urban Development* (London and Boston: Routledge and Kegan Paul, 1976). On Morocco, Madagascar and Indo-China, see Gwendolyn Wright, *The Politics of Design in French Colonial Urbanism* (Chicago: University of Chicago Press, 1991). On sub-Saharan Africa, see Liora Bigon, *A History of Urban Planning in Two West African Colonial Capitals: Residential Segregation in British Lagos and French Dakar (1850–1930)* (Lewiston, NY: Edwin Mellen, 2009).

22   The AOF, the federation of French West Africa, was created in 1895, alongside the federation of French Equatorial Africa (AEF), to facilitate the centralist decision-making process in Paris. The AOF's overall territory amounted to 4,633,985 sq km, and included eight colonies: Senegal, French Sudan (present-day Mali), French Guinea, Ivory Coast, Dahomey (Benin), Upper Volta (Burkina Faso), Niger and Mauritania. The resident population of Dakar was 1,500 in 1875. With the initiation of the 1885 railway and Dakar's new status, it grew to about 20,000.

23   The best source for an explanation of the politics behind Dakar's Médina in our opinion is still Raymond Betts, 'The establishment of the Medina in Dakar, Senegal, 1914', *Africa*, 41 (1971), 143–52. See also Elikia M'Bokolo, 'Peste et société urbaine à Dakar: l'épidémie de 1914', *Cahiers d'Études africaines*, 12:1/2 (1982), 13–46. The meaning of both words, 'Medina' and 'Plateau', is rooted in the vocabulary of French colonial urban planning in Africa; see Bigon, *History of Urban Planning*, pp. 198, 224–7.

24   Jean Bugnicourt, 'Dakar without bounds', in Brian Taylor (ed.), *Reading the Contemporary African City* (Singapore: Concept Media, 1982), pp. 27–42 (p. 30).

25   Archives Nationales du Sénégal, Dakar (hereafter ANS), P 167, Urbanism de Dakar, rues et places, etc. 1901–18. See also Marème Dione, 'Dakar au fil des plans', in Maurice Culot and Jean-M. Thiveaud (eds), *Architectures françaises outré-mer* (Liège: Pierre Mardaga, 1992), pp. 221–36 (p. 222).

26   Spiro Kostof, *The City Shaped* (London: Thames and Hudson, 1999), pp. 238, 240.

27   This element of 'pacification' of more liberal and anti-colonial metropolitan critics was noted by Sinou, without further reference: Alain Sinou, *Comptoirs et villes*

coloniales du Sénégal: Saint-Louis, Gorée, Dakar (Paris: Karthala, ORSTOM, 1993), p. 300.

28 Emile Lengyel, *Dakar: Outpost of Two Hemispheres* (New York: Random House, 1943), p. 30.

29 For more on the *villes nouvelles* and their relationship with the indigenous hubs in French North Africa, see Shirine Hamadeh, 'Creating the traditional city: a French project', in Nezar AlSayyad (ed.), *Forms of Dominance* (Aldershot: Avebury, 1992), pp. 241–60; Wright, *Politics of Design*; Prochaska, *Making Algeria French*; Zeynep Çelik, *Urban Forms and Colonial Confrontations* (Berkeley: University of California Press, 1997). See also chapter 1 in this book.

30 Janet Abu-Lughod, *Rabat: Urban Apartheid in Morocco* (Princeton, NJ: Princeton University Press, 1980), p. xvii.

31 The Wolof are a majority in Senegal. The Lebu are a Wolof sub-group. On the role of vegetation (trees) in their settlements, see David Gamble, *Peoples of the Gambia: The Wolof* (San Francisco: San Francisco State University, 1985); Eric Ross, *Sufi City: Urban Design and Archetypes in Touba* (Rochester, VT: Rochester University Press, 2006), pp. 176–215.

32 These Dakarois practices are evident from the early twentieth century. See, for instance, the testimony of elderly Fatim Diop in Philippe David, *Paysages dakarois de l'époque colonial* (Dakar: ENDA, 1978), p. 38; or the autobiography of Nafissatou Diallo, *A Dakar Childhood* (Harlow: Longman, 1982), p. 2. On 'cultural difference' as an excuse for segregationist colonial policy, see Assane Seck, *Dakar, métropole ouest africaine* (Dakar: IFAN, 1970), p. 132; see also Homi K. Bhabha, *The Location of Culture* (London: Routledge, 1994), ch. 7.

33 For instance, Christopher Winters, 'Urban morphogenesis in francophone black Africa', *The Geographical Review*, 72:2 (1982), 139–54 (143); Catherine Coquery-Vidrovitch, 'À propos de la cité-jardin dans les colonies', in Catherine Coquery-Vidrovitch and Odile Goerg (eds), *La Ville européenne outre mers* (Paris: l'Harmattan, 1996), pp. 105–26; Sinou, *Comptoirs*, pp. 307–8.

34 Jean Royer (ed.), *L'Urbanisme aux colonies et dans les pays tropicaux*, 2 vols (La Charité-sur-Loire: Delayance, 1932). For a monograph on the 1931 exposition, see Patricia Morton, *Hybrid Modernities* (Cambridge, MA: MIT Press, 2000).

35 E. Weithas, 'Rapport général sur l'urbanisme en Afrique tropicale', in Royer (ed.), *L'Urbanisme aux colonies*, vol. 1, pp. 111–14 (p. 112).

36 Weithas, 'Rapport', p. 113.

37 René Schoentjes, 'Considérations générales sur l'urbanisme au Congo belge', in Royer (ed.), *L'Urbanisme aux colonies*, vol. 1, pp. 170–88 (p. 178).

38 R. de Andrade, 'L'Urbanisation de Beira en Afrique orientale portugaise', in Royer (ed.), *L'Urbanisme aux colonies*, vol. 1, pp. 141–5 (pp. 144, 145). In this report the *cité-jardin* expressed colonial dreams as it had not yet been materialised.

39 For instance, ANS, 4P 169, Urbanisme au Senegal: services des parks et jardins, 1923; 4P 1461, Jardins publics de Dakar et Gorée: construction, 1921–22.

40 ANS, 4P 75, Plan d'aménagement de la cite jardin de Hann: pièces écrites et plans, 1957.

41 ANS, 4P 1461, Jardins publics de Dakar et Gorée: construction. Inside: Jardin des compagnies disciplinaires à Hann, 1870 (Génie, direction du Sénégal, petit atlas des batiments militaires); P167, Urbanisme de Dakar, rues et places, etc. 1901–18. Note par l'inspection de l'agriculture sur la plantation des avenues de Dakar, 28 September 1907.

42 For the French colonial 'romanisation' of African (communal) grounds, see Alain Dubresson, *L'Espace Dakar-Rufisque en devenir* (Paris: ORSTOM, 1979), pp. 105–6. For the issue of land ownership on Dakar's Plateau, see Seck, *Dakar*, pp. 122–31.

43 For more on the Office des Habitations Economiques, see Sophie Dulucq and Odile Goerg, *Les Investissements publics urbains en Afrique de l'ouest, 1930–1985* (Paris: l'Harmattan, 1989), p. 119. For the special terms given by the administration to French contractors, see ANS, 4P 272, Plateau, villas, 1922–23.

44 Cited in Sinou, *Comptoirs*, pp. 320–1.

45 Ann Laura Stoler, *Carnal Knowledge and Imperial Power: Race and the Intimate in Colonial Rule* (Berkeley: University of California Press, 2002); Michael G. Vann, 'The good, the bad, and the ugly: variation and difference in French racism in colonial *Indochine*', in Sue Peabody and Tyler Stovall (eds), *The Color of Liberty: Histories of Race in France* (Durham, NC: Duke University Press, 2003), pp. 187–205.

46 George Ribot and Robert Lafon, *Dakar: ses origines, son avenir* (Paris: Michels fils, 1908), p. 83.

47 For relations between the global economy and British metropolitan and colonial space, see Anthony D. King, *The Bungalow: The Production of a Global Culture* (Oxford: Oxford University Press, 1995). For similar developments in contemporary France see Green, *Spectacle of Nature*.

48 King, *Colonial Urban Development*, pp. 58–66.

49 For a detailed survey on Dakar's peripheral expansion in terms of economy and planning, see Alberto Arecchi, 'City profile: Dakar', *Cities*, 2:3 (1985), pp. 198–211. For an historiographic glimpse into this phenomenon, see Guy Mainet and Gérard Salem, 'Recherches de géographie urbaine en Afrique occidentale', *Espaces Tropicaux*, 12 (1994), 109–20.

50 ANS, P120, Bâtiments de Dakar, Hôtel du Gouverneur Général, 1902–06; K19, Sénégal ancien, travaux publics, jardin de gouvernement à Dakar, 1898.

51 ANS, P167, Urbanisme de Dakar, rues et places, 1901–18; 4P 169, Urbanisme au Senegal, services des parks et jardins, 1923.

52 ANS, P167, Urbanisme de Dakar, rues et places, 1901–18. For a general background about the origin and development of the French boulevards and avenues, see Kostof, *The City*, pp. 249–54.

53 Ribot and Lafon, *Dakar*, p. 28.

54 Rhodes House, Oxford, MSS. Brit. Emp., S. 99 1, 1901–16, papers (1914–16), on the removal of the capital of the Northern Province of Nigeria from Zungeru to Kaduna.

55 Sophie Dulucq, 'Les Ambiguïtés du discours et des pratiques urbaines: Afrique noire francophone (c. 1900–c. 1980)', in Coquery-Vidrovitch and Goerg (eds), *La Ville européenne*, pp. 217–34 (p. 222). She quotes from Alain Sinou, *Projets et pratiques d'espace à Bamako*, Mémoir de maîtrise d'urbanisme (Paris: n.p., 1980), p. 28 (my translation and analysis).

56 Maurice Ricord, *France Noire: Dakar, grand port impérial* (Marseilles: Sud editions, 1939), pp. 28–9 (my translation).

57 See, for instance, Derwent Whittlesey, 'Dakar and other Cape Verde settlements', *The Geographical Review*, 4 (1941), 609–38 (p. 631).

58 Catherine Coquery-Vidrovitch, 'The process of urbanisation in Africa', *African Studies Review*, 34:1 (1991), 1–98 (68–9, 71).

CHAPTER THREE

The 'plateau' in West African, French-speaking colonial towns: between garden and city[†]

Alain Sinou

The concept of the garden city, an idea initiated by Ebenezer Howard in England right at the end of the nineteenth century, would be put into practice in industrial Europe of the early twentieth century as a result of political concerns. Socialist politicians and town planners would use this concept to try to create an alternative to the insalubrious living conditions of workers gravitating to the big cities and crowding into slums. In France the main political activist of this movement was Henri Sellier, the socialist mayor of the Parisian suburb of Suresnes, and chairman of a government-subsidised housing company, the Departmental Office for Inexpensive Housing (l'Office Départmental des Habitations à Bon Marché). In the interwar years this would contribute to creating a dozen garden cities intended for workers. Up until today, this type of activity has remained closely associated with the concept of social housing.

There is therefore something rather paradoxical in examining the spaces created at the same time in the French colonies, intended for Europeans, the most privileged sector of society, using a concept that had evolved for social housing. Clearly, to explain this striking departure, we need to jettison the 'social' connotation, retaining only the principles of spatial organisation of the garden cities. These principles testify to a major development in the concept of creating urban areas and they would be employed in other metropolitan planning activities initiated by private developers for the wealthier classes. During the Second Empire, for instance, there were housing estates reserved for the middle class. The Vésinet project, undertaken in a town just west of Paris, is an emblematic example of this, and qualified, albeit retrospectively, as a garden city, thereby confirming the need to achieve a compromise with nature in urban settings.

All these projects, irrespective of whom they were intended for, shared several points in common. From a town planning point of view, they sought to create a model layout based upon an overall plan, initiated by a single client, that acquired and divided up parcels of land, which is contrary to what takes place in poor residential areas. In these areas, urban planning is largely the result of the actions of various landowners and small-scale developers. They purchase land on existing streets and round about, mark out a few roads that are extensions of existing ones, call the project 'subdividing into parcels', and then sell these parcels or put up buildings, depending upon pressure on property, without supplying infrastructure – water supply, drainage, electricity and above all public services (schools etc).[1] As against housing estates and company towns in industrial areas, set up during the nineteenth century by owners for the workers of a single company, where such principles did prevail, garden cities were targeted at a much broader urban customer base, testifying to a change in scale for town planning, which now operated at the level of an entire town. Nevertheless, contrary to England where this movement sometimes gave rise to the creation of new towns, on the continent it only developed at the level of the residential area. Having a single client for a project also led to the design of a homogeneous urban setting, designed by a single architect, who created the stylistic unity of the buildings put up by one or several developers, based upon a set of rules. Lastly, the influence of thinking about hygiene led to the area being organised upon several principles designed to improve the health and well-being of the residents: water supply and drainage networks prepared prior to the sale of the parcels of land, low construction density to ensure the free flow of fluids and access to sunlight, public services etc. Within this context town planners sought to introduce elements of nature into cityscapes, until then missing from towns or reserved for the 'exclusive areas' (*beaux quartiers*). Lines of trees were planted along the streets; recreation areas were encouraged on the parcels where homes were built; and, in addition, in a new area, one or more public gardens were laid out, open to all. Whether or not it had a social purpose, the garden city concept at the beginning of the twentieth century marked town planning thinking and contributed to developing a modus operandi in towns, in particular by requiring the reintroduction of 'nature' into the city.

What about colonial urban areas, bearing in mind that these were territories where many *villes nouvelles* were founded that are today considered as places where modernity was experimented with?[2] If the question of producing social housing was not on the agenda – irrespective of country or the nationality of the colonisers – the natural environment became the subject of many questions. Through the reconstruction of several areas reserved for 'whites' in sub-Saharan

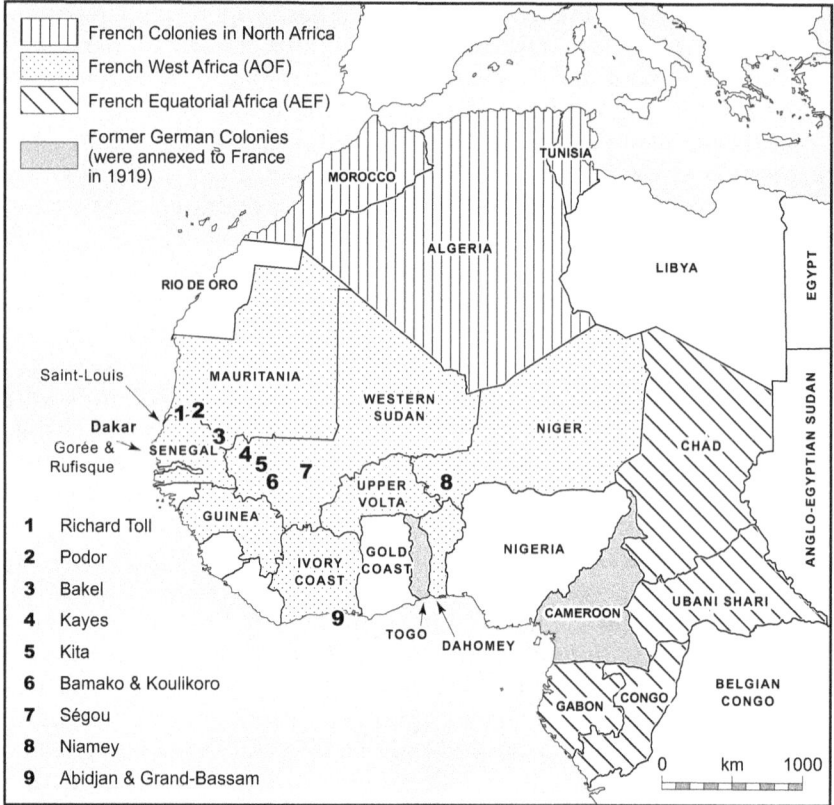

Figure 3.1 Places mentioned in the text marked on a map of French colonial Africa.

Africa, and especially the government town of Koulouba in Bamako (today the capital of Mali, formerly French Sudan), this chapter will expand the thinking of Liora Bigon on Dakar (chapter 2), by analysing the place accorded to greenery in other West African towns, and how it came about (for places mentioned in the text see fig. 3.1). These examples will allow us to assess if the garden city concept influenced these projects, and more generally, to try to identify a logic in the spread of urban models.

An enduring, hostile image of nature

The desire to make their colonial towns green required of the colonialists a 'positive' relationship with the natural environment, though until the beginning of the twentieth century this relationship was far from being achieved in sub-Saharan Africa. The relationship people have with the natural environment results at least as much from the image they have of it as from their physical experience, especially when it is a matter of new surroundings. Before they even ventured there, Westerners already had a particular image of Africa. Ever since Herodotus, sub-Saharan Africa had been synonymous with 'barbarism', that is, a world populated mainly by monsters and savages living in a climate inimical to people. Christian myths supported this viewpoint and its images of a land that God did not really have the time to fashion (six days is short!), which stimulated both excitement and fear. One had to wait until the eighteenth century, the Enlightenment and physiocratic thinking[3] for more reasoned descriptions of this region to be made by Western travellers, who only visited Africa's coastal areas. However, these travellers took badly to the climate, succumbed to 'fevers' and continued to give credence to the idea of a dangerous natural environment (both forests and deserts), which impacted on the behaviour of the local populations (adopting Montesquieu's theory of climate), and which would be conveyed later by the first colonists.

This omnipresent danger did not prevent certain specific cases of wonder, particularly in the humid tropical regions where nature was sometimes described as being 'luxuriant'. Naturalists, given the task of creating an inventory of the richness of these lands, missionaries and travellers emphasised the beauty of the vegetation, especially the silk-cotton trees and baobabs, whose size and shape fascinated them. Moreover, by the start of the nineteenth century, the question of exploiting the natural resources of these areas had become an issue – the rate of growth of the flora became an advantageous quality, and 'trial' gardens would be set up for 'economic botany' and for the examination of the growth of certain vegetable species.

As Westerners settled in Africa, these representations became more varied; however, they were continually marked by the fear of an environment that held both visible and invisible enemies. The desert repelled, even if it attracted certain romantic sensibilities. The Sahelian landscapes caused concern through their dryness, monotony and immensity. But while the flatness of the land prevented both travellers and soldiers from getting their bearings, these flat lands excited the imagination of officers who dreamed of conquering them and expanding the territory of the colonial empire. The dense forest of the tropical and equatorial regions was still 'impenetrable' and constituted the 'natural' refuge of ferocious animals and of tribes hardly less so.[4] And all these places, covered by the cult name 'the bush' (la brousse), represented an area where colonisers only ventured with caution.

The climatic conditions were hardly better perceived. The sun, heat and humidity, to which the colonisers were not accustomed, were deemed responsible by the medical officers of health for the proliferation of miasmas, for a long time considered carriers of fatal 'fevers'. As for the rains, even though they boosted agricultural production, their disturbing violence, the way they flooded the riverside areas where Europeans had settled and contributed to the spread of insects and mosquitoes, were all persistent disturbances to everyday life.

In this situation, how are we to understand that, at the beginning of the twentieth century, the areas where French civil servants would settle in the colonial towns of the empire would feature intense planting, which sometimes evoked the idea of garden cities? At first glance this would appear to be at odds with the medical theories about towns and the identification, right at the beginning of the twentieth century, of the carriers of tropical fevers which rather encouraged the elimination of damp environments, which were deemed pathogenic. In addition, in an epoch that saw the apogee of building nation states, where the United Kingdom was seen as an enemy and a competitor in colonial conquest, it might seem paradoxical that France was inspired by practices whose prototypes emanated from 'Perfidious Albion'.

The first settlements founded by Westerners, especially the French, along the West African coast between the sixteenth and nineteenth centuries – that is, the trading posts – did not seek to exclude any form of vegetation. In order to provide a food source, the directors of the trading companies in the forts caused the creation of kitchen gardens and orchards. Local production was cultivated, together with fruit and vegetables imported from Europe, not for purposes of export but simply to 'improve the ordinary'. On the other hand, while Western merchants appreciated, like the indigenous population, the shade and coolness provided by the trees, they did not encourage them being planted near their homes and even forbade it. These merchants feared attracting animal life that would disturb them, such as mosquitoes, and that might even attack them, such as snakes or wild animals. In the same way, they cleared the immediate surroundings of the forts and trading posts to protect themselves from the reptiles and insects that might be concealed there. This rejection of trees might also have occurred because some were considered holy by the local residents. In order not to be interrupted by ceremonies that might take place and to avoid disputes with members of animist cults, they preferred to see their homes surrounded by broad, tree-less areas, which had the additional advantage of being easily controllable.

The idea of home in the trading post was to a large extent inspired by the rules governing ships. All these men had spent many months at sea before reaching these coasts, and sometimes they organised trade from boats lying at anchor offshore, for fear of venturing on to the land. Naval officers and trading company representatives, who set up establishments, drew up the plans for their small forts based upon the spatial organisation of ships. Following this logic, it was consistent that most trading posts were set up on islands, sometimes in the sea (Gorée), but more often in estuaries (Saint-Louis of Senegal, Lagos).

The natural defences provided by this type of place were not always linked to a fear of being attacked by the locals, with whom the traders got on easily. It was also the result of a fear of settling on lands considered dangerous – because of men, beasts, climate and vegetation all combined – as though by partially isolating themselves they would be better protected from devastating fevers. This concern resulted from the image of a world still outside God's protection, as was 'proven' every winter season by the large number of Westerners living in the trading posts who were killed by fevers.

The very high mortality rate for whites in the tropics, where yellow fever and malaria were endemic, paradoxically resulted from their choice of where to settle. By setting up on estuaries edged with marshes, on flat land at water level which cannot wash away the rains and which suffers from the vicissitudes of the rivers, they had selected the very worst environment, because of the enormous number of mosquitoes in this humid area. However, in their ignorance, they were unaware that these insects were the carriers of these sicknesses, and sometimes had no choice on those sandy coasts, often bordered by broad lagoons.

The first plantations: Saint-Louis of Senegal

The Saint-Louis trading post, set up on an island in the estuary, brought together all these shortcomings. Yet it was selected at the beginning of the nineteenth century by the French administration as the capital of the new colony of Senegal, the bridgehead for the conquest of the Sahel. The concentration of the main body of troops and the civil administration here explains the scale of the efforts invested in changing the townscape and making it a symbol of a certain French civility. To this end an urban policy was adopted, modelled on what was being done in France, at first consisting of putting up buildings that symbolised the new colonial authority: a Governor's Palace was erected on the site of the former slave fort, together with a church, military barracks, hospital, school and even a mosque. At the same time the land was parcelled up, so as to facilitate control of expropriations by the occupants and to distinguish a public area under the control of the colonial authority from the private area, which the occupants could purchase, in accordance with the Civil Code, which was made applicable here (as at Gorée, Dakar and Rufisque).[5]

It is within this context that the issue of planting trees in the town will be discussed. In the centre of Saint-Louis, several government buildings and a few little islands covered by brick buildings comply more or less with a semblance of order, representing the newly introduced urbanism, while the further one gets away from here, the more the 'natural' regains the upper hand. The island is flat and covered with sandy soil, at best scrubby, where there are only indigenous 'straw huts', and it is inundated every time the water levels of the river rise. So how does one produce a long-term plan for the alignment of the allotment layout and allocations for the public areas on soil that in part needs to be remodelled after every flood? The systems invented in Europe – marking out plots, laying out roads, paving the streets, constructing pavements, setting up benches and other street furniture – cannot always be reproduced in Saint-Louis for lack of means, and the handful of streets that the government laid out, by clearing and flattening the ground, were quickly covered up again by sand and silt transported by the wind and the river water.

Planting trees was an attempt to fulfil the desire to carry out this draft plan for urban planning, while at the same time leaving on the landscape the imprint of authority, then something new in the society and economy of the trading posts. In practical terms, trees were planted at regular intervals, on both sides of the streets, especially on those not yet bordered by 'permanent' buildings. The purpose of the trunks and leaves was eventually to sketch out a new geometry in the town, creating vertical lines that would determine visual axes (as would the street lamps later on), and outlining vistas. These might escape up into the sky, precursors of future urbanisation, or just highlight a building or the porch at the end of the axis. These trees also served a physical function. They helped maintain the earth and stabilise the roads, especially along river banks, except where there were quays. The visibility of the road network is an essential condition for compliance with its rules and regulations, such as the prohibition on building there, the free circulation of people, and the prohibition on letting animals wander freely.

The choice of palm trees for these first tree-lined streets confirms that the authority's objective was not to provide shade for the pavements and improve the comfort of the passer-by. This tree with a tall trunk and few branches answered the sanitary concerns of the time. The palm trees, which poke through the jungle canopy, were much higher than the tallest buildings, then at most a single storey, and received the sea breeze. Their regular movement chased away insects and birds that might nest in the softest, dampest part of the trunk, from which the branches emerged. The palm tree also grows quickly in these climates, especially when planted near to water, which was the case on the island. Last but not least, this tree had no ritual significance for the local population, which preferred more majestic species such as the mahogany and the baobab. The choice of the type of palm tree was also significant: the one most frequently planted did not produce edible fruit, so as not to attract birds and insects, or 'natives' who would have been inclined to pick them. In addition, this choice did not require mobilising people to gather the fruit, so that they did not rot or attract vermin. There would nevertheless be some lines of coconut trees, whose coconuts would perhaps grace the tables of Westerners (figs 3.2, 3.3).

The planting in the following decades of lines of palm trees in various military camps, especially on Saint-Louis's 'Langue de Barbarie' (N'Dar Tout), testified to this same concern, to produce straight lines in a world where they were cruelly lacking. In a way, these trees were used as substitutes for posts or poles to introduce vertical lines into the landscape, rather than necessarily for greenery. This planting policy, however, was limited to certain situations and was not extended to residential or business areas. While other, larger trees were planted

Figure 3.2 Saint-Louis of Senegal, the central avenue of Guet N'Dar quarter. The regulated plantations of coconut trees on each side of the avenue contributed to the creation of the public space.

Figure 3.3 Saint-Louis of Senegal, the central avenue of Guet N'Dar quarter.

near such public buildings as churches and mosques to provide shade outside where people would gather to meet, they were banished from the residential quarters of both the Europeans and the 'natives'. Only the central square on the island of Saint-Louis, with the government building, was landscaped, which was carried out at the same time as the construction of the two military barracks during the 1830s. This helped to produce an urban ensemble made up of the planted esplanade, bordered on three sides by buildings, and on the fourth side open to the river and then the bridge linking the island to the 'Langue de Barbarie', a thin strip of sandy land squeezed between the river and the sea.

Colonial development at the beginning of the twentieth century: Bamako

From the very beginning of the twentieth century, at the end of the conquest phase, planning policies for all the conquered territories were put in place. These had two main objectives: to create the infrastructure required for the economic exploitation of these areas and to make the places where Westerners settled more salubrious. The towns would have a role to play in this process, especially those housing government bodies that were hubs of the communications network based on the rivers and railways.

In order to highlight the French presence in these new territories, senior members of the Ministry for the Colonies in France drew up directives to create an urban infrastructure that differed from those settlements set up both by the locals and also by Westerners, that is, the trading posts and military positions. The purpose of this policy was to attract the necessary number of Frenchmen for 'development' (*mise en valeur*), who were still fearful of venturing out into the 'lands of fevers'. It addressed first the new town of Dakar, which was the seat of the government of the federation, and was reflected in the 'greening' of its landscape, while also affecting the new administrative centres, or *chefs-lieux*, of the colonies. At the same time, an action plan was set up. The Ministry for the Colonies defined the directives and the broad lines of the policy. The federation governments created at that time, French West Africa (AOF, Afrique Occidental Française) and French Equatorial Africa (AEF, Afrique Equatoriale Française), were responsible for their implementation. The territories within each federation were governed by Lieutenant-Governors, who acted as Prefects and whose job it was to carry out the orders of the federation government. Yet this pyramid organisation was thwarted, especially in the first decades after it was set up, by the slowness and difficulty of communications and the low number of civil servants, which left a wide scope for manoeuvre for each level of authority.

This policy got going just as the urban planning debates were raging in Europe, yet colonial urban thinking was primarily influenced by several medical discoveries. Research carried out in both France and Britain since the 1880s on the carriers of yellow fever and malaria resulted in the identification of what spread both, certain types of mosquito.[6] In the tropical colonies decrees were issued forbidding the presence of stagnant water in both residential and public areas; health services were set up, which regularly inspected homes and required all receptacles containing liquids to be closed; they hired 'natives' to fill in the ponds. It was now realised that colonial settlements needed to keep a distance from the rivers, even if this was not always easy to implement, because they were often the only axis of communication. Rules were drawn up for the construction of residential quarters for the expatriate population, so that they should be better ventilated and protected from the causes of disease.[7] However, these steps were not sufficient to halt the epidemics, and more stringent measures that would completely restructure urban organisation would have to be employed.

Having failed to impose these sanitary rules on all the inhabitants, the AOF's colonial administration decided to create areas reserved for its own staff, where all the rules would be followed. The 'natives', whose lack of hygiene was now considered responsible for the spread of mosquitoes and more generally other bearers of infections – such as rats – and therefore of sickness, had to live far from this town, in their own areas. This policy would be systematised in the new colonial towns more than in Dakar, where notwithstanding the creation of the Médina quarter in 1914 following an outbreak of the plague, part of the local population continued to live within the existing town.

The planning of Bamako was testimony to this approach. This small village, set in a savannah with trees, borders the Niger River and included a small fort for the colonial troops, built at the time of the conquest. When this had been completed, several administrators suggested moving the capital of 'Upper Senegal and Niger' there, which was until then in Kayes, further west on the Senegal River. This place was considered particularly unhealthy, like the other posts set up along the Senegal: in 1881, for instance, about 40 per cent of the French garrisons at Podor, Bakel and Kayes were wiped out by yellow fever. In addition, Kayes was oriented towards the coast and could hardly symbolise French domination of the interior. The plain of the Niger answered this requirement, and the Bamako post was on the banks of the river and on the railway line then being built, which would connect the navigable reach of the Senegal to the Niger, which served the most distant, colonised areas on the borders of the Sahara.

Once it had been designated as the administrative centre of Upper Senegal and Niger (later to be called French Sudan, today's Mali) and after the railway had been completed, Bamako attracted much larger urban investments than other regional administrative centres such as Ouagadougou (Upper Volta, today's Burkina Faso) and Niamey (Niger). This town became the obligatory crossing point from Senegal for penetrating the centre of the continent. It was considered by the administration as the 'opposite number' of Dakar (with which it would be connected by railway in 1924), and as a showpiece of the policy being undertaken in the hinterland. It was also the recipient of particular care in planning, as testified by its 'greening' (*verdissement*), which was carried out in two ways – first in a new government quarter, Koulouba, and then in most of the lower town.

Koulouba: 'the inspired hill'

The term 'garden city', or its French variation *cité-jardin*, was never employed by the colonial governors who initiated the Koulouba project, the site of the Governor's Palace and, in post-colonial times, the home of the president of the Republic of Mali. It is the intensity of the vegetation that envelops the buildings that leads both visitors and guides to use the expression when referring to the government quarter.

The creation of this quarter stemmed from the wishes of Edgar de Trentinian, a soldier trained at Saint-Cyr, who was first in charge of this region before running the colony from a base in the town of Kayes.[8] In 1896 he recommended setting up the capital near Bamako, but was most critical of the unhealthy state of the banks of the Niger. Since the military post was situated on the plain of the Niger River, he proposed setting up the place of the new authority on the sandstone hills that dominated the plain. Being unable to prevent the 'natural' growth of the indigenous village, the Governor decided to arrange the new settlement on several sites. The commercial section developed in Bamako, where the railway station was built, hosting the French merchants from their trading companies and the natives, later removed to the outskirts, together with several colonial services related to the railway. The personnel who were running the colony would stay and work on the hill Point F, 160 metres above the village, where homes, administrative buildings and the Lieutenant-Governor's Palace would be built. The neighbouring little hill, Point G (still called this), would house the hospital. The troops would be garrisoned a few kilometres further north, in a camp set up on a plateau, near the village of Kati, which was also served by the railway. Lastly, the village of Koulikoro, in 1904 the terminus of the railway and a port of embarkation on the Niger, was also an area for development, and European traders set up there as well.

These multiple locations exactly met the concerns of the hygienists. The colonial administration was separated from the rest of the town, but it was also spread out to limit the risk of contagion from one area to another. The hospital was initially reserved for whites and for some government employees. It was isolated and was only accessible by a special road, so could be easily quarantined, as was the case of the two other establishments. The organisational principles employed in the layout of the hospital and of the military camps (construction of small buildings set apart from each other and each with a separate function or for a single pathology) were now applied at a new level, for urban areas. This dispersion of functions and of Westerners to different places, with the furthest about 80 km away, did not, however, seem to be the most efficient solution to the colonial town worthies. The plan to build on the hills was all the more complex to implement because it meant overcoming the sharp difference in height. In addition these hills lacked any springs.

Trentinian nevertheless insisted, and constructed on the highest point of Koulouba Hill a building which was intended to become his residence. It was only completed when he left the colony in 1899, and was not lived in for several years. Some even called it the 'Trentinian folly',[9] so mad did it seem to want to settle on this uninhabited, arid hill, covered in brush and broken up here and there by clumps of trees.[10] Yet from this high point Trentinian dominated the plain and could see the Niger in the distance, a view that suggested more the symbolic, ancient image of the conqueror dominating the lands where his finest battles had taken place than the need for security in a region that had been completely pacified (the main battles had taken place several hundred kilometres away). The location also met his sanitary concerns: these hills get the winds from the north, unlike the plain, and the ambient temperature is slightly lower (fig. 3.4).

The building project was confirmed in 1903 by the Governor General of the AOF, who had arrived in Dakar the previous year. Ernest Roume, a graduate of one of France's most prestigious universities and a member of the Council of State, recalled that it was best 'to occupy the high ground in order to be sheltered from the mosquitoes that spread the worst colonial sicknesses and to completely segregate the European population for the same reasons'.[11] The project manager on site would be Amédée William Merleau Ponty, in charge of organising the administration of the new colony. Initially Delegate

Figure 3.4 Panoramic view of the lower town of Bamako from the hill of 'Point F', today's Koulouba, where the Government Palace was erected.

of the Government General, then Lieutenant-Governor, Ponty would, between 1908 and 1915, become the Governor General of the AOF, and would retain a watching brief over everything that took place throughout the territory.[12] To achieve this, Roume and Ponty relied on a project management service within the colonial administration, based in Dakar and Bamako, and made up mainly of officers of the Engineering Corps. These drew their inspiration for drawing up the plans for sites and the architecture of buildings from rules issued by the Ministry and models drawn in the 'Atlas of Military Buildings', which made the rounds in all the colonies.[13]

The distances between each building in Koulouba, the geometric layout, and the separation between work and living areas, were not in and of themselves new principles of spatial organisation. They had already been applied in a good many places (hospitals, military camps and others), but here they were on an altogether different scale, that of a housing estate, even if the building density was quite a bit lower than other operations of this sort.[14] The initial plan called for putting up about a dozen buildings, of which only those along the large esplanade were of significant size, the others being much smaller, mainly single storey only, principally so as not to block the wind. This low building density, over some 25 acres, and the structure of the layout, built around a road leading to a palace, did not stem from garden city/*cité-jardin* policies or housing estates, even if the residential part comprised stand-alone houses on enclosed parcels of land. In addition, the integrity of the land was maintained; it was not sold as lots by a developer, but constituted a single, integrated entity belonging to the Colony. This combination of elements was more typical of parks, which in France harked back to an aristocratic tradition. Despite the Revolution, ever since the creation of Versailles this form had represented a point of reference that could not be ignored in the imagination of French builders and many sites of prefectures under both the Second Empire and the Third Republic drew inspiration from this model. Moreover, it is likely that the colonial officers, who were artisans on the ground of *la plus grande France*, also pushed for it,[15] especially in Koulouba where the greening might have been a means of obscuring a certain mundanity in the construction, caused by limited financial and human resources.

From this point of view, the 'luxuriant' vegetation set this area apart from other colonial settlements of the period, which were much less planted. The houses spread out among the undergrowth, the rectangular avenues, roundabouts, flowerbeds, fountain (facing the palace), the lines of trees that sketched out the views of the vegetation, groups of palm trees planted along the esplanade in front of the palace, the viewpoints, of which the most beautiful was reserved for the master of the place, embracing the horizon and the plain with the wide river that crossed it, were all elements recalling French-style parks, in a rather 'tropicalised' variation. In addition, in terms of both hygiene and comfort, the 'greening' of the residential and administrative areas offered various advantages: the colonialists also needed to protect themselves from the sunlight. The plant cover, therefore, which would overhang the residential administrative buildings and convert the roads into shaded avenues, cooled down the air much more than plain verandahs or arcades tacked on to the structures (fig. 3.5).

Yet the price to pay for this comfort and for the park was high, and for some was even out of due proportion. It required putting up buildings that offered assurances in terms of isolation against animals that might enter: raised above the ground, double-roofed, with a verandah going round the entire building, and doors and windows that closed hermetically,[16] all of which added considerably to the costs. The *tirailleurs noirs*, the African infantrymen of the French garrison, were requisitioned to do the work, but some refused, so prisoners of war were used to pave the road that came up to Koulouba and to cut the rocks that came from the hill. To avoid the *brousse* taking over again, continual work was required to drain the rainwater, prune the trees, clear the undergrowth from the hillsides, cut the grass and clear the ground. There were accordingly a considerable number of gardener-boys, who despite their efforts could not prevent a sleeping python from falling off a branch or some fine tarantulas from getting into a cupboard.

Moreover, the project's ambitions very quickly came up against reality, encountering many difficulties that were sometimes unforeseeable. The flooding of Kayes in the summer of 1906 and the yellow fever epidemic that followed it paralysed the works for six months, because the materials could not be brought in, traffic with the infected area having been cut to avoid the epidemic spreading.[17] The slow pace of the project led the colonial authorities to organise building down on the plain where the staff continued to live. The plans drawn up between 1900 and 1910 indicate the existence of an initial transportation network of roads linking the fort at Kati, Koulikoro and the river.[18] They also indicate the existence of various facilities such as housing, a shop and workshops – a geographical unit run by a commandant, a school, dispensary and native infirmary, a house for the doctor, post and telegraph office, market, housing for the assistants, a magazine for explosives, an abattoir and a *village de liberté*, a camp of 'liberated slaves' who were employed in forced labour.

Koulouba, an unusual form of garden quarter, was without question the 'greenest' in the AOF, even if it only grew on a small scale, perhaps for several different reasons. Building on a headland was not a colonial innovation, as the Acropolis reminds us. The new area for the exercise and representation of power dominated the town, like a fortress or

Figure 3.5 French administrative building on Koulouba.

rather more like a prince's palace, since considerations of defence were hardly paramount in this region at the time the project was decided upon. From this point of view, Koulouba incarnates an elitist concept of the colonial urban settlement, in which the decision-making minority (and not all the colonialists) lived among themselves, provided with superior comforts and separated from the indigenous population by a building-free zone, the slopes of the hill (today we would speak of a gated community). Indeed, this quarter combined the principles of privileged housing estates made up of individual residential units and of the French-style park, while meeting sanitary requirements. However, it was also part of the thinking that grants nature a place within the town, to which the garden city in Europe was a response. In this sense, Koulouba reflects a development in the attitude to the natural environment, no longer perceived as an enemy but as having the potential to serve as a tool.

It is, however, very unlikely that the contemporary governors had the time to read or even browse through the work of Georges Benoît-Lévy, published in 1904, which made known in France (or more precisely in Paris), among intellectual and scientific circles, the Anglo-Saxon concept of the garden city. These men had from the end of the nineteenth century started long colonial careers, and only went back to France for visits at best once a year. Furthermore, the garden city idea, which attracted certain French bourgeois and intellectual elites who were sensitive to English ways, was no doubt not to the taste of French military men, for whom everything emanating from England was inherently bad.[19] And they could not have known of several *cité-jardin* projects carried out in France, which would only be implemented in the 1920s. We need to consider other, less direct ways in which this concept was spread, and to examine the natural local conditions of these colonial players, especially the governors who promoted the Koulouba project.

The danger of fevers remained a trying reality for the colonisers, and for the French local governors who had seen epidemics up close, had even seen family members die from them.[20] They had intimate experience of disease, and ought to have been able to see that it was necessary to push the vegetation away as far as possible from colonial settlements. This reasoning, however, fails to take into account the particular experience of the military conquest in which these people had all taken part, and the relationship with the natural environment that this experience engendered. The military campaigns took the colonial governors for months on end into the interior of the continent, to places where the conveniences of the West were non-existent, and where they had to come to terms with this setting in order to survive. The long bivouacs gave them the opportunity to discover and appreciate certain landscapes, especially the many viewpoints over the Niger River – the kind that had made explorers dream for centuries. Without a doubt, these military men were visited by images of romantic heroes (as can be seen in the drawings by army cartographers who accompanied these expeditions, and who placed them in natural scenes that were in equal parts luxurious and menacing). More prosaically, they discovered the benefits of resting under clumps of trees, and had to be able to quickly identify those species that offered the best shade and under which animals, insects and vermin did not find shelter. By regularly sleeping under mosquito nets,[21] they protected themselves against the risk of fevers and discovered that they could survive in these climates, which proved to be less deadly than they had been told.

The Koulouba project also probably owed its existence to the political situation in which the colony's governors carried out their duties. Following the military-conquest phase, they were like pioneers. They also enjoyed full powers on account of their distance from the central authority and in the absence of any control over their actions when the new command and control institutions were being set up. Further, the governors were normally from the families of the office-holding middle classes, the gentry or military families, who 'went up' to the capital, attended the most prestigious Parisian institutions of higher education, and then entered the Civil Service or the military.[22] They were thus sensitive to ideas of progress as part of the French colonial *mission civilisatrice*, introducing 'civilisation' to the rest of the world. Their knowledge might have not been gleaned from books but rather from a variety of sources of current thinking on the place of nature in the city.

There were accordingly strong links with those involved in the Musée Social, in France, where new urban theories were being developed, together with some of the players in colonisation. The French politician, Jules Siegfried – author of the 1894 law bearing his name that encouraged the creation of 'inexpensive housing' and a member of the Garden Cities Association, founded by Georges Benoît-Lévy – was Minister for the Colonies between 1892 and 1893. There were also certain persons in the colonial project, even if moulded by the military, who might have been open to the idea of 'greening' parts of colonial towns, especially since for some of them the colonies were considered places specially suited for implementing modernity. It is not certain that they developed structured thinking on this subject, in the same way that some building traditions are passed on without the reasons behind them being known. Creating parks and gardens was also based on traditions that predated modernity, for instance those developed in France by the aristocracy,[23] and even earlier ones, which were developed in the Christian tradition, in which this type of space was associated with the image of paradise.

Moreover, in the colonial situation, creating a park such as that in Koulouba required human resources, provided by native forced labour, but did not need much finance: all the basic materials were available locally, free of charge. It can also be imagined that for these soldiers who wanted to refashion this territory and its nature in accordance with an ideal of modernity, this place, Koulouba, acted as a sort of secret garden, and in a way was where they could realise some of their dreams.

Conclusion: between plateaux and cités-jardins

The term 'plateau' is the generic name for the quarter where Westerners lived in colonial towns, normally referring to a higher and better-ventilated area. Yet in the areas discussed here the literal meaning of this term was far from fixed, as those towns were set up on flat ground, along the coasts and rivers. When in the 1920s colonial investment took off again, one of the authorities' challenges was to organise an urban area beyond Koulouba-type operations, intended to house and provide office space for several dozen civil servants. The colonial town was meant to become a place of trade and production, attracting locals and colonialists alike. Nevertheless, the growth of these new colonial towns needed to be more organised, both to affirm the colonial authority and to avoid the disorderly settlement of the European and African inhabitants, as occurred in the trading posts.

The planning of Bamako in the years 1920–30 testifies to this policy. A roadway and land parcels plan was drawn up for the entire town centre, intended for Westerners, whereas property for the natives, also organised in lots, was planned for the urban periphery. Koulouba would not benefit from this effort,[24] and the buildings were eventually surrounded by increasingly dense vegetation, making the impressive façade of the Governor's Palace invisible from the lower town. This policy was implemented by a new Lieutenant-Governor, Jean Henri Terrasson de Fougères, a civilian trained at the École Coloniale,[25] but who did not take part in the military conquest. De Fougères doubtless did not fully subscribe to the methods of his predecessor, who used and abused forced labour to build the colony's infrastructure.[26]

The First World War, in which thousands of Senegalese riflemen, or tirailleurs, fought, most of whom came from this region or the Mossi country, impacted on colonial policies and contributed somewhat to improving the status of the indigenous population. In this situation, urban planning could not be restricted to creating infrastructure for the government. The new Governor's actions testify to this development, as can still be seen in the layout of central Bamako.[27] This also explains the town's growth, greater than that of the other regional administrative centres in the AOF.[28] The African migrants grouped together on the plain, around the railway station and the old fort, and hardly at all around Kati and Koulikoro.

During his term of office, de Fougères systematically planted hundreds of tall trees along the new avenues laid out in the town of Bamako. The scale of operations was new and involved the entire urban space used by Westerners, though it was also open to 'natives', even if these were relegated to their own residential quarters. In this respect, the 'greening' of the urban centre contributed to the separation of the inhabitants. The planting of saplings and flower beds required a set of rules for the use of the public space. So that they could grow, it was necessary to prohibit animals (sheep etc.) from wandering around, and therefore these areas had to be separated from the African homes, in many of which animals were kept. While one of the purposes, as in Saint-Louis a century earlier, was to create a three-dimensional public domain, the mahogany and royal poinciana trees that blaze red for several months of the year were intended to delineate shady streets by creating 'bowers'. Planting was also carried out within the parcels of the quarters where the expatriates' villas and the administrative buildings were to be found, whose gardens would become as green as those surrounding the buildings in Koulouba.[29]

Such developments doubtless resulted from progress made in medicine and the prevention of malaria and yellow fever epidemics. Preventative use of quinine had become general practice among the colonisers. In 1934 a first vaccine was developed against yellow fever, though it would take years until all the colonisers, and later the colonised population, agreed to be vaccinated. Nevertheless, the yellow fever epidemics diminished and became less deadly. Applying sanitary regulations regarding the removal of stagnant water also contributed significantly to this improvement. Large-scale works were undertaken to fill in ponds and to dry out the marshy banks of the Niger. In this less pathogenic environment, which lent legitimacy to the colonial enterprise, trees provided both comfort and style to the town, which became known as 'stylish Bamako' (*Bamako la coquette*).

This policy, however, was not restricted to this town. Acacias in Senegal, badamiers in Grand-Bassam (Ivory Coast), franjipani and breadfruit in Abidjan, tamarisks and mango trees gradually provided shade for all the streets of the *plateaux* of the administrative centres of both the AOF (French West Africa) and AEF (French Equatorial

Africa).[30] The policy also appeared in other colonial towns, but to a lesser degree. Irrigation works started in the 1920s in the Niger Delta to develop cotton growing. This culminated in 1931 with the creation of the Office du Niger (Bureau of the Niger), an enormous project to work agriculturally the land bordering the river, on which the Ministry for the Colonies built great hopes of demonstrating the solid basis of colonial investment, at a time when this undertaking was being questioned back home by various economic players. As Britain had done in India, this region of the Sahel was meant to become a cotton storehouse, as indicated in the name 'the Black Indies' (*les Indes noires*) given it by colonial ideologues.

The old town of Ségou (also in formerly French Sudan) was meant, as part of this project, to grow and, according to some, even to become the future capital of the colony, when the railway line would be extended from Bamako, and a new quarter for the Office's functionaries would be built along the Niger. Its streets were all lined with trees, including mango, and the villas were set in the midst of densely planted parcels of land. The trees were sometimes right up against the façades, limiting direct sunlight and providing some natural cooling for the buildings. The river bank was intended 'at dusk' to become the place where the colonisers would go for a stroll. These urban ambitions, still restated in 1945,[31] would never be completed due to the economic fiasco of the agricultural project.

Less than forty years separated this project of settling the river banks from Trentinian's project, which, by contrast, sought to distance itself from the Niger River in favour of settling on the hills that dominated the plains. Sanitary conditions had in the meantime improved (at least for the colonisers), but the philosophy of urban planning had also considerably developed. The economic development of the French colonies played a key role for the government, whose mission was to produce an attractive working framework for both private investors and European personnel. This effort was reflected, as in Europe, in the production of 'basic' infrastructure (road and railway networks, ports, health, administrative and educational facilities). However, in the colonial setting, this included the creation of homes and residential districts for Westerners. In this sense the colonial authorities were to a degree in a similar position to the public developers of social housing projects in France, who played a role in property development in the absence of private parties that would develop this type of housing. In the colonial towns of the AOF and the AEF, no local player (they would in any case be inopportune), and especially no colonial business invested in residential developments for Westerners. In this sense, in practical terms, we could perhaps make an analogy with the public developers of garden cities, where a developer, the state, runs an end-to-end housing estate operation including the production of homes and facilities, and thereby defines a lifestyle.

Nevertheless, the issue of the place of nature in colonial towns never really enjoyed a consensus. The 1931 Conference of Colonial Urbanism in Paris had only one paper that specifically mentioned garden cities, in respect of the Zionist colonies in Palestine, then under the British Mandate.[32] The planting efforts carried out in the *villes nouvelles* of North Africa and the comfort provided by palm groves, two themes discussed at the conference, did not lead to a doctrine that supported the systematic planning of garden cities or *cités-jardins*, a term little used at the conference. From this point of view, the post-Second World War years marked a certain regression. The development of air-conditioning, as well as high-rise buildings, marked the abandonment of the urge to create a town that would try to come to terms, using local resources, with the rigours of the climate, and to use natural features to decorate it.

Notes

†   We would like to thank Alan Clayman for translating this chapter from the French. The meaning of the terms mentioned below– garden cities/*cités-jardins*, villes nouvelles, Musée Social, AOF and AEF – is as stated in Jelidi's chapter 1 and Bigon's chapter 2. (Editors)

1   Edouardo Mendoza, *La Ville des prodiges*, trans. O. Roline (Paris: Editions du Seuil, 1988).

2   Paul Rabinow, *French Modern: Norms and Forms of the Social Environment* (Cambridge, MA, and London: MIT Press, 1989).

3   Jean Erhard, *L'Idée de nature en France à l'aube des Lumières* (Paris: Albin Michel, 1994).

4   See the work of Joseph Conrad and especially his celebrated *Heart of Darkness*.

5   Alain Sinou, *Comptoirs et villes coloniales du Sénégal, Saint-Louis, Gorée, Dakar* (Paris: Karthala, 1993).

6   Ronald Ross and Charles Louis Alphonse Laveran, each of whom received a Nobel prize in medicine, in 1902 and 1907 respectively, identified the vectors of malaria; and Walter Reed, in 1901, discovered the vector of yellow fever.

7   The rules were mainly applied to models of construction, but also to lifestyle within the buildings, such as the systematic use of mosquito nets for rest and sleep.

8   This soldier, who, when appointed in 1898, aged 37, was the 'youngest General in the French Army', represents the very prototype of the colonial officer. Considered as a supporter in the colonial conquest to avenge the humiliating defeat of France in the Franco-Prussian War of 1870, he distinguished himself in the colonial combats in Macina, Bandiagara (today's Mali) and against Samory Toure, the Juula Islamic leader, in Guinea and its environs.

9   This recalls the eighteenth-century 'follies', which were identified with this colonial project in terms of the caprice of an aristocrat who wanted to transform parts of the bush into a garden, whatever this might cost.

10   It is hard to know the viewpoint of the local population, which was generally expected to be surprised by all this activity and its modes of building.

11   Quoted by Sébastien Philippe, *Une histoire de Bamako* (Brinon-sur-Sauldre:

Editions Granvaud, 2009). In Dakar the problem was partially solved by the incline of the rocky massif of Cap Vert.

12 His career is representative of the 'colonial destiny': this civilian and lawyer, who studied at the École Coloniale in Paris, was already in this region in 1894, where he assisted Colonel Archinard, responsible for the conquest. He then climbed very high in the civil service, always in the same region, where he would die in 1915.

13 The commander of the navy's Artillery Battalion, Louis Digue, carried out the survey of the settlement, which was approved on 15 December 1904 by the Government Council (see Philippe, *Une histoire de Bamako*). The commander of the Engineering Corps, Lepoivre, was given the task of carrying out the project.

14 Within an urban setting, and sometimes as guiding principles of new towns in England, garden city concepts and practices were generally carried out by property developers. The latter's preoccupation with profitability governed the size of the parcels and produced much greater density than in Koulouba, where the spatial constraints seemed to be dictated only by the steep slopes of the hills.

15 Many of the 'minor nobility' could be found among them.

16 The same building regulations were implemented by the British in their colonies, and these regulations influenced the French colonial administration. See Anthony D. King, *The Bungalow: The Production of a Global Culture* (London: Routledge and Kegan Paul, 1984).

17 Philippe, *Une histoire de Bamako*.

18 A variety of plans, not always accurately dated, indicate these developments, though they are hardly seen in contemporary photographic records, such as those of Fortier taken in 1905.

19 The Congress of Colonial Urbanism, held in 1931 in Paris under the aegis of the Minister for the Colonies, testifies to this ostracism; there was no report on the British colonial experience, which was by then much more developed than that of the French (the only exception was the last paper that dealt with the Zionist settlements in British Palestine; see also note 32 below).

20 Roume disembarked in Africa just after an outbreak of yellow fever. He had come to succeed the former Governor Ballay, who had been its victim.

21 The mosquito net effectively protects against malaria-carrying mosquitoes that mainly attack at night.

22 A classic career for social climbing during the Third Republic in France.

23 See Pierre Pinon, who shows how the engineers of the 'Ponts et Chaussées' envisioned the development of the colonial territory using the model of the garden. Pinon, 'Raisons et formes de villes: approche comparée des fondations coloniales française au début du xviii siècle', in Catherine Coquery-Vidrovitch and Odile Goerg (eds), *La Ville européenne outre-mers* (Paris: l'Harmattan, 1996), pp. 27–56.

24 Water conveyance and accessibility were always problematic; the gradients of the road, suited to pedestrians and horses, were too steep for the first vehicles that tried to drive uphill.

25 Succeeding the former, less prestigious version of the 'Cambodian School' (1885), the 'Colonial School' (created in Paris in 1889) offered training to colonial administrators, with particular regard to the Far East and Africa. (Editors)

26 Around 1905, in an ethnographic survey of the Avikam of the Ivory Coast, he opposed the methods of Governor General Marlin regarding implementing the census report, which served as a basis for forced recruitment of native workers.

27 Drawing up an urban plan in 1923; the grant of the status of a 'mixed commune' in 1920; the construction of a cathedral in 1923 and of the central market in 1925; the initiation of the flood-susceptible road leading to Sotuba; the creation of a colonial style for public buildings that was inspired by the local architecture of the Niger Delta and would be named 'neo-Sudanese', etc.

28 See Sophie Dulucq, *La France et les villes d'Afrique noire francophone, quarante d'ans d'intervention* (Paris: l'Harmattan, 1997). Dulucq suggests that in the previously sparsely populated region of the Mossi around Ouagagougou, it was the demand for services and amenities that was the cause of this significant growth.

29 Archives du Mali, 2 D 137, 'Rapport sur les travaux dans la commune mixte, 1925'.
30 Bernard Toulier, *Brazzaville la verte*, images du patrimoine, 62 (Paris: R Frey, 1996).
31 According to a plan for urban redevelopment and extension of the town, published in the journal *l'Architecture d'aujourd'hui* in the same year.
32 See Richard Kauffmann, 'Aménagement des colonies juifs en Palestine et principalement des colonies agricoles de l'organisation sioniste', in Jean Royer (ed.), *L'Urbanisme aux colonies et dans les pays tropicaux: communications & rapports du congrès international*, 2 vols (La Charité-sur-Loire: Delayance, 1932), vol. 1, pp. 224–38.

CHAPTER FOUR

The afterlife of the Lanchester Plan: Zanzibar as the garden city of tomorrow

Garth Andrew Myers and Makame Ali Muhajir

Henry Vaughan Lanchester was an important British architect of the late nineteenth and early twentieth centuries, and one of the prime movers in the professionalisation of town planning. Widely known for his work in England, Wales and India (he was the designer for Leeds University, the Cardiff Town Hall and the first formal town plan for Madras),[1] Lanchester also wrote the first comprehensive town planning scheme for the British Protectorate of Zanzibar's capital (also called Zanzibar). This plan was strongly influenced by Patrick Geddes and by the garden city movement more broadly. Despite its limited degree of implementation, Lanchester's 1923 plan for Zanzibar has cast a long shadow over planning in that small city. In this chapter, we detail the plan and its process of implementation, ending by highlighting several of the ways in which it lingers over contemporary planning in Zanzibar, especially planning associated with the ongoing Sustainable Management of Lands and Environment (SMOLE) programme.

From a locked, air-conditioned office on the third floor of a secured building housing part of the Revolutionary Government of Zanzibar's Ministry of Water, Lands, Construction and Energy, the SMOLE programme began, in 2006, to develop a GIS-based fiscal cadaster for Zanzibar and a digitised programme for land management in the new peri-urban satellite settlement of Tunguu. SMOLE, funded since 2002 by the Ministry for Foreign Affairs of Finland, began as a reformulation of an earlier Finnish project, the Zanzibar Integrated Land and Environmental Management (ZILEM) project (1989–96). ZILEM had also worked towards the aim of developing a comprehensive land information system for Zanzibar, with a pilot project in Jumbi, bordering on Tunguu, even closer to the edge of the city.

Both the Finns and the Revolutionary Government of Zanzibar represented these land management projects as dramatic improvements on previous planning in and around the city, as the means for fostering poverty reduction and greater democracy.[2] Indeed these projects both rose and fell during a time of dramatic transition in Zanzibar's political system and economic development framework. Zanzibar's socialist system remained intact from its 1964 revolution (and union with Tanganyika to form the United Republic of Tanzania) through the early 1980s. It has experienced a precipitous opening of its economy to a tourism boom and the reintroduction of multi-party politics over the last quarter-century.[3] This transformation had its parallels in urban planning, in programmes such as ZILEM and SMOLE.[4] Aid and technical support flowed from Western donors intent on a parallel loosening of state control on and proliferation of non-governmental community-based organisations or civil society institutions.[5] None of these programmes succeeded in their finite objectives, nor did they lead to the broader recreation of state–society relations envisioned under neoliberalism.

What is more, these institutional shifts, programmes and projects – and particularly ZILEM and SMOLE – have not proven to be as extraordinarily distinct as their proponents would immediately assume from their *colonial* antecedents, let alone from the avowedly socialist programmes and planning processes of the revolutionary era. In this chapter, we look back to Lanchester's 1923 plan to see what sorts of social relations and planning processes it modelled for the current generation, and to what extent one can really speak of 'moving beyond colonialism' in Zanzibari urban planning.[6] We argue that there are significant ways in which the manner and character of urban planning and urban and peri-urban land management retain similarities with those carried out in the implementation of Lanchester's ideas. We have, in separate works, each critiqued the connectivities between colonial planning in the post-Second World War era and that of Zanzibar's revolutionary socialist era that followed it.[7] Bill Bissell has recently documented the rhetorical deployment of the Lanchester Plan in the 1990s Master Plan for Zanzibar's Stone Town area, wherein the racist underpinnings of Lanchester's study are conveniently misplaced – even by Zanzibari planners.[8] In this chapter, we seek to analyse the colonial connectivities at the farthest ends of the formal planning timeline, those that reach from the beginnings of professional planning to contemporary planning under the rubric of good governance and sustainable development, particularly within one of Lanchester's crucial, as-yet under-examined priorities in his planning for Zanzibar, that of designing what he termed 'hutting grounds to the east' of the city. We seek to extend Bissell's argument, by contending that from Lanchester's time until this contemporary era, planning reforms have continued to be deployed within a system that lacks the sort of communicative social dialogue that might allow for genuinely participatory and integrated planning. Planning has never connected with ordinary people's lives, and programmes like ZILEM or SMOLE are likely to continue to fall short just as the Lanchester plan did 90 years ago, and for some similar reasons.

Back to the past: the historical geography of the Lanchester Plan

Zanzibar is an archipelago formed mainly by two major islands, Unguja and Pemba, which forms a semi-autonomous part of Tanzania. It is populated by close to a million people, about 40 per cent of whom are urbanised.[9] The built form of its city is dominated by informal planning and housing. Although a small fishing settlement existed by the twelfth century in the vicinity of the area known today as Stone Town, the modern history of the city can be dated to the establishment of a fort and formal trading post under Omani control in the 1690s, and it really only took off as a major urban settlement with the Omani Sultan Seyyid Said's decision to relocate his capital there early in the nineteenth century. A contest for influence with the Sultanate ensued among the major European powers for much of that century because of Zanzibar's importance in the control of long-distance caravan trading into the interior of East Africa, with Britain eventually emerging supreme and claiming Zanzibar as a Protectorate in 1890. After 73 years of colonial rule, Zanzibar re-emerged as a separate independent country in December 1963, only to go through a bloody revolution that began on 12 January 1964, and promulgated its union with Tanganyika to form the United Republic of Tanzania less than four months later, on 26 April. The political system in the islands retains a socialist flavour, but it is remarkable to see, at least in the realm of urban planning, just how much the British colonial era remains alive in policies, procedures and attitudes. The Lanchester Plan's afterlife is one example of this.

In 1931 Zanzibar's British Resident Richard Rankine began an unsuccessful loan application to the Colonial Office for town improvements by stating that 'town planning on scientific lines was first started in Zanzibar in the year 1922 when Mr. Lanchester visited the Protectorate and ... formulated a scheme'.[10] There had been some town improvements during the reign of Zanzibar's third Omani Sultan, Barghash (1873–88), and the British-run Public Works Department was over 25 years old by the time Lanchester visited the island. One British Consul, Gerald Portal, had drawn up a planning map of the town in 1892, just two years into the formal colonial era; in 1909 Consul Edward Clarke even started a Town Planning and Improvement Committee,

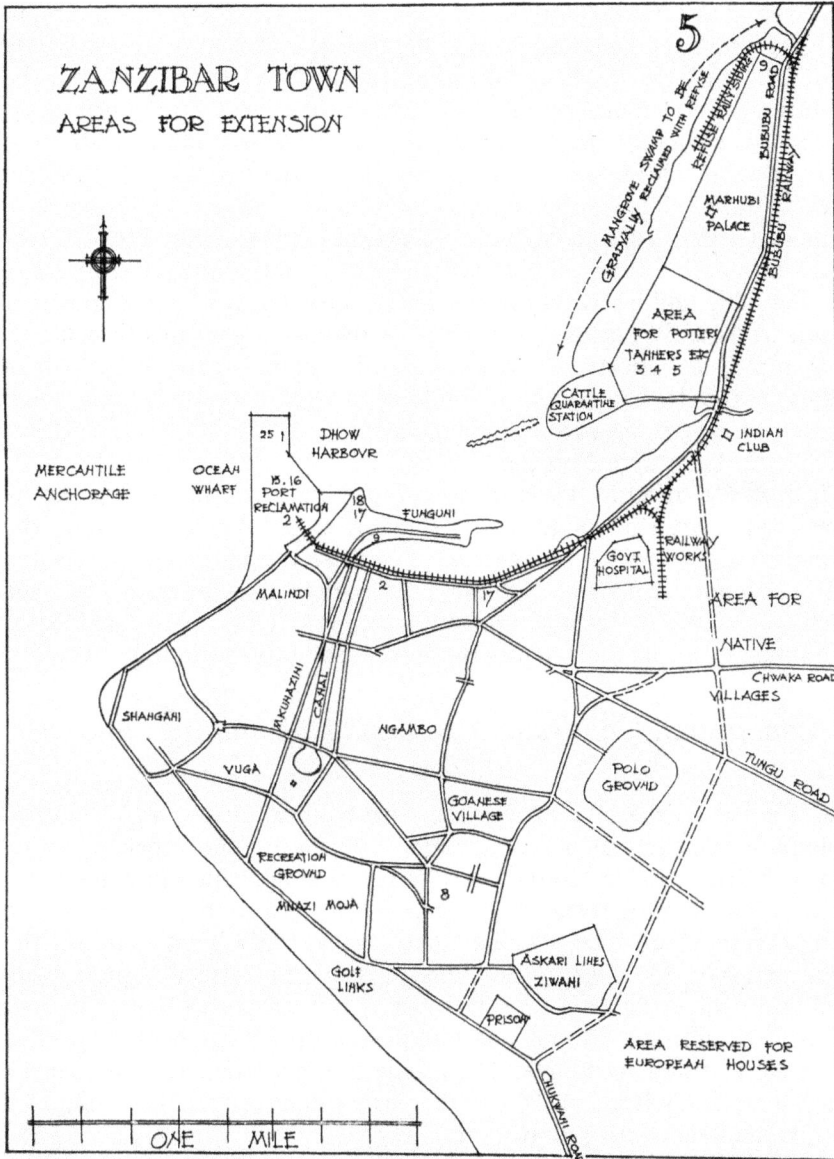

Figure 4.1 Lanchester's suggestion for 'hutting grounds to the east', segregated from new European suburbs (from Henry Lanchester, *Zanzibar: A Study in Tropical Town Planning* [Cheltenham: Barrow, 1923], p. 43).

though it apparently only met for a few months before disbanding in 1910.[11] Consul Clarke did take on the task of road improvement briefly in 1913. In 1916 the Secretary of State for the Colonies had told the administration that it should have a plan for the town to 'work up to; other wise [sic] the improvements of one period will not fit into those of the next'.[12] John Sinclair, who occupied various posts in the Protectorate from 1899 to 1924 (including British Resident from 1922 to 1924, the equivalent to a consulship or governorship after the Protectorate was transferred from Foreign Office to Colonial Office control), left a remarkable architectural imprint on the city, but his largest contribution to formal planning rested in his playing a part in the decision to employ Lanchester to create a plan for Zanzibar (fig. 4.1).[13] All of these points lead us to follow Rankine in arguing that formal colonial planning began with Lanchester's arrival.

More than anyone on the island at the time, Chief Secretary R. H. Crofton was intent on seeing that proper, modern European planning principles were introduced in Zanzibar, especially in Ng'ambo, the eastern 'Other Side' of Zanzibar city across a tidal creek from Stone Town, before it became 'too late'. He invited Lanchester to visit the island on his way back to England from service to the city of Madras in India, eventually arranging the formal invitation through Sinclair.[14]

Lanchester, Geddes and garden city planning concepts in Zanzibar

Lanchester's extensive experience with tropical cities and his professional credentials as a protégé and colleague of the urban planning guru Patrick Geddes convinced Crofton that the town planner could guide the administration's programme for urban development and improvement in what seemed to be a potentially bleak time for the Protectorate. As Bissell notes, the 'conservative surgery' approach to carefully de-densifying closely built urban areas, an approach that Geddes had made famous and had passed on to Lanchester, 'seemed precisely suited to address the problems' of Zanzibar: 'Lanchester's collaboration with Geddes over the years might seem to have prepared him well to apply this strategy in Zanzibar.'[15] This is mainly because of the high density, high plot coverage, poor ventilation and poor public health for which the city was known.

Economic issues had to be the first order of business on the planning agenda if it was to succeed with the higher-ups in the Colonial Office.[16] In this regard Lanchester had as his main task advising on the redesign of the port and the roads connecting it to the suburban clove plantations. These economic concerns were intertwined with political and strategic objectives. Maintaining the imperial connection with India depended still to some degree on watering British ships in Zanzibar. Lanchester noted that Zanzibar had 'the best water between Alexandria and the Cape', but his own goals were more terrestrial: 'to enhance the efficiency and amenity of Zanzibar as a civic organism'.[17]

Lanchester's notions of efficiency followed clearly from Geddesian ideas, which were then to be employed in the distribution and design of police stations as well as in an attempt at the reorganisation of social and economic activities. His goal was to make markets, shops, houses and neighbourhoods more in line with imperial ideas of health and more conducive to police surveillance. Lanchester's work can be seen as influenced not only by Geddes but by the garden city movement writ large – with that movement's obsessions, biases and ideological agendas: for all of its emphasis on parks, orderly suburbs and sanitation, it is still easy to see the plan as 'a strategy of power exercised ... to alleviate what were defined as social pathologies' in the interests of imperialism.[18] The primary influence, though, clearly came from Geddes, with whom Lanchester had collaborated extensively while serving as a key leader of the Royal Institute of British Architects.[19]

The result of Lanchester's three-week visit to Zanzibar was a fairly disjointed set of recommendations pulled together in a book called *Zanzibar: A Study in Tropical Town Planning*. The book itself included 79 pages of text, divided into six chapters. The first covered 'physiography and ethnology', while the second ran through Zanzibar's history – these initial 33 pages seem heavily dependent on the information and sources local British officials such as Crofton supplied to him, and particularly on F. B. Pearce's 1920 volume, *Zanzibar: The Island Metropolis of Eastern Africa*.[20] Nonetheless, these segments still represented an attempt at the sort of Geddesian sociological survey that Lanchester held up as a planning ideal. It is only in chapter three, on 'commerce and industry', that Lanchester turned to his own recommendations, particularly regarding the city's seaport, traffic engineering and the geographical reordering of economic activities. In chapter four, Lanchester focused on hygiene, with extensive attention to the public baths. Public health concerns also dominated his thoughts on housing in chapter five, with a focus on the layout and siting of new housing that took on the look, in a semi-organic fashion, of Ebenezer Howard's garden city ideals. Instead of concentric circle suburbs, the new areas would have been semi-circles crossed by wide, straight-line roads, but still well-spaced and separated by farms and gardens. The main 'garden suburb' Lanchester laid out in detail, however, was the 'European' suburb he intended for the southern third of the Stone Town peninsula.

In his brief concluding chapter, Lanchester touched on a few seemingly random, miscellaneous concerns – education, recreation, administration and building construction – that he could not find room for elsewhere. His maps, in the text itself and in a fold-out appendix, provide some further suggestions of planning ideas, typically without any further elaboration in the document. The slap-dash character of the conclusion adds to the evidence for Bissell's claim that the study was 'compiled out of bits and pieces ... and cut through with both lapses and inconsistencies'.[21] It was clearly meant as an attempt to carry out Geddesian ideals in Zanzibar, but under the severe handicap that the type of socio-cultural grounding and survey work Geddes would have expected (though he seldom accomplished it himself!) was simply not possible for Lanchester.

Implementing a secret plan

Although the book served as the main formal guide for town planning in Zanzibar until the late 1950s, it was never seen by more than a dozen or so colonial officers. When copies of the book were printed in early 1924, Sinclair told the East Africa High Commissioner in Nairobi that 'every precaution has to be taken from the time of Mr. Lanchester's visit to Zanzibar to obviate the possibility of any details of his town planning scheme becoming known to the public'.[22] When Lanchester told Crofton in 1928 that he still had plenty of copies available in England, he was advised to send a few, 'provided the copies are marked confidential and it is understood that they are not for communication to others'.[23]

Nowhere is it stated outright why such secrecy was necessary for such a very generalised, superficial survey of the town. Part of the cause may have been Lanchester's recommendation that all urban development be a 'government enterprise'.[24] He wanted to prevent speculators, particularly South Asian money-lenders, from finding out the areas selected for development by colonial officials and raising the prices of land prior to the beginning of any implementation of the scheme. Secrecy would enable the government to 'buy up quietly, without notice, ceremony, waste of time or revelation to speculators, any land required'.[25] This was an early instance in which the planning apparatus in Zanzibar recognised the vested interests controlling residential land as being major hindrances to the implementation of urban development schemes and tried to move around them.

It seems on first viewing that Lanchester's priorities concentrated in the Stone Town area – in part, that impression remains because the redesign of the port in Stone Town was one of the only large-scale parts of the scheme to be directly implemented. Infilling the creek that separated Stone Town and Ng'ambo, though it was technically not fully completed, was the other obvious success – Lanchester had proposed a controlled 'canal', and one was constructed in 1931, only to be filled during the 1940s. In part the impression of a Stone Town emphasis may have lingered because most of Lanchester's maps concentrate there. But in Crofton's 'secret memorandum' to fellow officers that was meant to guide the implementation process, he laid out, in order, Lanchester's top ten priorities for practical projects in the city, and the priority that came second to the 'harbour triangle' was that of 'hutting grounds to the east', in Ng'ambo, the city's Other Side. Lanchester saw improvements to and extensions of Ng'ambo as 'easier' by comparison to Stone Town: 'the provision of additional Swahili dwellings' from Ng'ambo through Tunguu 'and extending eastward as far as necessary' was, for Lanchester 'perhaps the simplest problem coming under the housing programme'.[26] This claim proved as inaccurate in Lanchester's time as it has in every planning scheme since.

The main landowners in Ng'ambo during the 1920s were the descendants of those who had controlled the land in the nineteenth century. What had changed was their relationship to their tenants and to the state.[27] The gradual change to the practical (yet contested) recognition of private property and its boundaries, and the collection of ground rents and premiums, had brought about a tense relationship between landlords and tenants. The administration had created and defended the earlier class of landlords, but by the 1920s several of the main landlords were no longer kindly disposed towards their colonial protectors. The inconsistencies and corruption rampant in the early days of the British-engineered Waqf Commission that had been created to deal with Islamic inheritance and property dedication cases, along with that of the Crown Lands Department, irritated the landlords. Particularly in the case of Ng'ambo's main landlords (the son and son-in-law of Tharia Topan and Lady Janbai, Mohammedhussein Tharia Topan and Jessa Bhaloo, and the sons of Remtulla Hemani, Mohammed and Gulamhussein), a deep mutual antagonism between state and landlord already prevailed.[28] There was ample reason for Crofton to suspect that the main landlords would be hostile to large-scale government intervention in their sphere of control.[29]

Another possible reason for keeping the Lanchester Plan secret may have had to do with colonial officials' opposition to the plan's financial implications; indeed, these other officials seem to have played a key role in reducing investment in its implementation – chiefly Sinclair's replacement as British Resident after 1924, Claude Hollis, who favoured the prioritisation of plantation agriculture's productivity.[30] We must also consider this concern in light of the overall attitude of colonial officers and consultants towards their subjects. Many officers of the time either openly or privately harboured highly negative views of the people for whom this scheme, ostensibly, was created – even those in favour of, or designing, the scheme. Another of Lanchester's reasons, for example, for arguing that government would have to be fully in charge was that 'having regard to the character of the majority of the present occupants of the area ... no general scheme of co-operative development would be feasible'.[31] In his book, Lanchester expressed the racist views of his colleagues in the Protectorate administration, views that were the underpinning not just of colonial rule but of the replacement of chattel slavery with wage labour by the Empire:

> Physically the Zanzibar Swahilis are well fitted for rough manual labour and are freely employed in loading and unloading ships, and in the transport of heavy goods. They work better in unison, and when extreme bodily exertion is required, than at less violent and isolated labour. Normally they are not energetic, and do not care as a rule to apply themselves indefinitely to one task.[32]

As his map of the 'racial distribution' of Zanzibar town shows, Lanchester was unwilling to categorise the people of Ng'ambo as anything more than 'natives' who 'work better in unison'. It is thus not surprising that he appeared so reluctant to reveal anything of his scheme to them.

The Lanchester Plan and the professional town planning mechanisms slowly established in its wake were designed to convey a particular vision of urban space to a Zanzibari audience, outside the hiding places of what James Scott called the 'hidden transcripts' of colonial authority.[33] Nowhere is this clearer than in what were seen all over the empire at this time to be the intimately intertwined spheres of housing and health.[34] Whether in southern or West Africa, the Middle East, South or Southeast Asia, this concern was, as Anthony King put it, more with 'health' than with health, because 'the exercise of prejudice regarding race, culture, and colour mixed up these [health] issues with racial and social issues. The culture and class-specific perception of health hazards more than the actual health hazards themselves was instrumental in determining much colonial urban-planning policy.'[35]

Lanchester saw the urban form of neighbourhoods associated with various groups in Zanzibar society as organic embodiments of a hygiene problem. Indians had 'overflowed into all the bazaars running eastward' while 'the real Swahili quarter' had 'irregularly scattered huts ... packed along irregular and narrow lanes'.[36] Irregularity, overcrowding and overflow in urban form were attributed to the 'ingrained habits' of poor hygiene among the non-white races.[37] Though 'in the matter of house accommodation the Swahili show[ed] his superiority over his pagan cousins the negro', the Swahili had 'bad housing', and it was badly arranged – and bad housing bred bad health.[38]

Lanchester's extensive proposals on housing revolved around four themes: 1) institutionalising and increasing the spatial extent of segregation of Europeans from 'natives' in the interests of health; 2) establishing stricter building codes to regulate, in particular, the sanitation systems of Ng'ambo; 3) using frequent fires in Ng'ambo as 'opportunities for remodelling the arrangement of huts' until a more comprehensive planned community could be organised; and 4) educating the public to affect 'a fuller appreciation of the possibilities of life resulting from better business organisation, improved housing and general facilities'.[39]

Against the wishes of Hollis, Crofton took on much of the work of enacting Lanchester's ideas in Ng'ambo. He maintained a warm correspondence with Lanchester for at least six years after the town planner's departure, and continually mined Lanchester's thin vein of expertise on Zanzibari urban development. From the readings Lanchester recommended to him, Crofton drew up the 'secret' memorandum for the members of the town planning board as a sort of introduction to their reading of the new plan. Before detailing Lanchester's ten priorities for the town to the board, Crofton highlighted two principles of European town planning theory which he felt would underlie any successful attempt to meet them: 'the English principle of betterment and the German principle of redistribution'.[40]

There is no reason to suspect that anyone paid particular attention to the Chief Secretary's memorandum itself in later years, and it is highly unlikely that the planners and technical consultants to ZILEM or SMOLE ever saw it. Yet these ideas that Crofton grafted on to Lanchester's plan became the *idée fixe* of planning's long unfinished symphony in Zanzibar. Beyond a general improvement of living conditions, betterment was also taken to mean that 'the town must pay for its own improvements'. Redistribution in the language of early twentieth-century continental urban management meant 'making plots regular' and using judicious and economical land acquisition by government as a 'means of civic control'.[41] These two principles, betterment and redistribution, continued to be publicly expressed goals in colonial town planning straight through to 1964. They have, indeed, persisted into the Finland-funded land reform programmes of 1989–96 and 2002–present. They are at the heart of what Bissell calls 'the secret life of the plan' that Lanchester wrote.[42]

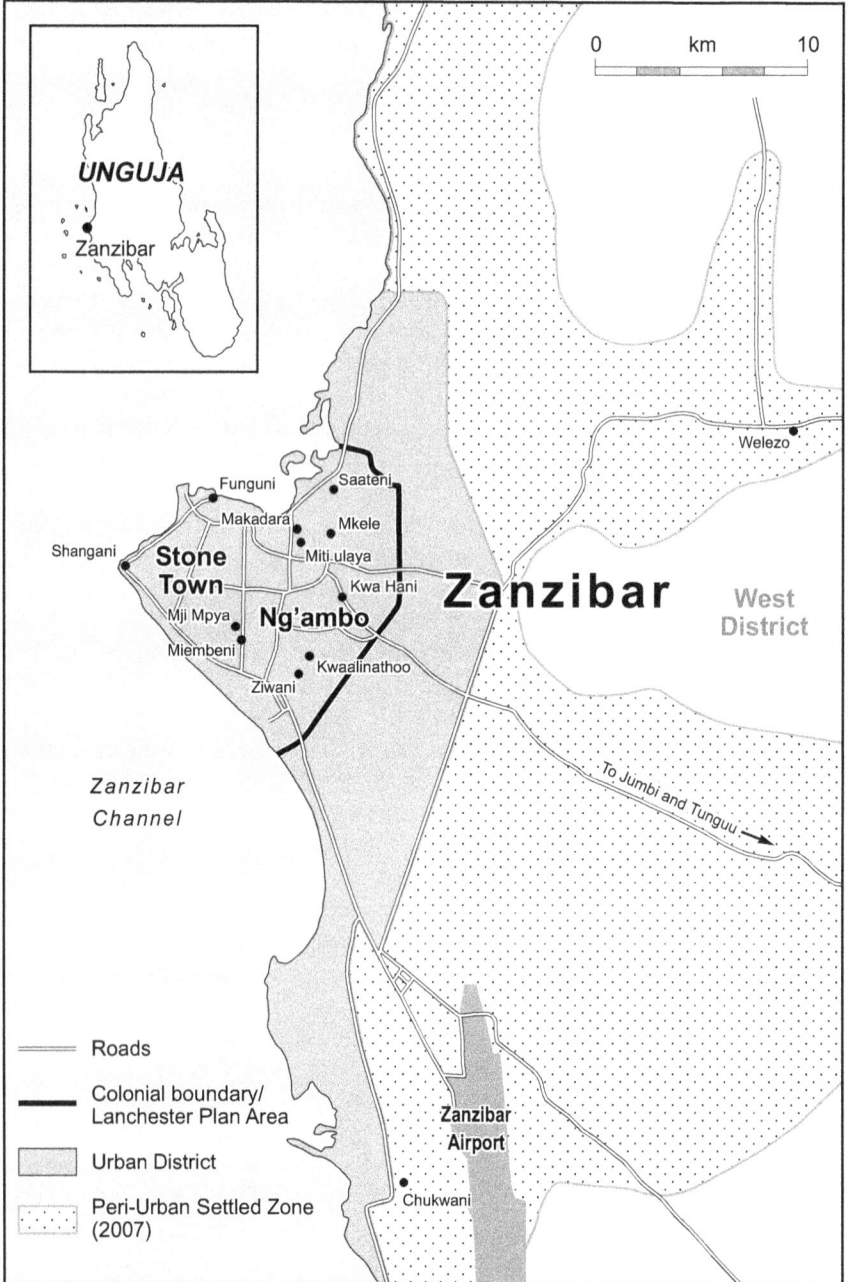

Figure 4.2 Zanzibar and its environs by the 2010s in relation to Lanchester Plan area.

Indeed, looking to the ten priorities Lanchester detailed for Crofton with fresh eyes in 2012, one can see that they have remained obsessions for Zanzibar's planners for nearly 90 years. Its port area has been reconstructed at least six times in the last 22 years. The modern versions of 'hutting grounds to the east' are the central priorities of ZILEM and SMOLE. The 'movement of noxious trades' became a priority of the Zanzibar Sustainable Programme of 1998–2005. Rebuilding the city market has been a conversation in Zanzibari planning for a century, even now despite the construction of a new market in the 2000s on the edge of the city. Although Lanchester's fifth and sixth priorities, for the embankment and reclamation of the Pwani Ndogo creek that separated Stone Town and Ng'ambo in the 1920s, would appear to have been somewhat accomplished, the Revolutionary Government sought to make the mouth of the creek into one of the world's largest swimming pools in the 1970s and oversaw the creation of a 'floating' mosque there in the 2000s, all the while continuing to struggle with the reappearance of the 'creek' in the floods of the rainy season that overwhelm the poor drainage system each year. Priority seven, through-roads for Ng'ambo, became central to the Ten Year Development Plan of 1946–55 and the Revolutionary Government's 1968 and 1982 plans. Priority eight, the renewal of 'Portuguese Street', the main shopping strip of inner Stone Town, became one of the key accomplishments of the Stone Town Conservation and Development Authority in the 1990s. The reclamation of the Funguni sand spit on Stone Town's north end, Lanchester's ninth priority in Crofton's translation, was a showcase project of the Revolutionary Government in the 1970s – the massive government-run Bwawani Hotel occupies Funguni today. The tenth priority, a road scheme for the Shangani area of Stone Town, was a core concern of the 1958 colonial Master Plan and the 1996 Master Plan for Stone Town, and the controversies over the implications of hotel construction for Shangani's roads are the central planning controversies of 2011 in Zanzibar. The 'secret life' of this plan is, indeed, a very long one (fig. 4.2).

How ironic, then, to note that Lanchester's plan was only marginally implemented by the administration, particularly between the world wars. This had to do partly with the fact that the internal organisations designed to take up Lanchester's concerns were changing structure and changing personnel on a regular basis. Constant shifts in the people involved in town planning appear to have been related somewhat to the skills and interests demonstrated by the particular officers involved. For example, the Medical Officer of Health from 1936 to 1939, S. W. T. Lee, took an active role in housing design and neighbourhood layout. The presence of a trained architect between 1938 and

1939 who had an interest in road design was quickly followed by his inclusion on the town planning board. But the continual adjustments and the lack of participation from any of the major players in colonial government suggest that the town's problems were a marginal concern to the administration.[43] Zanzibar was an export enclave almost totally dependent on plantation agriculture. The town was an administrative centre and a shipping and processing point; it was a secondary or even tertiary policy priority. Planning its urban and suburban land management has, indeed, remained an afterthought through to the Finnish era, despite various rhetorical flourishes to the contrary.

Controlling and racialising the 'hutting grounds to the east'

The actual work accomplished in town planning under the town planning board's leadership ebbed and flowed throughout the 1920s and 1930s. The whole enterprise seems to have been something like a favourite hobby of particular people rather than a serious attempt to improve the quality of life in the town – as it has been, essentially, ever since. Relations between the government and the more significant landlords were part of the problem, particularly in that second priority of Lanchester and Crofton, the 'hutting grounds to the east'.

One instance of the implementation of the Lanchester Plan for 'hutting grounds to the east' began in 1925, in a three-year-long negotiation with Ali Nathoo, a trustee of a Waqf estate in eastern Ng'ambo intended as a site for demonstrating good hut layout forms and public health measures. Ali Nathoo's land was adjacent to the barracks and training facilities of the Zanzibar police at Ziwani. When first approached by the town planning board with their plan for developing his swampy land as a housing estate, he expressed his eagerness to work with the administration if a lease or an exchange of land could be negotiated. He could not, he said, sell the land, as it was Waqf property, not to be sold.[44]

A suitable exchange was eventually arranged, only to be derailed by an internal memo from the police chief. His objections to a new neighbourhood adjacent to the police barracks included the threat of venereal disease ('no doubt very soon most of the huts would become brothels'), infectious disease ('a native village on the very borders of the camp [removes]... the advantage of isolation') and inadequate laws and by-laws about building that might protect the boundary of the police barracks from encroachment. Ultimately, Ali Nathoo was paid to release the swampier half of his property to the Ziwani barracks as a buffer zone with a tall barbed wire fence between it and what was termed the new African 'village'. He then submitted a grid-like neighbourhood design in accordance with new orderly precepts from the planning board, and the neighbourhood (*mtaa*, pl. *mitaa*) of Kwaalinathoo was begun.[45] Lanchester himself found the plan 'unduly rigid and monotonous', telling Crofton that 'probably, rectangular planning is best, but that does not necessarily imply covering large areas with long strings of huts in uniform parallel lines' – the layout of Kwaalinathoo to this day.[46]

Besides Crofton himself, only mid-rank health department officials consistently took planning seriously. Health officers often went beyond Lanchester in decrying conditions in the city and in using epidemiological metaphors: 'The town as a whole is a parasitic growth on the island', wrote one officer in 1935. The 'disarranged maze of huts' in Ng'ambo was seen to provide 'more acceptable material for the operations' of the department, apparently because of the physical ease with which neighbourhoods could be uprooted.[47] The experience in Kwaalinathoo, however, taught Crofton and the health officers that there were sometimes uncomfortable social relations problems in the way of that physical uprooting: the vested interests of land controllers. Their attention turned to developing other land in the eastern part of town directly controlled by the government. Two model villages (in Kwahani and Saateni) were laid out by the Medical Officer of Health in the late 1920s, with streets that followed a grid pattern, well-aligned houses and a local police post. These were followed by layouts in Miembeni (Mji Mpya – 'New City') and Mkele. A devastating fire in the late 1920s provided an opportunity to put some of the houses of Makadara in order on a wide, tree-lined street, in the *mtaa* known today as Mitiulaya (European Trees).

The lessons of Kwaalinathoo and the new semi-planned *mitaa* highlighted the clear need, from the administration's point of view, for the development of building rules and land development laws in the city. The work of surveying, developing and allocating new layouts was hindered by the unclear nature of tenure. The government was never really sure where it did and didn't own land. Landowners constantly claimed lands the government thought it controlled, or claimed each other's lands, and if questioned brought forth titles in court. Yet the titles were not fully surveyed, relying on landscape features (especially trees) that were in many cases long gone by the time of the dispute. In Miembeni, the government established a precedent it was to stick with for the entire colonial period: where government land was not available, the next best place to plan was on Waqf Commission land. Development of Waqf Commission properties theoretically eliminated the 'landlord problem', since trusteeship of these lands had supposedly been vested in the Commission, which had an official majority. Yet even here, trusteeship was being continually contested in the courts by the descendants of the Waqf dedicators and the poor and destitute peoples for whom the land had often been set aside.[48] Land tenure rules were written, and a few were passed by the British Resident's executive council in the late 1920s and early 1930s, but these were aimed mainly at rural areas and did little to clear up the problem in urban Zanzibar.

The Town Building Rules proved more significant in the struggle for controlling the urban setting. The building rules went through numerous drafts between Lanchester's suggestions in 1924 (which he had based on the laws of Mumbai and Calcutta, cities over 50 times the size of Zanzibar) and their passage through the newly established legislative council in 1929. These drafts did not significantly alter the core concepts of Lanchester's initial version. First and foremost, the building rules

> established a legal separation between the Stone Town, which was called 'Town', and Ng'ambo, which was considered one of a multitude of 'Native Locations' throughout the Protectorate. The distinction was predicated on a perception that there were simply two kinds of dwellings, a 'stone house' and a 'native hut'. The former belonged in Stone Town, and the latter in Ng'ambo.[49]

Jonathon Glassman has recently taken issue with the common tendency among both Zanzibari and especially foreign researchers to place undue emphasis on the role of colonial law in racialising political discourse in the city.[50] His point of caution is well taken, but the building rules very clearly delineated and fundamentally materialised a separation that had not really existed previously. Even if Zanzibaris on both 'sides' actively engaged in constructing racialised political discourse, it was the Lanchester Plan and its spinoffs in the building rules that in effect provided them with a map.

This separation, which Lanchester's report helped to solidify, carried over inequitably into realms well beyond housing, including infrastructure. Richard Burton had commented in 1872 about Zanzibar town that 'the dollar hunters from Europe are a mere floating population, ever looking to the deluge in prospect, and of course unwilling to do every man's business' by developing a drainage system.[51] A half-century later, Ng'ambo had become an urban drainage nightmare. Yet the early twentieth-century variant on Burton's species of dollar hunters, the ever-acquisitive Protectorate administration, still would have nothing of 'every man's business'. The Medical and Sanitary Department argued in 1924 that 'so far as the native population was concerned the main drainage system was not required', and no serious challenge to this view was offered until at least the 1960s.[52]

Nor was there an enormous effort to provide for an equitable educational infrastructure between the city's sides. The educational system for Zanzibaris was revised in the 1920s to train a diverse labour force. Four special educational tracks beyond primary school were established, corresponding to the four employment-generating sectors of the economy: agricultural, clerical, industrial and teaching.[53] Not only were Africans excluded from all but the industrial branch, but no government schools of any kind were built on the Other Side in the interwar years despite Lanchester's suggestion along these lines. No programme of economic development aimed at improving incomes or providing employment ever developed in tandem with Lanchester or Crofton's ideas for bettering the city. Africans did fit into the lower rungs of government employment, but many preferred day labour for private firms in the port, where at least a meal came with a day's work.

It often seemed that the real concern of the British was simply with having things under control. To use Mitchell's words, having the place 'contained' meant translating it into a spatial language they could 'read like a book'.[54] The most important translation of Ng'ambo's geography into planning language prior to 1945 'was quite literally a book: a set of twenty maps covering the entire area for use in all aspects of building control, town planning, rent collection, and sanitary engineering'.[55] This set of maps inspired by Lanchester's plan, the Ng'ambo Area Folder, served as a guide for a formal hut-numbering system for the police and the health office. The colonial power needed a system of streets and numbered houses to containerise the Other Sides in order for any further development programmes or planning schemes to go forward. This meant that a great deal of map and survey work lay in store. Being aware of the shortage of skilled manpower in the departments concerned led the Director of Medical Services to demand the latest technological application to town planning, an aerial photo.[56] Once the aerial surveys were complete in 1934, a painstaking process began to translate their details into cartographic form, with Ng'ambo carved into 37 named divisions. Although it set down the official boundaries between neighbourhoods (*mitaa*) as administrative areas,[57] probably the most important aspect of the Ng'ambo Area Folder was supposed to be its usefulness in building control through the delineation on its maps of limits of alignment (LOAs) as future roadways. The first official government architect, Lionel Bintley, drew up a road plan for Ng'ambo in 1938, incorporating the Health Department's sanitary lanes into the few pre-existing through-roads. Bintley's plan was then laid down on the maps of the Ng'ambo Area Folder, which showed the position of huts at the time of the 1934 aerial survey. According

[113]

to the aerial survey, the LOAs were obstructed by 475 houses, out of Ng'ambo's 7,730 huts, which were labelled and given numbered plaques in 1942. The plan was for the Health Department to utilise the building rules to deny permits for repairs or construction in these artificially devised lanes. Government would give hut-owners modest compensation payments until it had cleared the LOAs, and then would continue using the rules to keep them clear.[58] But the programme never really worked – homes had changed shape in the decade between the aerial survey and the LOAs, the government again failed to invest in carrying out the scheme, landlords did not cooperate with it, and in many instances neither did tenants. Thus the second priority of Lanchester, for 'hutting areas to the east', largely came to naught. And yet, like many of Lanchester's ideas, it haunts planning in Zanzibar nine decades later.

Another secret life? Planning for sustainable development and good governance

There is not enough space in a chapter of this length to detail the many parallels one finds between the 'lives' of the Lanchester Plan and the Finnish projects. As briefly as we can, in this final section, we develop an appreciation for several of these themes in ZILEM and SMOLE. There are numerous obvious differences, of course, between the planning mindset of the interwar years and that of the early twentieth century. For one thing, clearly the racist elements of the Lanchester plan are not a part of the planning landscape of the ZILEM and SMOLE programmes, at least explicitly.

Yet one of the key elements of Bissell's critique of Lanchester endures in the ZILEM and SMOLE plans, in what he terms the 'underside of external expertise': the thin base of local socio-cultural understanding upon which supposedly 'expert' views rest.[59] Lanchester's study emerged from his 'first visit to Africa. Like many development experts in the years to come, he had little familiarity with the social and historical specificities of the coast and understood not a word of either Kiswahili or Arabic.'[60] The same can be said of many of the Nordic technical advisors to ZILEM and SMOLE, including those whose residency in Zanzibar lasted for more than three years. To be sure, there is something very different from a colonial mindset at work in the Finnish Ministry for Foreign Aid's commitment to 'sustainable development' that 'incorporates the cross-cutting themes of environmental protection, gender equity and the protection of women's and girls' rights and the facilitation of the participation of those particularly vulnerable to exclusion'.[61] Like Lanchester, however, ZILEM and SMOLE consultants often proved 'astonishingly disengaged from social relations and realities on the ground',[62] nowhere more so than in the realm of local politics in the multi-party era that officially began in 1992 but had its immediate origins in public unrest in the late 1980s that directly corresponded with ZILEM's arrival.

The degree of secrecy and government heavy-handedness with which formal planning proceeds in the ZILEM-SMOLE era parallels that of the colonial regime of the 1920s and 1930s. We began this chapter with a suggestion of this. ZILEM and SMOLE's supposedly participatory land information systems and fiscal cadaster development out of remote sensing and digital orthophotography, like the efforts to produce the Ng'ambo Area Folder via aerial photography in the 1930s, are at the cutting edge technologically. But they are as wrapped in mystery as those earlier efforts, as far as ordinary people in Zanzibar are concerned. Access to the new computerised systems is as secret as Crofton's memorandum of the 1920s.

Four further parallels are worth noting; we discuss each briefly below. The first two concern the continued relevance, directly, of those principles of 'betterment' and 'distribution' Crofton gleaned from Lanchester. Third, the land control and civic control strategies of the interwar colonial regime are remarkably like those of the contemporary revolutionary regime. Finally, while segregation and segmentation are no longer explicit within the contemporary plans, inequitable infrastructure and revenue streams endure in the era of the new 'dollar hunters from Europe' of Zanzibar's twenty-first-century tourist industry.

The Crofton/Lanchester notion of 'betterment', meaning that 'the town must pay for its own improvements', is a fundamental theme of contemporary planning in Zanzibar, particularly in relation to SMOLE. The economic priority of SMOLE clearly focused around it – in emphasising the development of a fiscal cadaster, the project sought to enhance government revenues specifically to be ploughed back into urban planning and land management. The primary outcome of this reinforces the already existing inequalities of 'betterment' – Stone Town, which in the 1990s gained its own separate Master Plan and planning unit, the Stone Town Conservation and Development Authority, is in a far better position to 'pay for itself' than the rest of the city, where 90 per cent of the population resides. Unsurprisingly, SMOLE developed the fiscal cadaster first for Stone Town, and it has not proceeded with one for Ng'ambo.

Lanchester's idea of 'distribution', and of the importance of educating the public on the value of 'making plots regular', can be rather benignly and mundanely linked with the ZILEM and SMOLE programmes of rectangular land surveying and plot distribution in Jumbi and Tunguu. With the use of 'health' gone as an excuse for the racialisation of that orderly regularity, one might conclude that there is nothing wrong in making Zanzibar's new neighbourhood form regular. Yet there are elements of the hidden transcript of the colonial order and distribution that carry over negatively into the twenty-first-century version. For one, we can find the legal framework: despite the many revisions to Zanzibar's land laws in the last 20 years, both the building rules and the Town and Country Planning Act of the colonial era remain in force; in practice, these archaic laws are deployed by the contemporary regime more vigorously than any of the reform laws, when it suits the regime's political interests to do so. Moreover, the inequitable plot distributions in Tunguu, when coupled with the culturally alien design of the neighbourhood, show that the 'hutting grounds to the east' of the 2010s are as removed from the social understanding of ordinary residents as were those of Kwaalinathoo and other Lanchester-inspired new towns of the interwar years.

At first sight, it might seem that the relationships between the state and landholders are so dramatically changed from some 90 years ago as to be unrecognisable. Yet we can find numerous ways in which patterns endure and repeat. The revolutionary regime's capricious and cavalier pattern of interaction with Waqf holders remains very much that of the colonial regime: in one peri-urban area, Welezo, a Waqf-holder gave us a collection of 73 pieces of correspondence with the key lands officials (and on up to the President of Zanzibar) over the two decades of ZILEM and SMOLE, detailing his efforts to prevent his family's lands from being unlawfully parcelled and squatted, and yet some of the most powerful people in town ended up with the best plots on his Waqf.[63] The lack of clarity over who owns what not only persists, but has become worse, and the paltry achievements to date of reform-era registration and titling programmes hardly make a dent in the problem. Government continues to acquire land as a means of 'civic control': one needs to look no farther than the imposition of various institutions of state directly into the midst of 'new town' plans in Tunguu or Chukwani that disrupt more democratic and participatory alternative planning.[64]

Finally, we note the persistence of inequalities in the outcomes of planning that follow from the inequitable revenue streams noted above, as the 'dollar hunters from Europe' build profits – in collaboration with the islands' elites – from the blossoming tourism industry, an industry that essentially had its origins in the years of the Lanchester Plan. Over one hundred hotel projects have moved forward in Zanzibar since the beginning of the ZILEM project. Hotel development and tourism more broadly have heavily impacted Stone Town and Unguja island's east coast, and both areas have seen infrastructure and service provision improvements. Ng'ambo and the peri-urban areas of West District, just outside the municipal boundary, have experienced very little improvement in basic infrastructure and urban services, and even employment from tourism more broadly has bypassed the Other Side and its extensions in West District. The 'mere floating population' that Burton observed more than 150 years ago is still 'unwilling to do every man's business'.

Conclusion

Communicative or argumentative planning, with its participatory, democratic, decentralised and action-oriented rhetoric, has come to dominate planning discourse in many parts of the world by the early twenty-first century, and Zanzibar is no exception. Programmes such as the ZILEM and SMOLE projects have strong rhetorical commitments to democracy, collaboration and similar pillars of what are termed sustainable development and good governance. In certain respects, these contemporary plans do try to make these rhetorical commitments genuine and actionable. Yet in reaching back to the origins of professional planning in Zanzibar here, we have argued that other elements of the current planning agenda more than echo those of the interwar years.

Henry Lanchester and the British bureaucrats who attempted to implement his plans established patterns that have proved enduring in planning in Zanzibar. While the racism and segregationism explicit in his plans have generally faded from the scene, we contend that other key themes continue into the current era of sustainable development and good governance. The non-communicative planning of Lanchester's time, with its secrecy, draconian tactics, economistically skewed priorities, inequalities, obsession with order and regularity, and lackadaisical approach to the concerns of ordinary residents – particularly those in his 'hutting grounds to the east' – has bequeathed its inherently non-communicative core to the supposedly communicative planning of the early twenty-first century.

Notes

1 Charles Herbert Reilly, *Representative British Architects of the Present Day* (New York: Books for Libraries Press, 1931), pp. 112–25.
2 Government of Finland and Revolutionary Government of Zanzibar, *Terms of Reference for Consultancy Services* (Helsinki: Foreign Ministry, 2004).
3 Garth Myers, *African Cities: Alternative Visions of Urban Theory and Practice*

(London: Zed Books, 2011); Garth Myers, *Disposable Cities: Garbage, Governance, and Sustainable Development in Urban Africa* (Aldershot: Ashgate Press, 2005); Garth Myers, 'Peri-urban land reform, political-economic reform, and urban political ecology in Zanzibar', *Urban Geography*, 29 (2008), 264–88.

4　Myers, *African Cities*.

5　Garth Myers, 'Democracy and development in Zanzibar? Contradictions in land and environment planning', *Journal of Contemporary African Studies*, 14 (1996), 221–45; Myers, *Disposable Cities*.

6　Achille Mbembe, *On the Postcolony* (Berkeley: University of California Press, 2001).

7　Garth Myers, 'A stupendous hammer: colonial and post-colonial reconstructions of Zanzibar's other side', *Urban Studies*, 32 (1995), 1436–49; Makame Muhajir, 'How planning works in an age of reform: land, sustainability, and housing development traditions in Zanzibar' (PhD dissertation, University of Kansas, 2011).

8　William Bissell, *Urban Design, Chaos, and Colonial Power in Zanzibar* (Bloomington: Indiana University Press, 2011).

9　United Republic of Tanzania, *Population and Housing Census* (Dar es Salaam: United Republic of Tanzania, 2002).

10　Zanzibar National Archives (hereafter ZNA), AB 39/203, British Resident to Secretary of State for the Colonies, 25 March 1931.

11　Bissell, *Urban Design*, p. 129.

12　ZNA AB 39/203, Crofton, Chief Secretary, 'Secret memorandum on town planning', 1916.

13　Dean Sinclair, 'Field note: "memorials more enduring than bronze": J. H. Sinclair and the making of Zanzibar Stone Town', *African Geographical Review*, 28 (2009), 91.

14　The quotation comes from ZNA AB 39/203, British Resident John Sinclair's note of 28 May 1924 to British East Africa's High Commissioner, Robert Coryndon; Bissell, *Urban Design*, pp. 193–4.

15　Bissell, *Urban Design*, p. 202.

16　Garth Myers, 'From "Stinkibar" to "The Island Metropolis": the geography of British hegemony in Zanzibar', in A. Godlewska and N. Smith (eds), *Geography and Empire* (Oxford: Blackwell, 1994), pp. 212–27.

17　Henry Lanchester, *Zanzibar: A Study in Tropical Town Planning* (Cheltenham: Barrow, 1923), p. 2; R. H. Crofton, *Zanzibar Affairs, 1914–1933* (London: Francis Edwards, 1953), pp. 110–11.

18　Anthony King, *Urbanism, Colonialism and the World Economy* (London: Routledge, 1990), pp. 53–5; Crofton, *Zanzibar Affairs*, pp. 110–11; Lanchester, *Zanzibar*, p. 10.

19　Bissell, *Urban Design*, p. 197.

20　Bissell, *Urban Design*, p. 207.

21　Bissell, *Urban Design*, p. 209.

22　ZNA AB 39/203, Sinclair to Coryndon, High Commissioner, Nairobi, 29 April 1924.

23　ZNA AB 39/203, Crofton to Lanchester, 10 May 1928.

24　ZNA AB 39/203, Lanchester to Crofton, 29 April 1924.

25　ZNA AB 39/203, Crofton, 'Secret memorandum'.

26　Lanchester, *Zanzibar*, p. 70.

27　Garth Myers, 'Sticks and stones: colonialism and Zanzibari housing', *Africa*, 67 (1997), 252–72.

28　Myers, 'Sticks and stones'; Garth Myers, 'The early history of the Other Side of Zanzibar Town', in A. Sheriff (ed.), *History and Conservation of Zanzibar Stone Town* (Athens, OH: Ohio University Press, 1995), pp. 30–45.

29　ZNA, AB 34/1, Andrade to British Consul, 4 March 1914, in 'Inquiry into and reorganisation of the Wakf Department, 1913–15'; ZNA, AE 8/10, Muhamed Remtulla Hemani to British Resident, 26 July 1926, in 'Land at Mlandege claimed by Gulamhussein Remtulla Hemani'; ZNA, AE 8/11, Muhamedhusse in Tharia

[118]

Topan to Land Office, 11 December 1928, in 'Claim of land at Ngamboo by Mohammedhussein Tharia Topan, 1926–28'; and ZNA, AB 36/23, Shelswell-White to M-H.
T. Topan, 2 May 1933, in 'Ground rents in Ng'ambo, 1940–63'.

30 Bissell, *Urban Design*, pp. 247–50.
31 ZNA AB 39/203, Lanchester to Crofton, 29 April 1924.
32 Lanchester, *Zanzibar*, p. 15.
33 James Scott, *Domination and the Arts of Resistance: Hidden Transcripts* (New
    Haven, CT: Yale University Press, 1990).
34 For instance, Steven Frenkel and John Western, 'Pretext or prophylaxis? Racial
    segregation and malarial mosquitos in a British tropical colony: Sierra Leone',
    Annals of the Association of American Geographers, 78 (1988), 211–28; Maynard
    Swanson, 'The sanitation syndrome: bubonic plague and urban native policy in the
    Cape Colony, 1900–1909', *Journal of African History*, 18 (1977), 387–410.
35 King, *Urbanism, Colonialism*, p. 55.
36 Lanchester, *Zanzibar*, p. 13.
37 Lanchester, *Zanzibar*, p. 54.
38 Lanchester, *Zanzibar*, p. 70.
39 Lanchester, *Zanzibar*, pp. 58, 77.
40 ZNA, AB 39/203, Crofton, 'Secret memorandum'.
41 ZNA, AB 39/203, Crofton, 'Secret memorandum'.
42 Bissell, *Urban Design*, p. 254.
43 Garth Myers, *Verandahs of Power: Colonialism and Space in Urban Africa*
    (Syracuse, NY: Syracuse University Press, 2003).
44 See the two ZNA files, AE 4/10 and AE 4/18, entitled 'Negotiation about the
    property of Ali Nathoo at Ziwani, 1928–36'. ZNA, AB 39/203 and AE 5/1 (entire
    files).
45 Ibid.
46 ZNA, AB 39/203, Lanchester to Crofton, 15 March 1928.
47 Zanzibar Protectorate, *Annual Medical and Sanitary Report of the Health Depart-
    ment* (Zanzibar: Government Printers, 1935), p. 41.
48 See ZNA, AB 34/8, 'The Wakf validating decree of 1946'.
49 Myers, 'Sticks and stones', pp. 260–1; see also ZNA, AB 39/26, 'Town building
    rules, 1929–55'.
50 Jonathon Glassman, *War of Words, War of Stones: Racial Thought and Violence in
    Colonial Zanzibar* (Bloomington: Indiana University Press, 2011).
51 Richard Burton, *Zanzibar: City, Island and Coast* (London: Tinsley Brothers, 1872),
    p. 102.
52 ZNA, AB 39/203, MOH to Crofton, 12 August 1924.
53 Crofton, *Zanzibar Affairs*, pp. 20–44.
54 Timothy Mitchell, *Colonizing Egypt* (Cambridge: Cambridge University Press,
    1988).
55 Garth Myers, 'Naming and placing the other: power and the urban landscape in
    Zanzibar', *Tijdschrift voor Economische en Sociale Geographie*, 87 (1996), 237–46.
    See also ZNA, AW 2/100, 'The Ngambo Area'.
56 ZNA, AB 40/153, Director of Medical Services to Chief Secretary, 16 August 1934,
    in 'Aerial survey of Zanzibar, 1934–57'.
57 Myers, 'Naming and placing', p. 240.
58 See ZNA, AB 39/26, 'Town building rules, 1929–55', and AB 40/13A, 'Acquisition
    of property in Ng'ambo, 1940–54'.
59 Bissell, *Urban Design*, p. 206.
60 Bissell, *Urban Design*, p. 209.
61 Finland Ministry for Foreign Affairs, *Sustainable Development and Environment
    in Finnish Foreign Policy* (Helsinki: Foreign Ministry, 2006).
62 Bissell, *Urban Design*, p. 210.
63 Muhajir, 'How planning works', pp. 219–25.
64 Muhajir, 'How planning works', p. 295.

PART TWO

Garden cities in colonial and Mandatory Palestine (Eretz Israel)

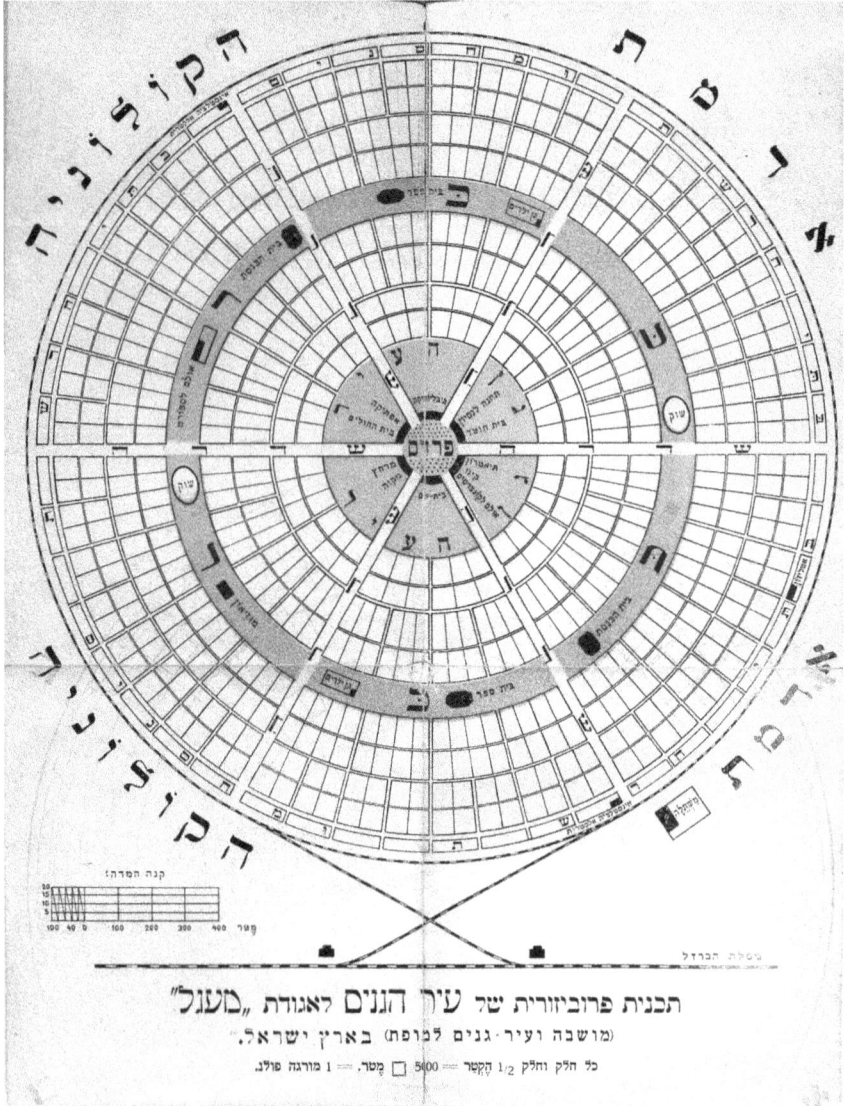

A proposal of the Association for the Founding of the Model Rural Settlement and Garden City in Eretz Israel (1917) titled 'Provisional Plan for Garden City by MAAGAL' (The Association for the Founding of the Model Rural Settlement, *Garden City in Eretz Israel*, p. 5).

CHAPTER FIVE

'May be solved by the construction of garden cities': German-Jewish literary proposals on garden cities in Eretz Israel

Ines Sonder

The garden city idea, pioneered in the late nineteenth century in Great Britain by Ebenezer Howard, was the first town planning model adopted by Zionist planners and architects for the Jewish homeland in Pales-tine.[1] First proposals and drafts were submitted by German-speaking Zionists in various publications, memoranda and Zionist newspa-pers. First clues can in fact be found in the writings of Theodor Herzl (1860–1904), the founding father of the World Zionist Organisation. Some of them made use of the literary genre which had started with Thomas More's essay *Utopia* (1516), depicting a fictional society in the future and its religious, social and political customs. Even Ebenezer Howard used this formula in the first chapter of his groundbreaking book *To-Morrow: A Peaceful Path to Real Reform* (1898), in which a garden city is described by means of a guided tour.

In 1902, the year when the second edition of Howard's book *Garden Cities of To-Morrow* was published, the *Deutsche Gartenstadt-Gesellschaft* (German Garden City Society) was founded in Berlin as the first garden city association outside Great Britain.[2] One of its founding members was the physician, social reformer and economist Franz Oppenheimer (1864–1943), who played a predominant role in the German settlement movement and *Freiland-Bewegung* (Free-Land Movement) as well as in the early Zionist colonisation of Palestine before the First World War.[3] The diffusion of the garden city idea in Germany influenced German Zionist planners and architects, and Zionist debates on the character of rural and industrial settlements. The ideological motivation for adopting Howard's urban concept was conspicuous as well.

A key figure in bringing the garden city idea to the Zionist public was the writer and economic theoretician Davis Trietsch (1870–1935). In 1905 he published the article 'Gartenstadt' (Garden City) in the Zionist monthly *Altneuland*, which became the starting point of his lifelong engagement with the Jewish garden city colonisation in Palestine. In numerous articles, pamphlets and lectures Trietsch recommended the garden city as the most appropriate urban form for agricultural and industrial settlements and the most adaptable to the predominantly 'urban Jewish immigrants' in Palestine. At the Twelfth Zionist Congress in Carlsbad in 1921, the garden city idea was finally adopted as the most important urban concept for Jewish settlement in Palestine.[4] It was subsequently realised in the 1920s in the construction of numerous Jewish garden suburbs on the outskirts of Palestinian cities and in plans for new garden cities and urban expansion, and was even applied to the layouts of agricultural settlements, which also reflected the principles of modern town planning.

This chapter concerns the most important German-Jewish writing on garden cities in Eretz Israel in the early twentieth century. This includes Theodor Herzl's vision of town planning and publications by Zionist planners and architects, among them Davis Trietsch, Wilhelm Stiassny and Alex Baerwald. None of these visions were realised. However, they reflected the beginning of modern Zionist town planning with far-reaching social, political, economic and architectural implications, partly influenced by well-known German architects and garden city planners. Moreover, this chapter reveals that town planning was not disregarded within the early Zionist movement,[5] but was part of a more comprehensive social concept in the building of a modern Jewish society in Eretz Israel.

Herzl's vision

Thousands of white villas gleamed out of luxuriant green gardens. All the way from Acco to Mount Carmel stretched what seemed to be one great park. The mountain itself, also, was crowned with beautiful structures … A magnificent city had been built beside the sapphire blue Mediterranean. The magnificent stone dams showed the harbor for what it was: the safest and most convenient port in the eastern Mediterranean.[6]

Theodor Herzl's vision of a prospective villa garden city on Mount Carmel in his programmatic utopia *Altneuland* (Old New Land, 1902) is impressive, as it had partially influenced Haifa's urban development in the 1920s, when the German-born architect Richard Kauffmann (1887–1958) planned various garden suburbs on Mount Carmel's summit and slopes,[7] and later when Haifa Bay was developed as a giant industrial and commercial centre, including the country's main port.[8]

A few years before, in 1896, Herzl had already imagined a possible urban shape for a future Jewish homeland for the first time. Then, when he was still a foreign correspondent for the great Vienna newspaper

Neue Freie Presse (1891–95) in Paris, he began – influenced by the anti-Semitic Dreyfus trial – to outline the literary architecture of his programmatic pamphlet *Der Judenstaat* (The Jewish State, 1896). On 8 June 1895 he wrote in note form in his diary: 'Create breathing spaces between towns. Every town like a big house located in the middle of a garden. In the free areas between the towns there must be only cultivated fields, forests, etc. By this I shall prevent hypertrophic cities, and the towns will look inhabited sooner.'[9] The following day he continued: 'City construction: The difficulty: a margin for expansion, and yet with an appearance of being inhabited. May be solved by the construction of garden cities.'[10] And some lines below, he discussed this idea:

> Since I want to establish garden cities, I face a dilemma: either to build the cities in forest clearings ... or plant trees between the houses, whereby I would lose the advertising appeal, the magic quality, but then I can develop the cities the way I want to; to be sure, they would look as if they were attending a tree nursery.[11]

Even before Howard's urban concept became common currency at the turn of the twentieth century, Herzl was familiar with the term 'garden city'.[12] In his later writings, he never used this term so explicitly again. However, it is remarkable that he not only envisaged the common idea that every house in the city should have a garden, but also the idea of a city being situated within a green belt of open countryside, as Howard did. According to Herzl, the construction of new towns and workmen's dwellings in a far-off Jewish homeland should reflect modern Western civilisation and town planning principles both in hygienic and social respects. Recourse to former development stages or attempts to 'overcome the troubles of Jews' solely by regenerating Jewish peasants Herzl considered 'artificial means' and an 'extraordinary mistake'.[13] In *Der Judenstaat* he wrote: 'If we wish to found a State today, we shall not do it in the way which would have been the only possible one a thousand years ago. It is foolish to revert to old stages of civilisation, as many Zionists would like to do.'[14]

Comprehensive drafts of building plans and about a hundred different types of houses would be designed by young Jewish architects prior to the mass emigration. Local groups in the Diaspora would have plans of the prospective towns so that the people might know beforehand where they were to go, in which towns and in which houses they were to live. The workmen's dwellings would resemble neither 'those melancholy workmen's barracks of European towns', nor those 'miserable rows of shanties which surround factories'.[15] They would present a beautiful uniform appearance, and the detached houses in little gardens would be united into attractive groups in each locality. 'The Temple will be visible from long distances.'[16] The land would belong to the Jewish Company, which was partly modelled along the lines of a great land-acquisition company.

In 1898, two years after he issued *Der Judenstaat*, Herzl visited Palestine as head of a Zionist delegation that met with the German emperor, Wilhelm II. Herzl's diaries speak eloquently of his horror at the squalor, neglect, foulness and 'levantinism' of the Palestinian cities, especially Jaffa and Jerusalem. During his stay in Jerusalem he wrote, on 31 October 1898:

> When I remember thee in days to come, O Jerusalem, it will not be with pleasure. The musty deposits of two thousand years of inhumanity, intolerance, and uncleanliness lie in the foul-smelling alleys ... If we ever get Jerusalem and if I am still able to do anything actively at that time, I would begin by cleaning it up. I would clear out everything that is not something sacred, set up workers' homes outside the city, empty the nests of filth and tear them down, burn the secular ruins, and transfer the bazaars elsewhere. Then, retaining the old architectural style as much as possible. I would build around the Holy Places a comfortable, airy new city with proper sanitation ... I am quite firmly convinced that a magnificent New Jerusalem could be built outside the old city walls. The old Jerusalem would still remain Lourdes and Mecca and Yerush-olayim. A very pretty, elegant town would be quite possible beside it.[17]

Later, he spelled out the details of urban renewal in his novel *Altneuland*. His literary vision, set in 1923, pictured the future Jewish homeland as a flourishing country, not explicitly a state but a new society based on cooperation, utilising all the accomplishments of science and technology, unencumbered by national chauvinism, tolerant and living in peace with its neighbours. The garden imaginary had a key role in Old New Land. New cities were to be constructed according to modern town planning ideas: 'Never in history were cities built so quickly or so well, because never before were so many technical facilities available.'[18]

Within the walls, Jerusalem's Old City had altered least. The Holy Sepulchre, the Mosque of Omar and other domes and towers had remained the same; but many splendid new structures had been added. A magnificent new edifice was the *Friedenspalast* (Peace Palace), where international congresses of peace-lovers and scientists were held. Outside the walls the picture was altogether different. Modern residential quarters were built, intersected by electric street railways, tree-lined streets and spacious boulevards, parks and gardens. There were various educational institutions, from kindergartens to the 'Zion University', as well as technical institutes and commercial colleges.

Jerusalem was no longer a neglected provincial town at the edge of the Ottoman Empire, only attractive as a religious centre, but 'a twentieth century metropolis'.[19]

The modern harbour town of Haifa – which by the end of the nineteenth century was only a small fishing village at the bottom of Mount Carmel – was Herzl's city of the future. A literary visit shows similarities to Howard's structural elements of the garden city. In the city centre lay an immense square – called *Völkerplatz* (People's Square) – bordered by arcades of large edifices which housed colonial banks and branch offices of European shipping companies. In the middle of the square was a fenced garden of palm trees. Both sides of the streets running into the square were bordered not only with palms, but also with electric lamps. The traffic was still lively but far less noisy; furthermore, an electric overhead train was installed. All over the city parks and cultivated green areas were planted. The larger the distances from the city centre were, the more rural and agricultural were the areas. The architecture in Haifa was 'fascinatingly varied':[20] magnificent edifices in the centre and elegant mansions in the residential quarters, 'surrounded by fragrant gardens'.[21] The dwelling houses with gardens were small and charming, intended for only one family. Several model plans were also made for pretty middle-class homes.

The gifted planner who built Old New Land's modern cities was the architect Steineck. As with other key figures of the novel, Herzl portrayed here one of his closest Zionist colleagues, the Viennese architect Oskar Marmorek (1863–1909), who was one of the founders of the Zionist weekly *Die Welt*, and was designated by Herzl as 'the first architect of the Jewish Renaissance'.[22]

As we know, *Altneuland* was far from being a successful utopian novel, particularly with regard to a prospective Jewish culture. Herzl was attacked by many adherents of the Zionist movement, especially Achad Ha'am (1856–1927), the founder of Cultural Zionism.[23] He was reproached for not being close to Jewish tradition and its values, including the Hebrew language and literature, deriving his visions almost exclusively from western European ideas. While in political and cultural respects his novel did not have a great influence on the development of Eretz Israel, some similarities in respect of town planning can be shown. In 1929 one of the best-known European journalists of his time, the Frenchman Albert Londres (1884–1932), wrote on Herzl's urban vision: 'Herzl, the prophet of the boulevards ... saw the first Jewish city in one of his dreams, rising gently from the Mediterranean shores, attracting the eye like a hill in spring. *Tel Aviv*, the spring hill.'[24] Although Herzl could never have anticipated the founding of Tel Aviv in 1909 – the first manifestation of a garden suburb in Eretz

Israel – his vision continues within the city's name: *Tel Aviv* (Hebrew: Spring Hill) is the title of the Hebrew edition of *Altneuland*.

The Jewish man and his capabilities

Although it is true that a good bit of our unnatural situation has resulted because we are not rural and that we are lacking farming professions, nothing would be as wrong as to convert our peddlers, craftsmen and industrial workers suddenly into peasants who should walk behind a plough in wide farm fields.[25]

The Zionist writer Davis Trietsch (born in Dresden and educated in Berlin) was a pioneer of practical Zionism and an early opponent of Herzl's Charter policy. In the 1890s he studied Jewish migration problems in the United States and attempted to get an endorsement for Jewish colonisation in Cyprus, especially for Romanian Jews.[26] After joining the Zionist movement, he tried to persuade the Congress to adopt his conception of a 'Greater Palestine', which was to comprise not only Palestine, but also Cyprus and El Arish, and he insisted on immediate practical settlement. After the Balfour Declaration, Trietsch fought for a 'Zionist maximalism', believing that a chance for large-scale immigration to Eretz Israel was at hand. Beyond his activities and writings regarding Jewish colonisation, Trietsch was one of the founders of the *Jüdischer Verlag* (Jewish Publishing House) and the *Orient Verlag*, as well as editor and co-editor of many periodicals (*Palästina, Ost und West, Volk und Land*). Later honoured as the 'pioneer of the literary summary of Palestine's economy'[27] by Otto Warburg, Trietsch's most popular book was the *Palästina Handbuch* (Palestine Handbook, 1907), which was translated into many languages and was often reissued.

As mentioned above, Trietsch was the first to suggest the garden city as the appropriate urban formula for Jewish colonisation in Palestine owing to its socio-economic needs and the character of the 'Jewish man and *his* capabilities'.[28] He regarded the Jewish colonisation of the Orient as a special case, fundamentally different from other cases of colonisation because of the nature of man, the land, the necessities and the means. Trietsch rejected the solely rural-oriented Zionist settlement ideology that was determined 'to thrust the plough back into the hand of the Jew who is weaned from agriculture'.[29] He aimed at a 'healthy professional stratification',[30] and proposed industrial development of the country in conjunction with small intensive rural farms, instead of extensive agriculture. This could be realised through independent garden cities as Howard had recommended. According to Trietsch, these offered the masses of the urban-industrial population both healthy labour *and* life conditions in the countryside; private houses and gardens for cheap rents compared with those of the urban industrial quarters, as well as easy access to job locations and food production facilities, which were partly managed as horticultural or rural family enterprises. Owing to its half-rural, half-urban character, the garden city provided a broad range of occupations ('industrial, cottage-industrial, mercantile, rural and other professions')[31] from the outset, in self-contained and healthy communities.

In his first article, 'Gartenstadt' (Garden City, 1905), in the monthly *Altneuland* Trietsch suggested two possible forms of Palestinian garden cities: one for the coastal region and one for inland plain regions. The latter refers to Howard's programme: a circular layout with several ring-roads, public buildings and squares located in the centre, backed by private houses with proper gardens (front gardens for flowers, back gardens for vegetables and trees) in the inner circle, and, beyond, a single or double external ring-road with factories connected by railway. The third, exterior ring-road is provided for bigger gardens and agriculture. The circle is intersected by four, six or eight radial roads. Similarly, a garden city in the coastal region should be developed, starting from the seaside along an inland road, parallel to the seafront. Near the harbour, the houses only have back gardens. In any case, the garden city land *should only be leased*, and never owned by individuals.

Town planning schemes played a minor part in his later writings on garden cities. As an economic theoretician, Trietsch increasingly focused on the problem of finding economic and financial bases for founding garden cities in Palestine, and discussed this with various potential industrial entrepreneurs. Until the beginning of the 1920s, numerous articles and memoranda on garden cities and the garden city movement were published by him.[32] Trietsch was a zealous collector of the publications of the German garden city movement. In a number of his writings one can find quotes from Hans Kampffmeyer (1876–1932), the first general secretary of the *Deutsche Gartenstadt-Gesellschaft*, and other garden city adherents. He repeatedly cited statistical data showing the positive results in respect of public health at the *Obstbaukolonie Eden* (the 'Eden' Orchard Settlement), a cooperative settlement founded in 1893 near Oranienburg, regarded as the forerunner of the garden city idea in Germany, as well as Letchworth garden city, the first English garden city founded on Ebenezer Howard's initiative in 1903. What is also remarkable is that Trietsch recommended the founding of a *Jüdische Gartenstadt Berlin* (Jewish Garden City Berlin) in 1918.[33]

In October 1920, while visiting Palestine as head of the so-called October-Commission intended to examine the feasibility of Jewish garden city colonisation, Trietsch was invited by the first High Commissioner, Sir Herbert Samuel (1870–1963), to present the commission's objectives. Afterwards he published a comprehensive report in the *Jüdische Rundschau*, in which he wrote: 'Firstly can I state that the idea of garden city colonisation has already been accepted in the whole country, and from now on it must be our task to clarify our requirements of this new form of colonisation and to propagate this clarity everywhere.'[34] In 1932, at the age of 62, Trietsch emigrated to Palestine and became one of the founding members of Ramot Hashavim, a self-sufficient settlement initiated by German-Jewish immigrants north of Tel Aviv. Here, a Trietsch Garden with a small memorial stone can be found in memory of this Zionist leader.

'A city within gardens': Viennese dreams of a Jewish colony in the Holy Land

The discipline of town planning is a particularly difficult science, the study of which can only be entrusted to a skilled and qualified technician endowed with practical knowledge. It requires a range of knowledge, specifically in local government politics, something which enables only a few technicians to work in this field.[35]

In Tel Aviv's town planning history, the Viennese court architect and *Baurat* (building officer) Wilhelm Stiassny (1842–1910) is well known for his draft 'Plan zur Errichtung einer städtischen Colonie für den Verein Achuzath Baith nächst Jaffa' (Plan to establish an urban colony for the Achuzath Baith Association near Jaffa), dated April 1909.[36] In November of the same year, Stiassny published a memorandum entitled 'Das Projekt zur Errichtung einer Kolonie im Heiligen Lande oder einem seiner Nebenländer' (The project to establish a colony in the Holy Land or in one of its neighbouring countries), which was the first proposal for a comprehensive plan for founding an urban Jewish settlement in Palestine according to the garden city idea, with far-reaching aims and numerous basic principles for its realisation, and with regard to regional and climatic conditions.[37] Although he never visited Palestine, Stiassny proves himself in his text not only very well-equipped with geographic, demographic and economic facts and statistics about the country, but also an expert on questions of Jewish colonisation. He acquired comprehensive knowledge about Palestine and the history of Jewish settlements in Eretz Israel not only from the Bible and its commentaries, but also from contemporary publications such as the description of Palestine and Syria in *Baedeker's Reisehandbuch* (Handbook for Travellers), and Davis Trietsch's *Palästina*

Handbuch (Palestine Handbook) and *Wirtschaftliche Tätigkeit in Palästina* (Economic Activity in Palestine). Familiar with modern urban planning principles,[38] Stiassny dreamed of 'a city within gardens' constructed according to the 'scientific regulations of town planning with consideration to the sun's position and prevailing winds'.[39] Unfortunately, his memorandum lacked a development plan or an illustrated depiction of the city's layout. However, his suggestions can be compared with his draft for Achuzath Baith.

In chapter 6 of the memorandum, entitled 'Unsere Kolonie' (Our Colony), Stiassny explained his planning ideas from social, cultural, industrial and political perspectives. The so-called 'city with its surroundings'[40] was to extend along the coastal line over a total area of 200,000 hectares (about 50 km long with an average width of 40 km); in its centre there was to be a river directly flowing into the sea. Similar to Herzl's *Altneuland*, Stiassny used the literary 'look to the future' that in his case covered ten years beyond the garden city's foundation. A flourishing Jewish community had emerged in which there was 'no house without garden, no street without stands of trees, no plaza without gardens and fountains'.[41] Street-gardens with shady avenues and arbours were planted in the middle promenades of the main roads. All streets were lined with front gardens with the exception of the broad market street, which was bounded by sheer endless rows of arcades. Every quarter had its own municipal garden; in the main district there was a city park of 25 hectares. North of the city, a 100–hectare forest park was planted which adjoined a city forest of about 2,000 hectares.

In accordance with Howard's ideas, Stiassny's garden city was functionally organised: pure residential quarters with detached houses were distinguished from districts in which trade and industry predominated. A building code regulated all building activities and was intended to prevent an unrestricted increase in property values. A great number of businesses and industries were present and flourished through trade with other Jewish settlements. A broad rural belt with fruit gardens and 'a wreath of thriving villages'[42] surrounded the city's outer ring, whose harvest would serve both the city's own consumption and the export trade. For transportation, the garden city was internally served by electric tram routes that also reached adjacent towns. The river flowing through the city had been made navigable and its branching system of canals also served as traffic and transportation routes. Furthermore, the entire city region was connected to coastal cities by a railway along the Levantine coastline, running through Port Said, El Arish, Gaza, Haifa (which had already grown into an important port), Akko, and farther towards Beirut and Tripoli. Numerous branch lines also led to other Jewish settlements as well as to the 'granary' of the Valley of Jezreel.[43]

As a coastal town the garden city also had a splendid sandy beach which naturally led to the development of a seaside resort. Resort guests in search of health, from all countries, classes and confessions, had been able to convalesce here in elegant guest houses and villas surrounded by exotically planted gardens and in the healthy sea air. Moreover, the city administration had acquired the curative sulphur springs, well known for more than three millennia, in whose environs swimming houses, hotels and villas were constructed.

On the day of the city's foundation, foundation stones were laid for three important institutions in the life of a Jewish community: a synagogue, a school and a cemetery. While Stiassny made no further remarks on religious life, his explanation regarding the educational system covered a broad sphere, including the founding of a 'University of the East'. Artists' settlements with numerous studios had arisen in the city's centre and its flourishing suburbs, and schools of architecture, sculpture and medallion craftsmanship were founded. Established in 1906, the 'Bezalel' art school in Jerusalem served as an arts and crafts institute. Stiassny's garden city had also developed into an important site of trade and industry for the entire area; large industry had been successfully settled, located in a special industrial area in the outskirts. After a decade of continuous and proactive planning development, a flourishing garden city had arisen on the shores of the Mediterranean, a city which in many respects – industrial, cultural and intellectual – formed the 'heart of all colonies' in Palestine. Although the memorandum's appendix contains a list of applications for the commencement of the project, which included sending a commission on an expedition to Palestine to choose suitable building sites, Stiassny's proposal was never realised. A few months after publishing his memorandum, in July 1910, he died.

The Nordau Garden City (1920): a view of colourful housing and new social society

A Palestinian garden city will and has to look different from such a city in Germany. The European has to learn if he is to appreciate and love the special character and beauty of the combination of flat-roofed houses with the Palestinian landscape.[44]

In summer 1920 the Jewish National Fund's Head Office published a brochure entitled *Eine Gartenstadt für Palaestina* (A Garden City for Palestine), which was one of the ambitious and comprehensive

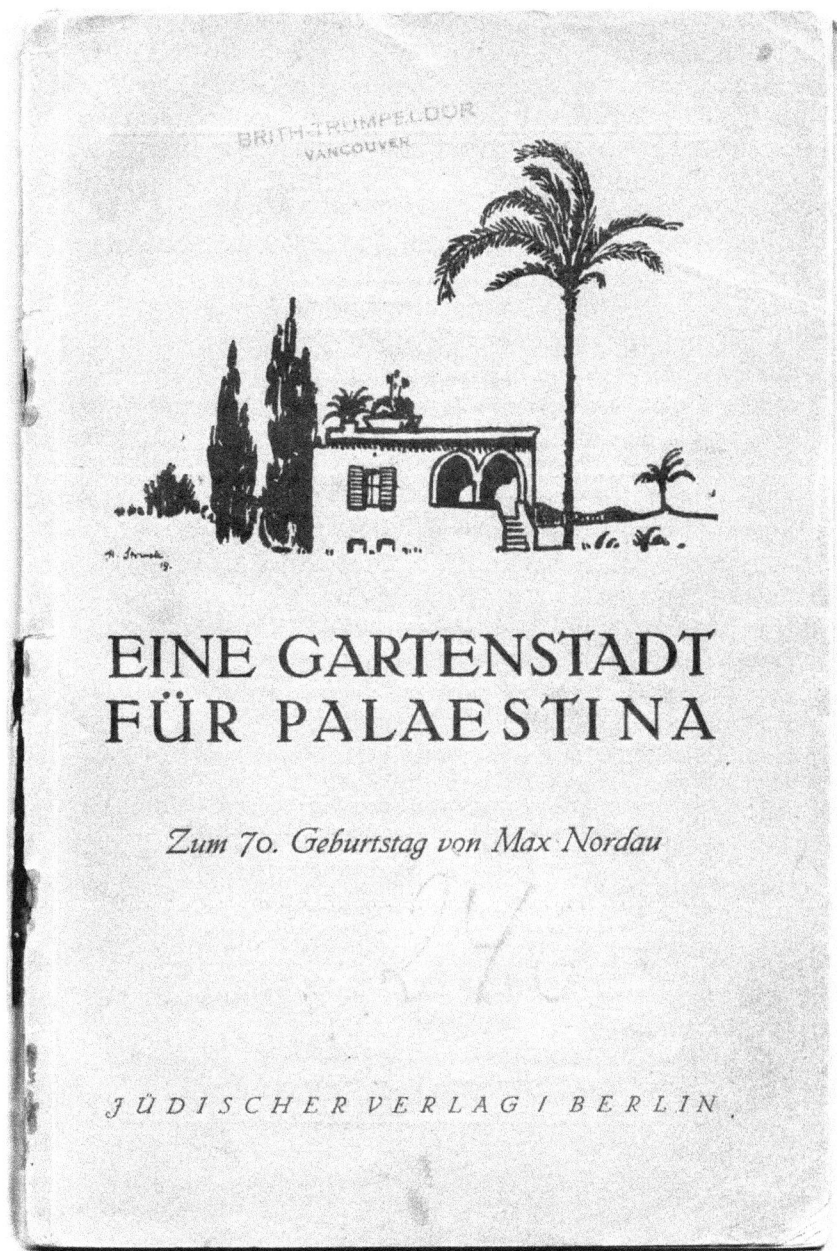

Figure 5.1 A Garden City for Palestine, front cover, with a sketch by Hermann Struck (*Eine Gartenstadt für Palaestina* [Berlin: Jüdischer Verlag, 1920]).

projects officially initiated by the Zionist Organisation in the field of urban planning after the First World War (fig. 5.1). In celebration of the seventieth birthday of the Zionist doyen and Herzl's confidant Max Nordau (1849–1923), the Zionist Inner Actions Committee (then based in The Hague), in cooperation with the Jewish National Fund, planned to establish a garden city in Palestine named after the well-known physician, cultural critic and writer.[45] It was the first time that a team of chosen experts was officially charged with outlining a garden city according to socio-economic and town planning principles.

The editor of the brochure was the writer and Herzl's first biographer, Adolf Friedemann (1871–1932); the painter and etcher Hermann Struck (1876–1944) designed a vignette, 'Nordau Garden City'; the sociologist and economist Franz Oppenheimer discussed common socio-economic questions in his essay 'Garden City'; and the Prussian Government Builder and architect Alex Baerwald (1877–1930), prominent for his design of Haifa's Hebrew Technical Institute (Technion), wrote an essay on architectural and constructional aspects of the garden city and designed the draft 'Zukunftsbild der Nordau-Gartenstadt aus der Vogelperspektive' (Future image of the Nordau Garden City from bird's-eye view, 1919) (fig. 5.2). Finally, the English Zionist Israel Cohen (1879–1961), from the World Zionist Organisation, spoke about the principles and duties of the Jewish National Fund. The brochure ended with Nordau's autobiography. For the realisation of the project, a special fund was incorporated to collect ten

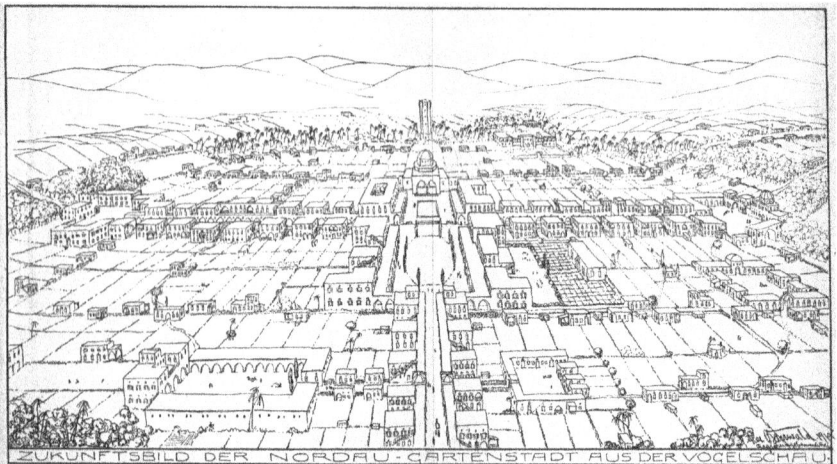

Figure 5.2 Alex Baerwald, 'Future Image of the Nordau Garden City from a Bird's-Eye View' (1919) (*Eine Gartenstadt für Palaestina* [Berlin: Jüdischer Verlag, 1920], appendix).

million francs in Jewish communities worldwide in the course of one year.[46]

Alex Baerwald's essay 'Die Nordau-Gartenstadt in architektonischer und bautechnischer Beziehung' (The Nordau Garden City in architectural and constructional respects) was written as an imaginary dialogue between a Jewish family from Germany who visited the Nordau Garden City in spring 1922 and a city clerk serving as their guide and explaining the principles of town planning and architecture. In it Baerwald used the same literary genre as had Howard: a journey through the future city. At that time, in spring 1922, 400 families comprising 2,000 people, plus about 300 individuals, were living in the new community, and approximately 100 new people per month moved in. The garden city was located on the coastal plain near a harbour town, with a railway station on the 'Egypt–Haifa Line'. The garden city's land belonged to the Jewish National Fund, private houses were leased for a hundred years, and life was based on cooperative ideas. The urban draft shows an orthogonal grid; the vantage point in Baerwald's sketch is identical to the elevated railway station of the Nordau Garden City, and a water tower appears on the horizon. Similar to Howard's concept, the urban nucleus is surrounded by a green belt with an agricultural zone; the industrial area is located beyond. The hills in the background are the Judean Hills.

The crossing point of the two main streets consists of a vast square, called Nordau Square, which is dominated by a dome-shaped synagogue, flanked by two monumental structures: the Beth Ha'am as the administrative centre of the new community, and the *Gesellschaftshaus* (Community Centre) as the cultural centre comprising a concert hall for 500 people. The big synagogue, as the religious centre, is considered the 'crown of the garden city' according to the urban concept *Stadtkrone* (City Crown) put forward by German expressionist architects, and championed in particular by Bruno Taut (1880–1938). In line with Howard's ideals, Taut published his book of the same title in 1919, which envisaged garden cities with green spaces and fantastic buildings in the centre as an expressionist iteration of a cultural acropolis, with impressive scale and notions of social restructuring.[47] The architect Richard Kauffmann, the first Zionist town planner in Palestine from 1920, was also inspired by Taut's urban concept and designed most of his later garden suburbs, *kibbutzim* and *moshavs* (cooperative settlements) with a so-called *Siedlungskrone* (Settlement Crown).

The shapes of buildings, streets, public spaces and gardens in the Nordau Garden City were of homogeneous design. The standard housing types of varying size (one- or two-storeyed) and density reflected a symbiosis of modern Western engineering and hygiene on the one hand, and regional architectural characteristics on the other. While the private houses had mostly flat roofs with roof terraces, most of the public buildings had domes. Further architectural characteristics were arches and ventilation holes above the windows for air circulation, which are typical of local Arab building traditions. Visiting the Nordau Garden City, the family father from Germany shouts out enthusiastically: 'How beautiful is the Arabian building style with its flat roof terraces corresponding to the Palestinian landscape!'[48]

To avoid architectural monotony and uniformity, the private houses were distinguished by their coloured façades or shutters. The use of colour as a design principle is an interesting detail in Baerwald's draft, because he had never applied it to his Palestinian architectural plans before (nor later), nor suggested it in other writings, for example his article 'Ein Siedlungshaus für Palästina' (A settlement house for Palestine, 1920), written at about the same time.[49] However, this again alludes to the architect Bruno Taut, who had already in 1913/14 designed the German garden city of Falkenberg near Berlin with coloured houses, doors and window frames, which were the first example of the use of colour on mass housing estates and became known in the vernacular as 'Tuschkastensiedlung' (Paint Box Estates).

Furthermore, Baerwald's Nordau Garden City was inspired by another influential German architect, Hermann Muthesius (1861–1927), who was known for promoting many of the ideas of the English Arts and Crafts movement within Germany. As one of the pioneers of German architectural modernism, Muthesius had been a member of the Artistic Advisory Board of the German Garden City Society since 1909, and had designed many small-scale and model houses for various German garden cities, among them the first German garden city, Hellerau, near Dresden. Baerwald quoted Muthesius regarding the economic factors of building, and pleaded like him for stone buildings instead of 'surrogate' buildings and shanties, because they would have permanent value despite higher costs.[50]

Accompanying Baerwald's proposal, Franz Oppenheimer wrote an essay, 'Gartenstadt' (Garden City), in the same volume, about socio-economic issues.[51] Both men were old acquaintances in the early Zionist movement, working together when the first experimental agricultural settlement (*Siedlungsgenossenschaft*) at Merchavia in the Valley of Jezreel was established in 1910 according to Oppenheimer's cooperative principles, with Baerwald as the actual planner.[52] In his essay Oppenheimer primarily dealt with economic questions and social justice, principles of public land ownership and the symbiosis between urban and rural settlement – themes he repeatedly discussed as a settlement promoter, believing the monopoly of land to be the central evil of capitalist society. Oppenheimer had become interested in social issues at the end of the nineteenth century when he practised as a physician in the poorer quarters in northern Berlin (1886–95), and was inspired by the social ideas of Henry George (1839–97) and Theodor Hertzka (1845–1924). As a founding member of the German garden city movement, Oppenheimer regarded Howard's urban concept as 'flesh of my flesh and blood of my blood',[53] as he wrote in the foreword to the first German translation of Howard's book, *Gartenstädte in Sicht* (Garden Cities in Sight, 1907).

Besides the socio-economic issues Oppenheimer discussed in his essay, he also dealt with the urban planning of a garden city which he called *Genossenschaftsstadt* (Cooperative City). Adopting in general Howard's concept of segregation of land use and alternating arrangement of residential zones, he regarded the predetermination of area and population as 'Künstelei'[54] (artificiality). This is because new social cities and self-contained communities with public ownership of land would not resemble the big Western capitalist cities. Embedded in spacious green surroundings, the city's physical frame should be designed as a whole work of art that expresses its essential values as a cooperative society. He preferred terrace houses because of economic and formal architectural factors which were aimed at achieving a 'general aesthetic impression'.[55]

Oppenheimer saw his urban ideal in modern revivals of the most beautiful naturally growing cities and little towns that arose from the 'best architectural period in our history, the Middle Ages'.[56] As an example of such a contemporary new creation according to the principles of modern town planning, he referred to the layout of the German garden city of Staaken, near Berlin-Spandau. This was planned by Paul Schmitthenner (1884–1972), in a way which would satisfy both the *Künstler-Architekt* (artist-architect) and the economist. Staaken garden city was built for the employees of the armaments factory in Spandau from 1914 to 1917 by order of the Ministry of the Interior of the German Reich. Schmitthenner strived for an idyllic small-town atmosphere, to be created by gardens, narrow streets and small squares – although the two- and three-storeyed terrace houses were built with standardised ground plans and prefabricated parts. The curved and crooked roads and squares could be conceived as imitations of medieval towns.

With his preference for medieval towns with their picturesque curved streets, Oppenheimer stood in significant contrast to Baerwald's orthogonal draft for the Nordau Garden City, which is based on geometric principles and 'ideal city' planning.[57] In this they represent the two major opposing trends in modern town planning within the

German garden city movement – reflecting a controversy that subsequently had an impact on town planning in Eretz Israel. However, in some details Oppenheimer's *Genossenschaftsstadt* (Cooperative City) is also opposed to Baerwald's proposal in the brochure *A Garden City for Palestine*; apparently they had not synchronised their essays as had been intended. Whereas in Baerwald's draft the railway station is located outside the urban centre, in Oppenheimer's it is situated in the middle of the town, as in the draft of the first garden city, Letchworth, founded by Howard and planned by Barry Parker and Raymond Unwin in 1903. It is no less interesting to note that with regard to cultural, religious and regional aspects one can hardly identify Eretz Israel or a Jewish social community in Oppenheimer's essay; for instant, he used the term *Gotteshäuser* (Houses of God) instead of synagogues, which would have been more obvious.

Despite great efforts and the endorsement of the Zionist leadership, the Nordau Garden City was not realised. In February 1923, the year of Max Nordau's death (he died in January in Paris), a residential quarter on Jewish National Fund land was established in the then northern area of Tel Aviv, and in honour of the Zionist leader it was named 'Nordiyah'. Alex Baerwald emigrated to Palestine in 1924, and became the founder and one of the first teachers of the Faculty of Architecture at the Technical Institute in Haifa. Planning a lot of public structures and private buildings, for example for the aforementioned Hermann Struck, Baerwald is regarded the doyen of the pioneer architects in Eretz Israel.[58] Franz Oppenheimer, who had officially renounced Jewish nationalism before the First World War, gave some theoretical courses to the leaders of the labour movement in Palestine from 1934 to 1935. In 1936 he was appointed an honorary member of the American Sociological Association and in 1938 he emigrated, via Tokyo and Shanghai, to Los Angeles.

Towards Jewish garden suburbs

Although garden suburbs were not originally part of Howard's plan, they became the most frequent form of suburban construction in early twentieth-century Europe.[59] This is also true regarding Zionist town planning, starting with Tel Aviv in 1909 as the first Jewish garden suburb in Eretz Israel. Among the Zionist proposals by German-speaking architects we also know about designs for a garden suburb near Haifa, submitted in 1919 by Alexander Levy (1883–1942),[60] the founder of the *Palästina-Baugesellschaft* (Palestine Building Society). Another design was that of Fritz Kornberg (1889–1944),[61] who was later involved in planning the Hebrew University on Mount Scopus, Jerusalem. Both

ARCHITEKT ALEXANDER LEVY

VOM BAUEN UND WOHNEN
IM NEUEN PALÆSTINA

MIT EINEM VORWORT VON
PROF. DR. OTTO WARBURG
UND 53 ILLUSTRATIONEN

ANHANG:
ERNST HERRMANN, HAIFA:
ÜBER DIE AUSSICHTEN DER BAU-
TÄTIGKEIT IN DEN JÜDISCHEN
NIEDERLASSUNGEN PALÄSTINAS

1 9 2 0

HERAUSGEGEBEN VON DER PALÄSTINA BAUGESELLSCHAFT
WELT - VERLAG / BERLIN

Figure 5.3 Alexander Levy, *On Building and Housing in the New Palestine,* front cover (*Vom Bauen und Wohnen im neuen Palästina* [Berlin: Welt-Verlag, 1920]).

[139]

drafts were published in the comprehensive memorandum entitled *Vom Bauen und Wohnen im Neuen Palästina* (On Building and Housing in the New Palestine, 1920), edited by Levy the following year (fig. 5.3).[62] It was in fact the first proposal for housing estates in a garden suburb of Haifa, but it was also never implemented.[63] However, it is significant to note that a publication that was endorsed 'Gedruckt als Denkschrift für die Leitung der Zionistischen Organisation in London' (printed as Memorandum to the Leadership of the Zionist Organisation in London) was written and foreworded by Otto Warburg (1859–1938). He was the chairman of the board of directors of the Palestine Building Society, and this publication thus gained the status of a quasi-official Zionist document.

Alexander Levy, who later designed the renowned so-called *'Pagoda House' (1924)* in Tel Aviv, was involved with the German garden city movement and was a warm admirer of Bruno Taut and his utopian writings. In November 1919 Levy wrote to Richard Kauffmann, who was also close to Taut's ideas:

> One pet idea of mine for Palestine that was recently inspired by a programmatic article by [Bruno] Taut is: Dissolution of the cities! But also not 'villages' in the old sense. For this complexity of ideas, I have worked out the formula: 'Palestine: a garden' – of God if you want, neither town nor village is suitable for us Jews and for the New Man at all. The city is too much inherent in us, the village too little.[64]

Conclusion

The first two decades of the twentieth century were in a sense a utopian era of modern Zionist town planning. Although the Zionist movement declared agricultural settlement as one of its primary tasks, the urban sector was also the focus of planners and architects, especially those who made claims for an industrial development of the country and a healthy professional stratification. Howard's concept of combining the advantages of both town and country was regarded as the proper urban formula for the resettlement of the Land of Israel and the founding of a new Jewish society. Not least was it intended as an antithesis to the unhealthy living and housing conditions of both the European ghetto and the neglected Ottoman cities. The supporters of the garden city idea within the Zionist movement attempted to adapt Howard's concept to the Palestinian environment: its local architectural tradition to be combined with a modern 'Hebrew style' – envisaged as a so-called Eretz Israeli style – and the regional climate. They developed their designs not primarily in terms of town planning, but with particular attention to socio-economic and cooperative aspects, as well as to political and socio-cultural contexts. Ultimately, they failed because of a lack of capital – the most important problem within the Zionist movement until the 1920s – and of available land, as well as many other basic and external factors.

Finally, although most Israeli towns were established after the founding of the state in 1948,[65] Israeli town planning was apparent in the visions and blueprints of European planners and architects decades earlier. Most of them were of German-Jewish descent or trained in German schools of architecture, and were familiar with the reformist ideas of well-known German architects and garden city planners before and after the First World War. Their writings and architectural visions for a 'New Zion' can be seen as part of the European literature of 'town planning utopias', but envisaged for a new urban society that expressed modern technology and ideas of social justice in the rural Zionist landscape in Palestine.

Notes

1   Ines Sonder, *Gartenstädte für Erez Israel: Zionistische Stadtplanungsvisionen von Theodor Herzl bis Richard Kauffmann* (Hildesheim: Georg Olms Verlag, 2005).
2   A precursor of the garden city idea in Germany was Theodor Fritsch (1852–1933), a rampant anti-Semite, who contributed visions of *Die Stadt der Zukunft* (The Town of the Future, 1896) and *Die neue Gemeinde* (The New Community, 1903). Because of their ideological position these works had no sustained impact on the German garden city movement.
3   Alex Bein, 'Franz Oppenheimer als Mensch und Zionist', *Bulletin des Leo Baeck Instituts*, 7:25 (1964), 1–20.
4   *Stenographisches Protokoll der Verhandlungen des XII. Zionisten-Kongresses in Karlsbad vom 1. bis 14. September 1921* (Berlin: Jüdischer Verlag, 1922).
5   Eric Cohen, 'The city in Zionist ideology', *The Jerusalem Quarterly*, 4 (1977), 126–44.
6   Theodor Herzl, *Old New Land*, trans. Lotta Levensohn (New York and Princeton, NJ: Markus Wiener Publishers, 1997 [1902]), p. 58.
7   For Richard Kauffmann's complete works, see Uriel M. Adiv, 'Richard Kauffmann 1887–1958. Das architektonische Gesamtwerk' (PhD dissertation, Technische Universität Berlin, 1985).
8   In fact, Haifa's modern deepwater port was built by the British Mandatory Administration. Opened in October 1933, it was later enlarged by the State of Israel.
9   Raphael Patai (ed.), *The Complete Diaries of Theodor Herzl*, trans. Harry Zohn, vol. 1 (New York and London: Herzl Press and Thomas Yoseloff, 1969), pp. 45–6.
10 Patai (ed.), *The Complete Diaries*, vol. 1, p. 59.
11 Patai (ed.), *The Complete Diaries*, vol. 1, p. 60.
12 The term 'garden city' was known before Howard adopted it for his urban concept. In the 1860s, for example, Chicago was called a garden city because of the many cultivated gardens and groups of trees within the city.
13 Theodor Herzl, *The Jewish State* (Boston: Borgo Press, 2008), pp. 64–5. *The Jewish State* was originally published by the American Zionist Emergency Council on the occasion of the fiftieth anniversary of the publication of *Der Judenstaat* in Vienna, 14 February 1896.
14 Herzl, *The Jewish State*, p. 69.
15 Herzl, *The Jewish State*, p. 76.

16 Herzl, *The Jewish State*, p. 76.
17 Raphael Patai (ed.), *The Complete Diaries of Theodor Herzl*, vol. 2 (New York and London: Herzl Press and Thomas Yoseloff, 1969), pp. 745–7.
18 Herzl, *Old New Land*, p. 68.
19 Herzl, *Old New Land*, p. 247.
20 Herzl, *Old New Land*, p. 67.
21 Herzl, *Old New Land*, p. 68.
22 Letter from Theodor Herzl to Oskar Marmorek, 18 May 1897, cited in Markus Kristan, *Oskar Marmorek: Architekt und Zionist, 1863–1909* (Vienna: Böhlau, 1996), p. 28.
23 Achad Ha'am, 'Altneuland', *Ost und West*, 4 (April 1903), 227–44.
24 Albert Londres, *Ahasver ist angekommen. Eine Reise zu den Juden im Jahre 1929* (Munich: Deutscher Taschenbuchverlag, 1998), pp. 163–4.
25 Davis Trietsch, 'Gartenstadt', *Altneuland*, 11/12 (November 1905), 351. All translations from the German are by the author.
26 Oskar Rabinowicz, 'Davis Trietsch's colonization scheme in Cyprus', *Herzl Year Book*, 4 (1962), 119–206.
27 Otto Warburg, 'Davis Trietsch zum Tode', *Jüdische Rundschau*, 11 (5 February 1935), 5.
28 *Stenographisches Protokoll der Verhandlungen des XII. Zionisten-Kongresses*, p. 371 (emphasis in the original).
29 Trietsch, 'Gartenstadt', p. 351.
30 Trietsch, 'Gartenstadt', p. 351.
31 Trietsch, 'Gartenstadt', p. 357.
32 For bibliography, see Sonder, *Gartenstädte*.
33 Central Zionist Archives (hereafter CZA), A104 /67, 'Zum Projekt einer jüdischen Gartenstadt bei Berlin'; Ines Sonder, 'Gibt es eine jüdische Gartenstadt?', in Michal Kümper et al. (eds), *Makom. Orte und Räume im Judentum. Essays* (Hildesheim: Georg Olms Verlag, 2007), pp. 49–55.
34 'Davis Trietsch über die Lage', *Jüdische Rundschau*, 6 (21 January 1921), 36.
35 CZA L1/51, letter from Wilhelm Stiassny to Otto Warburg, 2 November 1908. All translations from the German are by the author.
36 Ines Sonder, 'Wilhelm Stiassny und der Bebauungsplan für Tel Aviv (1909)', *David. Jüdische Kulturzeitschrift Österreichs*, 58 (2003), 38–41.
37 Ines Sonder, 'The project to establish a colony in the Holy Land: the Viennese architect Wilhelm Stiassny (1842–1910) and his building program for Palestine', *Assaph. Studies in Art History*, 9 (2004), 135–60.
38 While planning Achuzath Baith, Stiassny recommended an extensive list of contemporary books on town planning, especially by German architects, as well as Howard's first German edition of *Gartenstädte in Sicht* (Garden Cities in Sight, 1907). CZA L1/51, letter from Wilhelm Stiassny to Otto Warburg, 2 November 1908; CZA L2/71, letter from Otto Warburg to Arthur Ruppin, 6 November 1908.
39 Wilhelm Stiassny, *Das Projekt zur Errichtung einer Kolonie im Heiligen Lande oder einem seiner Nebenländer* (Vienna: Verlag des Jüdischen Kolonisations-Vereins, 1909), p. 38.
40 Stiassny, *Das Projekt*, p. 37.
41 Stiassny, *Das Projekt*, p. 39.
42 Stiassny, *Das Projekt*, p. 41.
43 It is a remarkable preview of the later agricultural developments, because the Zionist Organisation was able to acquire land in the Valley of Jezreel only at the beginning of the 1920s.
44 CZA KKL1/584, letter from Alex Baerwald to KKL, 8 December 1919. All translations from the German are by the author.
45 The idea of honouring Max Nordau with the foundation of a garden city in his name was first proposed for July 1909 in celebration of his sixtieth birthday, but never realised. CZA L51/83, and CZA L2/21–1, Entwurf zur 'M. Nordau Kolonie' (8 February 1909).
46 CZA KKL1/584, For the 'Zehnmillionenfonds' (Ten million funds).

47 Bruno Taut, *Die Stadtkrone*, with contributions by Paul Scheerbart, Erich Baron and Adolf Behne (Jena: Verlag Eugen Diederichs, 1919).

48 Alex Baerwald, 'Die Nordau-Gartenstadt in architektonischer und bautechnischer Beziehung', in Adolf Friedemann (ed.), *Eine Gartenstadt für Palästina. Festgabe zum 70. Geburtstag von Max Nordau* (Berlin: Jüdischer Verlag, 1920), p. 39.

49 Alex Baerwald, 'Ein Siedlungshaus für Palästina', *Neue Jüdische Monatshefte*, 4:9/10 (1920), 208–14.

50 Baerwald, 'Die Nordau-Gartenstadt', p. 61.

51 Franz Oppenheimer, 'Gartenstadt', in Friedemann (ed.), *Eine Gartenstadt*, pp. 24–37.

52 Myra Warhaftig, 'Siedlungsgenossenschaft Merchavia von Alex Baerwald nach Franz Oppenheimer', in Sonja Günther and Dietrich Worbs (eds), *Architektur-Experimente in Berlin und anderswo. Für Julius Posener* (Berlin: Konopka, 1989), pp. 164–71.

53 Franz Oppenheimer, 'Geleitwort', in Ebenezer Howard, *Gartenstädte in Sicht* (Jena: Eugen Diederichs, 1907), p. iii.

54 Oppenheimer, 'Gartenstadt', p. 25.

55 Oppenheimer, 'Gartenstadt', p. 33.

56 Oppenheimer, 'Gartenstadt', p. 30.

57 Helen Rosenau, *The Ideal City: Its Architectural Evolution* (London: Studio Vista, 1974).

58 Myra Warhaftig, *They Laid the Foundation: Lives and Works of German-Speaking Jewish Architects in Palestine 1918–1948* (Berlin: Ernst Wasmuth Verlag, 2007).

59 The first example was Hampstead Garden Suburb, founded in north-west London in 1907. The master plan was prepared by Barry Parker and Raymond Unwin.

60 Edina Meyer-Maril, 'Alexander Levy – ein deutsch-jüdischer Architekt zwischen Berlin, Tel Aviv, Paris und Auschwitz', in Julius H. Schoeps, Karl E. Grözinger and Gert Mattenklott (eds), *Menora* (Bodenheim: Philo, 1998), pp. 315–38.

61 Warhaftig, *They Laid the Foundation*, pp. 44–53.

62 Alexander Levy, *Vom Bauen und Wohnen im neuen Palästina* (Berlin: Welt-Verlag, 1920).

63 Gilbert Herbert and Silvina Sosnovsky, *Bauhaus on the Carmel and the Crossroads of Empire* (Jerusalem: Yad Izhak Ben Zvi, 1993). A couple of years later, Richard Kauffmann planned various garden suburbs on Mount Carmel near Haifa.

64 CZA A 175/150B, letter from Alexander Levy to Richard Kauffmann, 5 November 1919. Translation from the German by the author.

65 Erika Spiegel, *Neue Städte: New Towns in Israel* (Stuttgart and Bern: Karl Krämer Verlag, 1966); Zvi Efrat, *The Israeli Project: Building and Architecture, 1948–1973* (Tel Aviv: Tel Aviv Museum of Art, 2004) (in Hebrew).

CHAPTER SIX

Urban development and the 'garden city': examples from late Ottoman-era Palestine and the late British Mandate

Yossi Katz and Liora Bigon

Since the early twentieth century, much attention has been paid to Ebenezer Howard's well-known book *Garden Cities of To-Morrow*. The aim of this chapter is to examine the reception of Howard's widely disseminated ideas in early twentieth-century Palestine and their influence on Ottoman-era urban development (up to 1917), particularly in Tel Aviv, Haifa, Tiberias and Jerusalem (for places mentioned in the text see fig. 6.1). We shall also offer some glimpses of garden city development during the British Mandatory regime (1922–48), most notably in the 1920s and during the Second World War. This chapter draws heavily on primary sources and its contribution to the part of this book dealing with Palestine lies in the synoptic view it offers of various case studies by means of brief comparisons. Thus, it bridges the gap between chapter 5 with its purely literary conceptualisation of garden city ideas for Palestine and chapter 7 which presents the particular historical circumstances of an actual case study, namely, the establishment of Tel Aviv as a garden city.

The garden city idea and the success of the garden suburb in Europe

Howard's revolutionary essay sought solutions for the complex problems facing the cities and towns of Europe in the wake of the Industrial Revolution, above all, the difficulties caused by overpopulation and lack of proper planning. To this end he proposed the establishment of new towns that would take every possible aspect of life into account and offer a whole range of employment opportunities. These towns were to be surrounded by a green belt, with an advance limit set on the number of houses in each, with large areas designated as open parks and private gardens and a strong emphasis on the preservation of natural beauty and healthy living conditions. All in all, Howard's concept of the garden city

Figure 6.1 Places mentioned in the text marked on present-day map of Israel.

was diametrically opposed to the conditions then prevailing in the old cities of Europe.[1]

Ideas similar to Howard's had been propounded by other reformers, and he clearly made use of studies by earlier writers such as James Buckingham, Robert Pemberton and Benjamin Richardson.[2] However, they described utopian cities, while Howard succeeded in transforming his vision into reality.[3] This is why, even today, Howard's book remains important both in terms of research and theory and with regard to the application of his ideas. From a practical point of view, the impact of his book was immediate and brought about the foundation of a movement whose object was the establishment of garden cities. A Garden City and Town Planning Association, which later changed its name to the Town and Country Planning Association, was established in England in 1899. Its aim was to implement the principles expressed in Howard's book and to bring about the establishment of garden cities.[4]

In England, the construction of Letchworth, the first garden city, began in 1903. Letchworth demonstrated the feasibility of Howard's ideas. It was mainly due to the influence of the garden city movement that the 1909 town planning legislation in England, which set out clear population limits, gained momentum.[5] Yet the movement for garden cities spread far beyond the British Isles, and quite rapidly in the case of Europe and the West. This was particularly notable in Germany, where at the beginning of the twentieth century a German Garden City Association was established in cooperation with its sister movement in England. The German movement also published a book similar to the one published in England.[6]

Despite the spread of the garden city movement and its modernising influence on urban planning, only two garden cities were actually established by 1920: Letchworth and, also in England, Welwyn.[7] Before the late 1920s, the impact of Howard's novel ideas on town planning found expression mainly in the establishment of garden suburbs, although these were not mentioned specifically in his book. At the same time, one of the objectives of the Town and Country Planning Association was to encourage the creation of garden suburbs in order to ease the immediate situation of existing towns, although the movement continued to insist that the overall solution lay in creating garden cities.[8]

The first garden suburb planned and created using Howard's ideas was Hampstead, near London, in 1907. The ideas incorporated in Hampstead included the allocation of large areas for parks and gardens around the houses; limiting the area allocated for private building; separating businesses from inhabited areas; and taking comfort, natural beauty, aesthetics and hygiene into consideration. The planning phase began in 1905 and by 1911 over 1,000 houses had been constructed which were occupied by over 4,500 people.[9] Hampstead was utterly different from the typical English suburb. Thomas Adams, an advocate of Howard's ideas, wrote in one of his articles: 'Hampstead Garden Suburb is probably the best planned of modern neighbourhoods in the London region. Its features have been regarded as a model in other parts of Great Britain, as well as abroad.'[10]

Culpin, the secretary of the Town and Country Planning Association, noted in a report from 1913 that dozens of plans for garden suburbs had been submitted and that some of these were in the process of being built and occupied.[11] Culpin, it would seem, had mixed feelings on the subject: 'The Garden Suburb succeeds the more quickly. The child outstripped the parent, and in the same degree the great truth has been in danger of becoming overshadowed by the lesser truth.'[12] Similarly, in Germany, 'the child outstripped the parent'. Although not one garden city had been built by the 1920s, a number of garden suburbs were created, such as Ratshof near Königsberg and Hellerau near Dresden. There were also contemporary plans to build additional garden suburbs.[13]

Howard's ideas reach Palestine: the establishment of Tel Aviv

Prior to 1917, Palestine had been under Ottoman rule. The Jewish immigrants to Palestine preferred, for the most part, to settle in towns such as the port of Jaffa rather than in agricultural settlements. This preference, particularly for Jaffa, was the result of the town's location as a port city, as well as the immigrants' natural desire to remain in the port of their arrival. Jaffa was also situated at the centre of the Jewish agricultural settlements founded during the 1880s and 1890s; this immigrant population in Jaffa was also more liberal than the mainly Orthodox population of Jerusalem. Such social conditions suited the new immigrants and constituted another reason for staying in Jaffa (fig. 6.1).[14]

Housing conditions in early twentieth-century Jaffa were hardly adequate. The streets near the haphazardly developed port were narrow and unclean, the houses small and crowded together, without a direct water supply. In general, a person coming from an established town in Europe would find living conditions there rather difficult.[15] Moreover, because of the large number of Jewish immigrants reaching Jaffa, it was hard to build apartments or even rent them, and what was available was very expensive.[16] These conditions spurred the Jewish immigrants of Jaffa to organise and establish a modern suburb nearby.[17]

The plan they chose as their model was that of the garden suburb, the most up-to-date European concept in contemporary town planning. They had learned of Howard's model and the English and German literature written about it while still in Europe, or through Zionist leaders and other individuals in Germany who sent the literature to their representatives in Palestine.[18] However, those Jaffan Jews who banded together to build a new suburb wished not only to accommodate material needs but also to promote Zionist aims by participating in the development of rural and urban settlement in Palestine. Thus, they emphasised the cultural and social aims of the suburb as well as its physical character.[19]

According to the plan, the suburb was to be parcelled into lots measuring at least 600 sq m on which fully detached houses were to be built. The houses were to cover not more than 30 per cent of the site, the remainder serving for gardens and trees. Areas were to be earmarked as public gardens; roads and pavements were to be designated and paved. The houses were to have sewers and a water pipe system as well as pipes for watering gardens. Drinking water was to be drawn from wells rather than collected from rainwater and the streets were to be illuminated.[20]

In addition to these general principles pertaining to all garden suburbs, there were also characteristics stemming from Zionist objectives. Thus, Hebrew schools and other important institutions providing public services were to be built at the heart of the suburb as a way of signifying their importance.[21] It should be noted that in Hampstead as well as in Howard's model, public buildings were also located in the centre, although usually as a matter of convenience. It was likewise decided that the proposed inhabitants of the suburb should all be Jewish and it was forbidden to sell or rent houses to non-Jews, Muslim or Christian. The aspirations of the inhabitants to develop a society that reflected their Zionist-nationalist values determined this approach.[22] Regarding the geographical location of the suburb vis-à-vis the old town of Jaffa, they decided to build it some distance away as an autonomous Jewish unit. The intervening space, they felt, would protect the Jews from problems of overpopulation and provide an area where they could gather together and nurture their national values, speaking Hebrew in Jewish educational and cultural institutions, and developing a national public life and an independent community. Such a vision was realisable only through the geographical separation of the Zionist-nationalist community from Jaffa.[23]

Garden suburbs in Palestine: from Tel Aviv to Haifa and Tiberias

The garden suburb of Tel Aviv – initially called Ahuzat Bayit (house or housing estate) – was built in accordance with this programme. In March 1908 the Ahuzat Bayit Association purchased an area of 85,000 sq m about two kilometres distant from the centre of Jaffa in a north-easterly direction. The land, owned jointly by a group of Jewish real-estate dealers from Jaffa and Jerusalem, was sandy, almost useless for agriculture. The contract gave the association an option to purchase additional areas bordering this plot, thus securing the possibility of expanding the suburb in the future. Difficulties raised both by Arabs from nearby Jaffa and the Ottoman authorities resulted in a year's delay, and the official purchase did not take place until March 1909.[24]

The construction of Ahuzat Bayit thus began in 1909, and by the end of that year some fifty homes had been built to house 500 people. In the middle of the suburb stood the Herzliya Gymnasium (the Hebrew High School) which remained for many years the centre of all Zionist-nationalist life in Tel Aviv. The final plan, however, allocated only 25 per cent of the area for public use as compared to 40 per cent in the original plan for this suburb.[25] There was a reduction in the extensive areas allocated for parks and public gardens. Realistic economic forecasts were taken into account at the expense of the ideal programme, since ignoring the financial constraints might have endangered the whole project. Nonetheless, the inclusion of parks and public gardens within the urban sphere and the allocation of only 30 per cent of the building plot to the house itself represented a fresh approach to green spaces, the last word in urban planning. This inspired even the Ottoman regime, which for centuries had been more interested in felling trees for various uses than in planting them. The Ottomans embarked on various planting projects around the country, as the German Templers had done in the 1860s, in both urban and rural areas. One of the highlights in this Ottoman endeavour to improve the urban landscape in Palestine during the First World War was the planting of 'Jerusalem Boulevard' in Jaffa in 1915. Oriented towards contemporary Tel Aviv (originally named Djamal Pascha Boulevard and later King George Boulevard), this street was 30 m wide and 800 m long. It was lined with Washingtonia trees that were tended by pupils of the Mikve-Yisrael agricultural school.[26]

During its first years, Tel Aviv was a true garden suburb, with the town of Jaffa serving as its central city. A little later, however, Tel Aviv began to transform itself spontaneously into what would become a city. Each year more land around the suburb was bought up by Jewish agencies, and the number of houses and residents continued to grow. By 1914 Tel Aviv covered 570,000 sq m, as opposed to 85,500 sq m in 1909, and the number of houses totalled 204, with some 2,000 residents.[27] Tel Aviv began to take on various functions and commerce flourished there. Even prior to the First World War, there was a general feeling that the suburb was turning into a town.[28] Indeed, in 1921 Tel Aviv was officially proclaimed a local council and in 1934, a city, the first Jewish city in Palestine, and it was so called with good reason.

The success of the first Zionist-Jewish garden suburb in proximity to a well-established old city was recognised even in 1910, and stimulated the establishment of similar garden suburbs in the Jaffa–Tel Aviv area and near other, older towns with large Jewish populations. Thus, organisations were established and private initiatives were undertaken with the aim of creating garden suburbs near Haifa on Mount Carmel, and in Tiberias, Safed, Gaza, Hebron, Ramla and Jerusalem. It should be noted that Jerusalem neighbourhoods outside the Old City walls began to develop in the mid-nineteenth century, well before the crystallisation and spread of Howard's ideas.

The idea of establishing garden suburbs throughout Palestine caught on through the familiar process of diffusing a hierarchical form. The focal point was Tel Aviv, where information was received from abroad, and the agents who propagated the ideas were private entrepreneurs and, more particularly, companies created by the Zionist establishment for this purpose.[29] This process was commented on in the newspaper *HaOlam* (The World) in its 26 January 1911 edition: 'The aspiration to build special Jewish suburbs can now be found in other towns as well.'[30] In *Die Welt* of 7 February 1913, the following statement is found: 'Tel Aviv's success has led to a situation in which plans are being worked out everywhere with the object of founding similar neighbourhoods and the model for emulation is the new town of Jaffa.'[31]

Haifa was the second location following Jaffa–Tel Aviv that implemented the idea of the garden suburb. An association called Agudat Ahim (Society of Brothers) was formed towards the end of 1906, and three years later it established the Jewish garden suburb of Herzliya, named after Theodore Herzl. The suburb was situated on Mount Carmel, a few kilometres away from the port around which the mainly Muslim old town of Haifa was built. The garden suburb of Herzliya became the nucleus for the larger suburb of Hadar HaCarmel (Carmel's Glory).[32] The latter developed in the 1920s on Mount Carmel and became the Israeli town of Haifa – a sort of Tel Aviv analogous to Jaffa. In the centre of Herzliya a technical college, the Technion, was founded along with the Reali high school, which, like the Herzliya Gymnasium, became the centre of national Zionist life in the new town.[33] Beyond the material aims of these projects was the concern for a national Zionist life with spatial implications. In the garden suburbs of Haifa – such as Hadar HaCarmel and Bath Galim (Daughter of the Waves) by the sea – land reserved for public use made up between 40 and 50 per cent of the site.[34]

An association was also formed in the summer of 1907 that aimed at establishing a garden suburb near Tiberias. In 1914 the association succeeded in purchasing land which lay north-west of the wall of the Old City. At the beginning of the 1920s, a garden suburb called Ahuzat Bayit, later renamed Kiryat Shmuel, was founded. The Jewish and Zionist population of Tiberias in particular gradually moved to the suburb and the Jewish town of Tiberias developed around it later on.[35] Prior to the First World War, there had been plans to build garden suburbs near Gaza, Hebron, Ramla and Safed as well, but they were not feasible owing to the small number of Jewish inhabitants in those cities and a general lack of means.[36]

Figure 6.2 Kauffmann's original plan for Talpiot, 1921 (from the collections of the Central Zionist Archives, Jerusalem, MM\24\15).

Figure 6.3 Beyth Ha-Kerem's 'Crown' from one of its first streets, showing the David Yellin teachers' seminar dating from 1913, Jerusalem.

Garden suburbs in Jerusalem

Tel Aviv's success led the bank of the Zionist Organisation and the Company for the Purchase of Urban Land (*Palästina Immobilgesells-chaft*) to decide on the establishment of a garden suburb near Jerusalem. Towards the end of 1912 these institutions purchased some 170,000 sq m of land south of Jerusalem along the main road from Jerusalem to Hebron. They also initiated the establishment of an association called Talpiot, whose members were to be the inhabitants of that suburb.[37] The local press in 1912 reported on the establishment of the association: 'It is said that the new association called Talpiot, which was formed in order to create a large and beautiful neighbourhood like the one in Tel Aviv-Jaffa, or one even more beautiful than the latter, will begin work next spring.'[38] The construction of the suburb commenced in 1922.

Talpiot was established on a hill that dominated the western side of the Bethlehem Road, and from its summit a panoramic view of Jerusalem opens up: from the Old City to the Jordan Valley, from the Dead Sea to the mountains of Jordan. It was planned by Richard Kauffmann, who came to Palestine from Germany in 1920 at the invitation of Arthur Ruppin, a Zionist thinker and leader, and one of the founders of Tel Aviv. Under the British Mandate Kauffmann was one of the chief actors in the planning of agricultural and (sub)urban Jewish settlements. It was in this context that garden city inspiration was most evident in Palestine, especially from the 1920s onward.[39] Kauffmann planned more than 150 settlements, *kibbutzim*, suburbs and towns. Following Patrick Geddes in 1919, he was involved in the 1922 planning of Hadar HaCarmel, to which Talpiot bore some resemblance: Talpiot's hill was crowned by several public structures, such as a school and a synagogue, alongside a park. Circular roads were laid out in accordance with the hilly topography of the site and planted with strips of greenery. Although Kauffmann's original plans were not fully implemented, they bore the influence of garden city rhetoric and an explicit vision of Talpiot as a 'suburban garden city' (fig. 6.2).[40]

Additional garden suburbs like the one in Talpiot sprang up around Jerusalem in the 1920s and the 1930s, including Rehavia, Bayit VeGan (House and Garden) and Beyth Ha-Kerem (the House of the Vineyard), where most of the Zionist-Jewish inhabitants lived.[41] Beyth Ha-Kerem, for instance, which was also planned by Kauffmann, was similar in its configuration to Talpiot: the summit of a hill crowned with public buildings such as a community centre and a Jewish teachers' seminary, annexed to a model school (fig. 6.3). Along its circular roads, residential plots were allocated, with a park and sports grounds in the lower, fertile area of the hill.[42] In fact Kauffmann's application of the concept of a 'city crown' in his suburban planning for Haifa and Jerusalem was directly influenced by the ideas of Bruno Taut (the *Stadtkrone*), as discussed in chapter 5. Yet it was not Taut's architectural detail that inspired Kauffmann as much as his principles: a prominent public structure at the highest point of a site, fronted by a hillside square with an adjacent park and surrounding roads that rise with the site's elevation lines.[43]

Jerusalem's Arab garden suburbs

By the first quarter of the twentieth century a number of Arab 'garden suburbs' had been built outside the walls of the Old City of Jerusalem, though nothing of the kind existed in Jaffa. Among the first of these were Mas'udiya, Babe s-Sahira, Wadi el-Joz, Huseini, Esh-Sheikh Jarrah, Baq'a and Talbiya.[44] These suburbs were, among other things, a manifestation of the modernising trend within traditional Arab society visible elsewhere in the Middle East, after the region opened up to Western influences at the turn of the nineteenth century.

By contrast to the Jewish garden suburb developments, the new Arab residential neighbourhoods bore a definite upper-class character. They were built only by and for members of an affluent class with social status and influence, educated in the new European schools of Jerusalem and at American universities. Large sums were allocated to build splendid villas surrounded by gardens enclosed by high stone walls. The initiative to build such neighbourhoods came from individuals, not from collective organisations. They were not suburbs in the real sense of the term, since they had not been planned from the outset by authoritative bodies that could supervise their building and management once they were established. These neighbourhoods were built along frontage roads or within a framework of building lots established by the owners of the land. Moreover, no public buildings or services, no mosques, churches, community centres or libraries were planned for the benefit of the residents.[45]

This building of new neighbourhoods coincided with the introduction of reforms and improved education in Palestine. Besides the wish to enjoy better living conditions, their construction was meant to show off the material wealth and social status that the owners had accrued – a display of ostentation that ran contrary to traditional precepts of modesty in the Arab home. At the same time, the new neighbourhoods reflected conservatism in their preservation of the social fabric, the family framework and the patriarchal way of life. Over the years, the marked upper-class character of the Arab neighbourhoods did not become diluted but, on the contrary, grew stronger. The tone of social prestige was also preserved. Architectural forms were eclectic in their derivation, incorporating elements of traditional Eastern design from different periods and countries, and modern elements, also from different countries, which combined to create a style with a distinctive decorative character. At the same time, the structures used models of Islamic architecture from Jerusalem and elsewhere, which constituted an important source of inspiration.[46]

Indeed, while the general appearance of these neighbourhoods was quite green, any direct reference to Howardian concepts in this context is vague at most. It is only in the early Mandate era and especially from the mid-1920s to the late 1930s that a modernist International Style is evident among the eclectic designs of these Arab suburbs. Nevertheless, modern influences as such first appeared in building materials and styles, and only later involved overall planning conceptions. Up to 1917, under the Ottoman regime, there was no explicit planning policy and, thus, complete anarchy in matters of planning. Construction outside the old walls was carried out as a private enterprise in the Arab sector, without any interference from organised communal bodies. The abundance of vegetation in these neighbourhoods originated in the private courtyards that normally encircled the buildings – in addition to, or instead of, an inner, more traditional, courtyard. Built-up areas often covered only about one-quarter of the total area of the plot, which was carefully walled with a guarded entrance gate. Some of the courtyards included decorative fountains, and were planted mostly with palm trees, orange trees, lemon trees and oaks. The presence of bougainvillea was, and still is, noticeable in these areas, especially to the left of the main entrance of the building, and in some of these private gardens a pair of palm trees was planted on either side of the main gate (fig. 6.4).[47] There was no similar planting of bougainvillea and palm trees in the contemporary Jewish quarters. These Arab neighbourhoods, however, were not 'garden suburbs' per se as conceptualised in the equivalent urban developments of the Jewish sector.

Suburban developments inspired by the garden city idea in the Jewish sectors of Jerusalem – such as Talpiot, Rehavia, Bayit VeGan, Beyth Ha-Kerem, and also in Haifa or Tel Aviv – were established with the material objective of improving living conditions but also with Zionist ideological motivation. The ideological element was central to their development. Particularly in Tel Aviv, the initial middle-class character of some of these developments was only marked in the first year or two. Very soon, workers and other residents with limited means built new suburbs in Tel Aviv as well as Haifa, adopting smaller

Figure 6.4 One of the first Arab houses in Talbiya, Jerusalem.

building plots and plans that reflected only their functional needs. As the class composition became more mixed, the exclusive garden suburb character dissolved into a more gregarious town-like ambience. After the First World War, the process intensified until these quarters burgeoned into full-grown cities.

Early twentieth-century Palestine underwent a variety of changes characteristic of regions receiving large numbers of European immigrants. Processes of modernisation within traditional societies in a traditional environment were accompanied by social and spatial polarisation. By contrast, modernisation within a Western population in a traditional environment was associated with decreasing social and spatial polarisation.

Plans for garden cities in Palestine following the First World War

On the eve of the First World War, various Zionist circles proposed basing urban development in Palestine on Howard's model of the garden city.[48] During the war, a period during which attempts to develop the Land of Israel came to an enforced halt, and immediately following the war, the Zionist leadership in charge of settlement discussed different methods of settling the land once the war was over, in light of new knowledge. They did not believe it would be possible to send arriving immigrants who wished to settle in the cities to the older towns where development had been spontaneous and inadequately planned, with all the problems this implied. Instead, they decided to construct new towns, planned according to Howard's conception of the garden city. The advantage of garden cities and the feasibility of Howard's ideas was evidenced by the fact that Letchworth had been built and Welwyn was in the process of construction. Thus, they held, it was of particular importance that a public organisation made up of future inhabitants should be responsible for the construction of the garden city. Further-more, they believed, the land on which their city was built should be publicly owned, which would prevent land speculation, a general characteristic of new towns, particularly those housing large numbers of immigrants, as had occurred even in Tel Aviv on the eve of the First World War.[49]

It would seem, therefore, that the garden city concept had many advantages in the Zionist context. In the first place, the idea that the land of the garden city should be in public possession was very similar to the Zionist idea that the entire land of Palestine belonged to the Jewish nation. Secondly, the garden city combined aspects of both city and country life and was thus in tune with Zionist ambitions to base the economy as well as the society of the Jewish homeland on agricul-ture. The garden city also eased the transition from city life to country life for immigrants who wished to change their method of earning an income from urban employment to agricultural labour. The coopera-tive elements in Howard's ideas also fitted in with other concepts that were beginning to emerge in Zionism such as the emphasis on cooperative trends in land settlement.[50]

A first attempt to implement plans for a garden city in Palestine was made towards the end of the First World War by a group of Zionists from Warsaw. They had joined together in 1917 for this specific purpose, establishing the Association for the Founding of the Model Rural Settlement and Garden City in Eretz Israel, a name that was abbreviated in Hebrew to MAAGAL (a transliteration that also means 'circle').[51] The group even contributed to the purchase of land east of Tel Aviv in order to build a garden city there. The architectural plans used by this group were almost identical with the ones that had appeared in Howard's book, except that they incorporated typical Jewish institutions such as the synagogue and Mikve (ritual bath) (fig. 6.5). By embracing this plan, the group sought to unify the benefits of country life – perceived by its members to include good health, fresh air, food at low prices and low taxes – with all the conveniences of town life, such as economic profit, accessibility to labour markets, spiritual institutions and urban recreation.[52]

The logo designed by the Association for the Founding of the Model Rural Settlement and Garden City in Eretz Israel is interesting: its framework emphasised the radial conception of the original garden city idea, with the name of the association inserted in Hebrew inside. The internal circle of the logo consists of the Star of David, together with the Hebrew letters spelling MAAGAL, and symbols of agricultural work (a sickle, foliage, sunrise) and tools of manual labour (a hammer). This logo represented contemporary Zionist imagery and aspirations together with the role assigned to the garden city model. That is, the garden city was to soften the transition from city to country, and enable the Jewish people to return to the natural values of an agricultural way of life as opposed to the industrial and commercial urban life of Europe.

Like other garden city 'urban utopias' in contemporary Europe as well as in Palestine, objective problems and particularly financial difficulties prevented the realisation of the MAAGAL plan.[53] For the same reason, contemporary plans to establish garden cities in Palestine had to be abandoned, even those that preceded the first plan to be actually realised in 1921 – the circular model of the agricultural settlement of Nahalal, as conceived by Kauffmann. Yet in the urban sphere, Kauffmann's master plans for a city in Palestine never eventuated. In Palestine, as in England and Germany, 'the child outstripped the parent', and while garden suburbs proved highly successful, garden cities did not. In fact, not a single garden city was built at this time.[54]

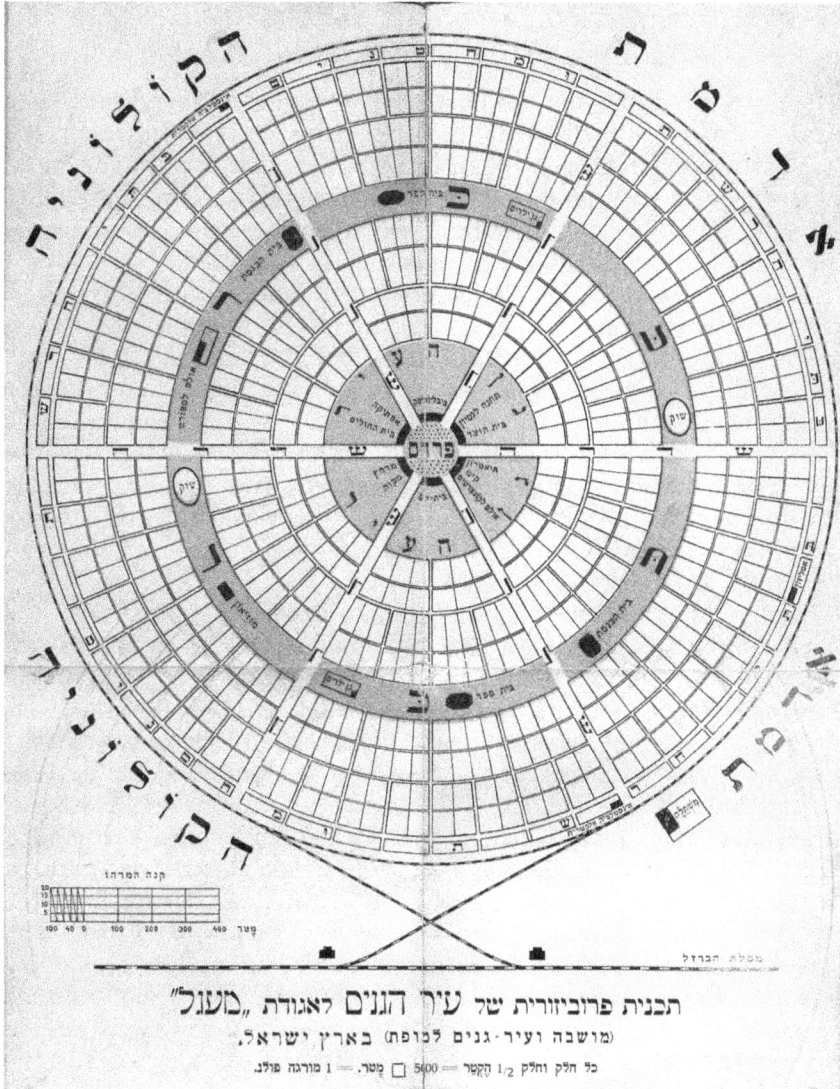

Figure 6.5 A proposal of the Association for the Founding of the Model Rural Settlement and Garden City in Eretz Israel (1917).

Garden city plans in Palestine during the Second World War

The years 1940–45 were shadowed by restrictions on land purchases exercised by the British over the Jewish National Fund (JNF). The JNF thus intensified its previously created frameworks of collaboration with private capital, to provide a source of income that would boost land purchases. The bulk of the effort involved private capital raised in England and Ireland to create what were called 'Farm Cities' or 'Garden Cities'.[55] The garden city plan was intended to produce a direct increase in contributions to the JNF from holders of private capital, and especially from those who had not been involved in its projects before. The JNF was well aware of the widespread movement for establishing garden cities and garden suburbs in various locations throughout the world; thus it is not inconceivable that the very use of the term 'garden city' by this organisation was intended to increase the number of British Jewish subscribers. This was despite differences between the original British garden city ideas and the model plan which the JNF sought to develop.[56]

Under the plan, the JNF would grant interested contributors the option of receiving a 49–year lease on a plot of land 2,500 sq m in area intended for a house and a small auxiliary farm. The JNF assumed responsibility for drafting the plans for such settlements as well as linking them to main roads, and planting trees in suitable areas, but the expense involved in preparing the area for settlement would devolve on the contributors. The small farm in the garden city plan was not intended to support its owners, but was suitable for a vegetable garden and fruit trees that would provide for the family's needs, and perhaps enable it to sell the surplus and enjoy additional income. In some cases, the farm was not intended to generate any income for its owners 'and their entire work in the garden would be only a leisure activity and a source of spiritual satisfaction'.[57] The contributor had to decide whether he wished to establish his house in the garden city within ten years of the time of his contribution. He also had the option of turning the house over to relatives or renting it out.

The JNF's garden city plan was enthusiastically received in England and Ireland. Aside from the attractiveness of the plan, it constituted a reliable source of income for the JNF. By the end of 1943, it was reported that over one thousand families had joined the plan and were organised within the framework of regional and national associations affiliated mainly with the Palestine Farm City Association. Most of the subscribers came from London, Glasgow and Manchester. Nonetheless, in the latter half of 1944, pursuant to clarification of the military situation in Europe and the feeling that the end of the war was approaching, private individuals in Britain lost interest in this plan, as did the JNF for various reasons.[58]

The JNF had decided to allocate areas in five locations which it owned for the establishment of garden cities, on the sea coast south of Nathanya (1,973,000 sq m) for example, and near Beit She'arim (665,000 sq m). It began to examine programmes for garden cities in early 1943, and only then sought to clarify the crucial issues involved. Were the garden cities to be independent urban units or would they rely on other cities? Were the places allocated for garden cities suitable for this purpose? Could the JNF's concept of garden cities be put into practice? From their deliberations it became clear that not all sites were suitable. Furthermore, it emerged that in principle the cities would be independent units offering all the required services. As a consequence, the JNF realised the need for a minimum of a few hundred families in each city to create the requisite conditions for developing educational institutions, food supplies and markets and for maintaining infrastructure on an economically feasible basis, without encumbering the residents. Other questions arose concerning the date for the construction of the garden cities. Would this be before or after the owners had migrated to Palestine? Were the lands at the various locations suitable for the types of gardens that had been planned? What income level could be derived from the gardens?[59]

Solutions to all these issues were not found, but in early 1944 the JNF entrusted the implementation of detailed planning for the garden cities to the architect Alexander Klein. It also opened negotiations with construction companies, which took another couple of years. In addition, it emerged that most participants in the programme had not decided whether they would actually migrate and build their homes in the garden cities. 'The activity in its entirety suffers from a lack of clarity. Not all the participants, especially those in the outlying towns, are aware of all the details involved in their contracts, and especially the obligations incumbent upon them. Furthermore, two companies – Farm City Association and the Company headed by Mr. Shen – are conducting parallel activity which causes difficulty.'[60] The JNF decided not to be directly involved in implementing the plans for fear that the confusion created in the public mind regarding its goals would bring about a lessening in contributions. It would only assist by connecting the organisations in Britain with the construction companies in Palestine.

In fact, until the end of 1946, only the garden city of Beit She'arim reached the stage of completion and construction. Planned by Klein as an independent unit which was conceived as a garden city, its plots were organised on both sides of the main curved roads, which followed the physical layout of the site. Cordons of open areas encircled the settlement and connected the concentrations of residential plots. In Beit She'arim (today's Tivon) about 200 homes were erected before the end of 1946, mostly by British Jews.[61]

Conclusion

The publicity that Howard's ideas had received by the early twentieth century reached Palestine shortly after they were first published and long before the British Mandate, which began in 1922. These ideas, adopted by Zionist immigrants from Europe, determined the Zionist model for urban settlement. Both at the planning level and at the level of their enactment, Howard's ideas were implemented within a framework of garden suburbs, incorporating certain elements. Based on Zionist aspirations to establish garden suburbs in Palestine, the universal model of the garden suburb was used to segregate the two nationalities of Palestine, Jews and Arabs, in order to provide the conditions which then seemed necessary for developing a national Zionist society within the cities of Palestine. The implementation in Palestine of Howard's original idea of the garden city encountered difficulties similar to those it had faced in Europe.

Tel Aviv was the first garden suburb to be built in Palestine. Although it was planned as a suburb, Tel Aviv quickly developed into a budding city despite its proximity to Jaffa. The reasons for this were its unique location, the fact that it became the national and urban centre of the country, and that the inhabitants of the new suburbs planned around Tel Aviv insisted that it should be a Jewish city, separate from neighbouring Jaffa. Tel Aviv, it seems, is the only garden suburb built under the influence of Howard's ideas ever to become an independent city.

Tel Aviv's success encouraged the development of similar garden suburbs in Tiberias and Haifa. Both formed the nucleus around which the Israeli towns evolved; these, however, did not become independent cities. The geographic conditions and advantages which had helped Tel Aviv transform itself into a city were not applicable to the other suburb cities in Israel. Today, as a result of the growth of Tel Aviv and the fact that it has become the centre of a metropolis, it is impossible to discern its origins as a garden suburb. The same is true for Haifa and Tiberias. Only in Jerusalem did no Jewish urban centres grow out of the garden suburbs. The reason for this is that historical Jewish centres existed outside the walls of the Old City prior to the creation of the garden suburbs. Since the garden suburbs were built at a distance from the central thoroughfares, they had no chance of competing with the local centres and have therefore remained garden suburbs to this day.

From the very beginning, the incorporation of garden city ideas into the urban development of Zionist settlement in Palestine was not merely morphological or aimed at the amelioration of living conditions. Garden city concepts offered more than an alternative to the industrial cities of Europe, the like of which did not as yet exist in Palestine. They provided relief from unsuitable living conditions in the old towns after centuries of haphazard planning by the Ottoman regime.[62] Yet these modern garden city concepts served Zionist ideological aspirations and practical needs long before their application in Palestine by the British regime. Due to the importance accorded by Zionism to an evolving national life and cultural community, large tracts of land were allocated for communal institutions, usually at the hub of the planned urban area or on its highest ground. Though public buildings in Howard's model were centrally placed as well, they were there as a matter of convenience rather than as being symbolic of ideology and spiritual life. In the Zionist context, the Howardian model was useful in terms of communal land ownership values in urban as well as rural development, alongside active involvement by communal representative bodies in planning and supervision. The latter elements were missing from contemporary Arab neighbourhoods outside Jerusalem's Old City walls, for instance, where greenery was abundant but only an inkling of garden city ideas existed prior to the 1920s.

During the 1940s – by which time garden city notions in Palestine had been absorbed both by the British and the architects of the Zionist enterprise – the term 'garden city' was taken up by the Jewish National Fund. It acquired land for a series of new urban settlements called garden cities, and used this term to serve the purely practical end of recruiting contributions from British Jews, and involving them in post-Second World War JNF initiatives. While planning features in one settlement might be ascribed to garden city influence, the use of this term by the JNF was largely opportunistic.

Notes

1 Ebenezer Howard, *Garden Cities of To-Morrow*, ed. F. J. Osborn (London: Faber and Faber, 1946 [1902]).
2 James Silk Buckingham, *National Evils and Practical Remedies with the Plan of a Model Town* (London: Peter Jackson, 1849); Robert Pemberton, *The Happy Colony* (London: Saunders & Otley, 1854); Benjamin Ward Richardson, *Hygeia: A City of Health* (London: Dodo Press, 1875).
3 John *Rockey, 'From vision to reality*: Victorian ideal cities and model towns in the genesis of Ebenezer Howard's garden city', *Town Planning Review*, 54 (1983), 83–105.
4 Ewart Gladstone Culpin, *The Garden City Movement up-to-date* (London: The Garden Cities and Town Planning Association, 1913), pp. 5–6.
5 Culpin, *The Garden City*, pp. 5–6, 16–17; Thomas Adams, *Recent Advances in Town Planning* (London: J. & A. Churchill, 1932), pp. 37–43. See also D. Hardy, 'War

planning and social change: the example of the garden city campaign, 1914–1918', *Planning Perspectives*, 4:2 (1989), 187–8.

6   Willy Lange, *Land und Gartensiedlungen* (Leipzig: J. J. Weber, 1910), pp. 189–92; Walter L. Creese, *The Search for Environment: The Garden City Before and After* (New Haven, CT: Yale University Press, 1966), pp. 300, 311–12.

7   Robert Fishman, *Urban Utopias in the Twentieth Century* (New York: Basic Books, 1979), p. 23.

8   Culpin, *The Garden City*, pp. 10–13.

9   On Hampstead, see Raymond Unwin and Baillie Scott, *Town Planning and Modern Architecture at the Hampstead Garden Suburb* (London: T. Fisher Unwin, 1909); Creese, *The Search*, pp. 219–54; Culpin, *The Garden City*, pp. 25–7.

10   Adams, *Recent Advances*, pp. 40–1.

11   Culpin, *The Garden City*, pp. 16–37.

12   Culpin, *The Garden City*, pp. 12–13.

13   Lange, *Land und Gartensiedlungen*, pp. 189–92; Creese, *The Search*, pp. 311–12.

14   Yossi Katz, 'Ideology and urban development: Zionism and the origins of Tel Aviv, 1906–1914', *Journal of Historical Geography*, 12:4 (1986), 402–24; Yehoshua Kaniel, 'The conflict between Jerusalem and Jaffa over leadership of the Yishuv in late Ottoman times, 1882–1914', in *Shalem, Studies in the History of the Jews in Eretz-Israel (Palestine)*, vol. 3 (Jerusalem: Shalem, 1981), pp. 185–212 (in Hebrew).

15   David Smilanski, *With My Fellow Countrymen and Townsmen* (Tel Aviv: Yedidim, 1958), pp. 482–4 (in Hebrew).

16   *Hazman*, 6 June 1906; *Hazman*, 17 May 1906 (both in Hebrew).

17   Central Zionist Archives (hereafter CZA), L51/52, letter from the Ahuzat Bayit Association to the Keren Kayemet (the Jewish National Fund), 19 February 1907.

18   Akiva Arie Weiss, *The Beginning of Tel Aviv* (Tel Aviv: Aynot, 1957), pp. 65–6 (in Hebrew); CZA, L2/71, Warburg to Ruppin, 6 November 1908; *Jerusalem*, vol. 1 (Jaffa, 1913), pp. 20–7 (in Hebrew); A. Gabstein, 'Urban building in Palestine', *Eretz Israel* 7:8 (1918), 45–6 (in Russian).

19   Lange, *Land und Gartensiedlungen*, pp. 189–92.

20   Alter Droyanov, *Tel Aviv Book* (Tel Aviv: The Book Committee, together with the Municipality, 1936), p. 75 (in Hebrew); Weiss, *The Beginning*, p. 85; CZA, L2/578; Tel Aviv Municipality Archives (hereafter TAMA), the protocol file of the Ahuzat Bayit Association, 3 June 1907.

21   TAMA, articles in *Tel Aviv*, vol. 2 (unpublished, in Hebrew); Smilanski, *With My Fellow*, p. 525; Weiss, *The Beginning*, pp. 115–23; *HaOlam*, 31 August 1909, p. 15 (in Hebrew); Yossef Eliyahu Sheloush, *The Story of My Life* (Tel Aviv: published by the author, 1931), p. 139 (in Hebrew; reprinted Tel Aviv: Bavel Publishers, 2005).

22   TAMA, the Prospectus of the Ahuzat Bayit Association, 31 July 1906; TAMA, the protocol of the meeting of 3 June 1907 (both in Hebrew); Weiss, *The Beginning*, p. 85; Yechiel Tshlenow, *Five Years of Our Work in Eretz Israel (Palestine)* (Moscow: n.p., 1913), p. 55 (in Russian); CZA, L18/105/4.

23   CZA, L51/52, Ahuzat Bayit Association to the Jewish National Fund, 19 February 1907; TAMA, Ahuzat Bayit protocols file, protocol from 3 June 1907; Droyanov, *Tel Aviv*, p. 84.

24   Droyanov, *Tel Aviv*, pp. 85, 92, 94; Smilanski, *With My Fellow*, p. 485; *HaOlam*, 4 May 1909, p. 15; Curt Nawratzki, *Die Juedische Kolonisation Palästinas* (Munich: Ernst Reinhardt Verlag, 1914), pp. 380–1; Sheloush, *The Story*, p. 131; TAMA, file of Ahuzat Bayit Association, minutes of meetings, 9–20 October 1907, 16 January 1908–9 November 1908, 9 January and 4 March 1909; CZA, L51/52, letter from Levontin to Ruppin, 24 May 1909.

25   TAMA, Unit 1, file 40, letter from Treidel to Weiss, 8 January 1909, and letter from Treidel to Weiss, 9 January 1909; TAMA, file of Ahuzat Bayit Association, minutes of meetings, general meeting, 17 and 20 February 1909; CZA, L2/633, letter from Ruppin to the Keren Kayemet, 15 February 1909; *HaOlam*, 4 May 1909, p. 15.

26   Nili Liphschitz and Gideon Biger, *Green Dress for a Country: Afforestation in Eretz Israel, The First Hundred Years 1850–1950* (Jerusalem: KKL and Ariel, 2004), pp.

42, 47–9. See also Elli Schiller, *Jaffa and its Sites* (Jerusalem: Ariel, 1981), vol. 15 (in Hebrew).

27 *The Development of Tel Aviv in Diagrams* (Tel Aviv, 1924), p. 10 (in Hebrew); *HaOlam*, 2 February 1911, p. 15; *Die Welt*, 5 October 1912, pp. 570–2; Droyanov, *Tel Aviv*, pp. 340–1; TAMA, Ahuzat Bayit protocols file, protocol of 23 February 1909; CZA, L18/68/2.

28 TAMA, Ahuzat Bayit protocols file, protocols of meetings from 15 September 1909, 17 November 1909, 25 May 1910, 8 August 1910, 12 June 1912, 4 December 1913, 25 March 1913, 14 October 1913, 24 April 1914; *HaPoel Hatsair*, 1 November 1912, p. 21; *HaPoel Hatsair*, 26 December 1912, pp. 11–12; *HaZman*, 17 January 1914, p. 4; *HaOlam*, 5 February 1914; *HaHerut*, 27 May 1914, p. 1; *HaHerut*, 25 June 1914, p. 2 (all in Hebrew).

29 Yossi Katz, 'Diffusion of the urban idea: the suburb of Tel Aviv as a model for programmes for modern suburbs in Israel at the end of the first decade of this century and up to the First World War', *Horizons: Studies in Geography*, 11/12 (1984), pp. 108–27 (in Hebrew). On the model of diffusion in a hierarchical form, see Lawrence A. Brown, *Innovation Diffusion* (London and New York: Methuen, 1981).

30 *HaOlam*, 26 January 1911, p. 4 (in Hebrew).

31 *Die Welt*, 7 February 1913, pp. 169–72.

32 For more details about the urban development of this neighbourhood under the early British Mandate, see Gilbert Herbert and Silvina Sosnovsky, *The Garden City as Paradigm: Planning on the Carmel, 1919–1923* (Haifa: Technion, 1986).

33 Yossi Katz, 'The founding and beginning of the Herzlia neighbourhood, the first Hebrew neighbourhood on Mount Carmel (Haifa)', *Horizons: Studies in Geography*, 8 (1983), 49–56 (in Hebrew); see also Haim Aharonovitz, *Hadar HaCarmel* (Haifa: Vaad Hadar HaCarmel, 1958) (in Hebrew).

34 Richard Kauffmann, 'Aménagement des colonies juives en Palestine et principalement des colonies agricole de l'organisation sioniste', in Jean Royer (ed), *L'Urbanisme aux colonies et dans les pays tropicaux* (La Charité sur Loire: Delayance, 1932), vol. 1, pp. 224–38 (pp. 228–9).

35 CZA, L2/71, the AhiEzer Association to Ruppin, 3 June 1911; *HaOlam*, 13 May 1913, pp. 11–12; *Hatsfirah*, 12 June 1914, p. 13 (in Hebrew); CZA, L18/98/6, reports of the *Palästina Immobilegesellschaft* for the years 1910–11; *HaPoel Hatsair*, 7 August 1914, p. 15; CZA, L2/9, the Palestine Office to the Zionist Bank (APC) in Tiberias, 2 June 1914.

36 Katz, 'Diffusion of the urban idea'.

37 *Teruma LeCohen* (Tel Aviv, 1926), pp. 68–9 (in Hebrew); CZA, L18/98/6, reports of the *Palästina Immobilegesellschaft* for the years 1911–13; Arthur Ruppin, *Chapters from My Life*, vol. 2 (Tel Aviv: Am Oved, 1947), pp. 162–3 (in Hebrew).

38 *Hamoriah*, 7 November 1912, p. 2 (in Hebrew).

39 Alona Nitzan-Shiftan, Marina Epstein-Pliouchtch and Tal Alon-Mozes, 'Richard Kauffmann: between architectural and national modernisms', *Docomomo Journal*, 35 (2006), pp. 48–54; Marina Epstein-Pliouchtch and Michael Levin, *Richard Kauffmann and the Zionist Project* (Tel Aviv: Hakibbutz Hameuhad, forthcoming).

40 Kauffmann, 'Aménagement des colonies juives', p. 228.

41 CZA, A34/12, protocol of the second annual meeting of the directors of the Zionist Bank (APC) on 21 October 1913; *HaZman*, 20 June 1913, p. 2; Gideon Biger, 'Garden suburbs in Jerusalem: planning and development under early British Rule, 1917–1925', *Cathedra*, 6 (1978), 108–32 (in Hebrew).

42 Kauffmann, 'Aménagement des colonies juives', p. 228.

43 Simon Stern, 'Richard Kauffmann as a town planner in the Jewish settlement of Eretz Israel in the early Mandate era', in Zeev Safrai et al. (eds), *Hikrei Eretz: Studies in the History of the Land of Israel, dedicated to Prof. Yehuda Felix* (Ramat Gan: Bar Ilan University Press, 1997), pp. 365–90 (pp. 386–8) (in Hebrew).

44 After the 1948 war and the partition of the city most of the Arab homes in the southern parts of the city were deserted (e.g., in the last two aforementioned

suburbs) while the main building projects of this sector were (and still are) concentrated in the east and the north-east parts of the city (i.e., the other aforementioned suburbs).

45   See Ruth Kark and Simon Landman, 'Muslim neighbourhoods outside the Jerusalem city walls during the Ottoman period', and Gideon Biger, 'The development of Jerusalem's built up area during the first decade of the British Mandate, 1920–1930', both in Yehoshua Ben-Arie (ed.), *Jerusalem in the Modern Period* (Jerusalem: Information Centre, 1981), pp. 174–211, 267–72 (in Hebrew).
46   For an architectural analysis of these modern urban developments, without reference to the parcelled lot and gardens, see Ron Fuchs, 'The Palestinian Arab house reconsidered, part II: the changes of the 19th century', *Cathedra*, 90 (1998), 53–86 (in Hebrew). See also David Kroyanker, *Jerusalem Architecture, Periods and Styles: Arab Buildings outside the Old City Walls* (Jerusalem: Keter, 1985), pp. 227–376, 456–8 (in Hebrew).
47   Kroyanker, *Jerusalem Architecture*, pp. 83–4.
48   R. Binyamin (the literary name of the writer Yehoshua Radler Feldman), 'Garden Cities', in *Jerusalem*, vol. 1 (Jaffa, 1913), pp. 20–7 (in Hebrew).
49   Akiva Ettinger, *Companies for the Settlement of Eretz Israel (Palestine)* (Jerusalem: JNF, 1920), pp. 73–94 (in Hebrew); Gabstein, 'Urban building', pp. 45–6.
50   *HaOlam*, 1 April 1908, pp. 177–8; *HaOlam*, 20 May 1908, pp. 265–6; *HaOlam*, 27 May 1908, p. 282; Moshe Smilanski, *The Palestine Land Development Company* (Tel Aviv: The Palestine Land Development Company, 1952), pp. 10–11 (in Hebrew).
51   See the brochure: The Association for the Founding of the Model Rural Settlement (i.e., Model Moshava) and Garden City in Eretz Israel (Palestine), *Garden City in Eretz Israel (Palestine)* (Warsaw: Bnei Zion, 1917), pp. 1–19 (in Hebrew), pp. 20–39 (in Yiddish).
52   The Association for the Founding of the Model Rural Settlement, *Garden City in Eretz Israel*, p. 5.
53   Yossi Katz, 'Plans for the establishment of "garden cities" in Eretz Israel during the second decade of the twentieth century', *Cathedra*, 15 (1980), 198–200 (in Hebrew).
54   Katz, 'Diffusion of the urban idea'; Biger, 'Garden suburbs'.
55   CZA, KKL10, 24 March 1942; JNF Report, 1947, pp. 127–9.
56   Yossi Katz, *The Battle for the Land* (Jerusalem: Magnes Press, 2005), p. 247.
57   For citation, see CZA, KKL5/12689, in no. 217. See also CZA, KKL5/13870, KKL5/13862, various publications on garden cities; JNF Report, 1947, pp. 128–9.
58   CZA, KKL5/12688, talk with Kollek concerning garden cities and collaboration with private capital, 1 February 1942; CZA, KKL5/12687, letter from Mohilewer to Granovsky, 12 May 1943, concerning the collection of the agreements, lists and accounts of the garden cities; CZA, KKL5/13862, letter from Weiss to Granovsky, 13 October 1944; JNF Report, 1947, pp. 128–9.
59   Maps in CZA, KKL5/11789; KKL5/13867; KKL5/13860; KKL5/12689, letter from Borochov to Epstein, Danin and Matrikin, 15 February 1943; KKL5/12687, the following documents: summaries of meetings regarding garden cities, 28 April 1943; 'Opinion of the Honorary Committee regarding Garden Cities', 7 April 1943; letter from Mohilewer to Borochov, 24 June 1943.
60   CZA, KKL5/15571, report by Foeder on his visit to Britain and Holland in May–July 1946. Leopold Shen was responsible for the circulation of the plan in Britain on behalf of JNF and he initiated the establishment there of the Keret Company, whose purpose was similar to that of the Palestine Farm City Association Ltd.
61   CZA, KKL5/13867, letter from Mohilewer and Weiss to Ussishkin, 17 April 1944; CZA, KKL5/1382, letter from Weiss to Granovsky and Epstein, 13 October 1944; JNF Report, 1947, pp. 58, 128–9. See also Katz, *The Battle*, pp. 247–53.
62   For a different view, however, on the state of urban planning under the (late) Ottoman regime in Palestine, see Salim Tamari, 'Confessionalism and public space in Ottoman and colonial Jerusalem', in Diane E. Davis and Nora Libertun de Duran (eds), *Cities and Sovereignty: Identity Politics in Urban Spaces* (Bloomington: Indiana University Press, 2011), pp. 59–82.

CHAPTER SEVEN

Garden cities and suburbs in Palestine: the case of Tel Aviv

Miki Zaidman and Ruth Kark

Zionist historiography has often referred to Ahuzat Bayit, the Jaffa neighbourhood from which Tel Aviv developed, as a unique phenomenon. Today there is a tendency to place even unique phenomena within the context of universal ideas and trends. The proximity in time between the appearance of the first 'garden city' (1903) and the first 'garden suburb' (1907), both in the UK, and Ahuzat Bayit (1909), as well as some physical similarities, has led researchers to seek a connection between the two, and to term Ahuzat Bayit a 'garden neighbourhood'. At first, the garden city movement was a social-anarchist one, whose objective was to extend the suburban standard of housing, until then the province of the middle class, to the entire population. This movement gave birth to modern town planning.

Ahuzat Bayit, on the outskirts of Jaffa, was established as a suburb with middle-class aspirations, including class, ideological and ethnic segregation following European middle-class suburbs and colonial models of separate residential areas for Europeans and the native population. However, local conditions, including a society comprised of residents of similar socio-economic position, and the mechanisms for its establishment, including building by-laws, in addition to concepts of the early Zionist movement which shared a similar ideological platform with the garden city movement, transformed Ahuzat Bayit into a unique local model for the diffusion of suburban life in Palestine.

In this chapter we shall examine how the Ahuzat Bayit neighbourhood in Jaffa, soon to develop into Tel Aviv, related to the 'garden city', 'garden suburb' and 'middle-class suburb' models of urban settlement. Ahuzat Bayit is justly considered to be the pioneer of a revolutionary urban culture in Palestine and a model for later neighbourhoods and cities. In addition, an attempt shall be made to ascertain to what extent the ideas of the international garden city movement influenced the founders of Ahuzat Bayit. This is a subject of great significance for understanding the history of the settlement ideology of the Zionist movement in Palestine. Garden city ideals were gradually adopted by the Zionist movement after being introduced to German Zionists by Franz Oppenheimer in 1903 and promulgated in an article published by Davis Trietsch in 1905.[1] The concept was first broached in Palestine in relation to Jewish settlement in 1911 by Arthur Ruppin (1876–1943), who visited Palestine from May to September 1907, and arrived again in the country from Germany in 1908 to head the Palestine office of the Zionist Organisation. He mentioned it in connection with the Kerak peninsula on the southern shore of the Sea of Galilee.[2]

The garden city idea was adopted as the leading principle for almost all Jewish urban settlement in Palestine during the first half of the twentieth century. The physical layout of Ahuzat Bayit and 'garden city' concepts were the two most influential factors on town planning in Palestine.[3]

'Garden city' beginnings and their distinctive features

The garden city movement, like political Zionism, was born during the final decade of the nineteenth century.[4] The first realisations of garden city ideas in England, designated mainly for the working classes, were inspired by the villa estates (detached or semi-detached houses in suburban or residential areas). These estates, since the 1830s, had been characteristic of the form of housing through which the middle class tried to differentiate itself from the working class. In Letchworth, established in 1903 and planned by Raymond Unwin,[5] the plots were much smaller than in the middle-class suburbs (two houses per 1,000 sq m as compared to an average of 0.2 houses per 1,000 sq m in the middle-class suburbs). This increased density, together with a network of public institutions and places of employment in commerce and industry, enabled a lively communal life in the garden city that was lacking in the middle-class suburb.

The suburban appearance of the garden city contributed to its popularity, since it reflected the aspiration of the lower classes to adopt the lifestyle of those above them on the social ladder in a process known as stratified diffusion. However, it also produced a focus on spatial aspects and the physical infrastructure, pushing aside the social objectives. This tendency was reinforced in 1907, when Unwin planned the first 'garden suburb' in Hampstead, about 5 km from London.[6] While similar to the garden city from the point of view of physical layout, housing density and its social objectives, Hampstead's location near the big city and the omission, by its planners, of independent industrial enterprises blurred the differences between the garden city and a middle-class suburb.

The garden city idea was interpreted on three different levels by various groups of people – we shall use these three interpretations in the subsequent case study of Tel Aviv. The narrowest definition was precisely set down in the publications of the International Garden City and Town Planning Association, based on Ebenezer Howard's book, and was exemplified in two garden cities established in England. A wider definition, adopted by professionals, scholars and some members of the garden city movement in various countries, included several related aspects such as 'garden suburbs', 'model communities' and the like. These variants reflected an environmental perception that developed gradually throughout the nineteenth century. It maintained that in order to solve the social problems caused by the Industrial Revolution, a drastic change in the milieu in which the lower classes lived in the big cities was needed. Towards the end of the century this definition also adopted anarchist principles, calling for the dismantling of the big city and for communal ownership of land. The physical form of the area in all such planned settlements was grounded in the 'green and natural' image of the middle-class suburb, which in the nineteenth century was considered as the very opposite of the densely populated and soot-filled city. In effect, this was an effort to apply the suburban lifestyle, by which the middle class aspired to differentiate itself from the working class, to the entire population. In reality, what differentiated between garden suburbs and middle-class suburbs were smaller plots and the establishment of many public institutions to make communal life possible.

Finally, the widest interpretation of the garden city idea was that held by the public at large. It included not only garden cities, but all suburbs, communities of detached houses and cities having a 'green' image. The general public was led astray by the adoption by the garden city of the physical spatial layout of the middle-class suburb. Thus, it widely applied the term 'garden city' to a form that concentrated solely on physical aspects, ignoring all the social and communal content which was part of the original concept of garden cities.

Ahuzat Bayit: the first modern Jewish suburb

In addition to its Zionist aspects, the establishment of Ahuzat Bayit should be seen as part of urban development in the Ottoman Empire in general, and in Jaffa in particular.[7] During the second half of the nineteenth century, the Ottoman Empire underwent constitutional, economic and demographic developments that led to a break from traditional urban frameworks. The Tanzimat reforms of 1839 and 1856 paved the way for privatisation and changes in land ownership patterns, even enabling – to a certain degree – land acquisition by foreign citizens. Changes in the economy included improved transport links with Europe, leading to an increase in trade and tourism, a significant rise in agricultural production, and the first signs of industrial development. Significant demographic developments included a decline in the death rate and migration into the cities. These tendencies resulted in the physical expansion of certain cities beyond their walls and to the creation of urban foci side by side with the ancient city. In most cases, these new neighbourhoods were populated by foreigners, migrants, minorities and the upper classes of the local population. Often, these new areas adopted European-style construction which was quite different from the old 'Middle Eastern' city.[8]

The roots of the initiative to establish the new neighbourhood of Ahuzat Bayit should also be sought in the make-up of the newcomers to Jaffa. Among its Jewish residents were a relatively large number of immigrants who had recently arrived from Europe, imbued with Zionist ideals. The founders of Ahuzat Bayit were all middle class, and though they did not have particularly large amounts of capital – even by the inferior economic standards of early twentieth-century Palestine – they considered themselves as bourgeoisie and held aspirations characteristic of that class. Arthur Ruppin described them in 1907 in the following terms: 'There are sixty families in the Ahuzat Bayit Society, all of them wealthy people, from Jaffa and the area.'[9] They wished to express their middle-class status[10] through ownership of property, above all of land. Furthermore, they wanted to distance themselves, culturally and geographically, from the lower classes. The founders of Ahuzat Bayit, who claimed to represent progressive European culture, willingly opted for leaving the old city in favour of the establishment of middle-class suburbs of free-standing homes. Many of them were also motivated by Zionist ideals; they intended to make strenuous efforts to build a new society, and were quite open to new ideas.

Additional factors in the establishment of the new neighbourhood in Palestine were also reflected in its physical layout. Some were prosaic and practical, such as the decline in the amount of available living space in Jaffa. Others were influenced by urban developments resulting from the Industrial Revolution in Europe. Not all these ideas were openly expressed by the founders. Zionist historiography, too, preferred to portray Ahuzat Bayit as a unique phenomenon, and thus in many cases ignored its relationship to contemporary developments in European cities.

The founders of Ahuzat Bayit, products of a progressive Western civilisation, brought with them innovative ideas that left their mark on the shaping of the new neighbourhood, turning it into something different from the ancient city of Jaffa. Ahuzat Bayit also differed from other Jewish neighbourhoods established in Palestine since 1865, even though these were also new and original for their times in both international and local terms. Three elements contributed to the shaping of the neighbourhood during the planning stage: the residents, the planner and the representative of the Zionist Organisation. First of all were the initiators, the settlers who intended to plan a neighbourhood that would reflect their ideals and aspirations. It should be noted that the situation of the settlers being the major force influencing the character of the settlement is unique to Ahuzat Bayit and similar neighbourhoods established in Palestine prior to and immediately after the First World War. In Europe, capitalists or philanthropic organisations were the initiators of garden cities or suburbs, not the future residents themselves. Later, in Palestine, this initiative passed to the Zionist Organisation which employed professional town planners – a profession that became firmly established from the second decade of the twentieth century – to plan residential areas for prospective immigrants.

The status of the future residents as European 'colonists' in the Levant deepened their desire to establish neighbourhoods separate from 'the native population'. During the last decade of the nineteenth century such segregation became the official policy of the British colonial administration, under the influence of Sir William John Ritchie Simpson, who considered Orientals to be immoral and unhygienic. For security, cultural and especially health reasons, separate 'European neighbourhoods' were created in many colonies, physically separated from the old cities by a park or a belt of agricultural land. They included contemporary modern systems for the improvement of public health, such as water supply and sewage infrastructures. Among the characteristics of such neighbourhoods was low housing density, with a preference for free-standing and well-ventilated houses, large gardens and wide and straight streets – a reflection of rationalism and order.[11] Edward Said noted a similar process when he analysed the phenomenon of 'Orientalism'.[12]

Hygienic conditions cropped up time and again in the discussions relating to the establishment of Ahuzat Bayit. Just as in the classic colonialist conception, this was often accompanied by a demand for national and cultural segregation. In one of his studies, Yossi Katz quoted Jehiel Tschlenow (1913):

It is difficult to cure all of Jaffa and all of Tiberias, but it is possible to create healthy surroundings in a neighbourhood of our own. For us it was more important to create a national atmosphere with the very establishment of a new life, and finally it is important to enhance our prestige in the country, and this is easier to do when we concentrate our forces rather than when we spread them out among the much larger local population.[13]

The Zionist-nationalist outlook of the founders added weight to their need for physical segregation from Jaffa, a city of mixed population. Already in 1907, Arthur Ruppin wrote:

I attach great importance to the establishment of a Jewish quarter, both in Jaffa and Jerusalem, that will not be negligible within the neighbourhoods of the other ethnic communities, and will not be lacking, from the standpoint of sanitation, all that is lacking in the existing Jewish quarters in Jaffa and Jerusalem. The streets are narrow, the filth and the odd manner of building in these urban quarters are a downright disgrace to the Jews and discourage many good people from settling in the country. As for Jaffa, it is very important to build splendid and healthy houses for the Jewish middle class. I do not think I am exaggerating if I say that the establishment of a Jewish neighbourhood is the best way for the Jews to gain economic control of Jaffa.[14]

Competition with the Arab population motivated the founders of Ahuzat Bayit to build it as a 'model settlement', one that would be innovative and different in relation to Jaffa. Akiva Arieh Weiss, one of the founders, maintained: 'The efforts of the society must be aimed at proceeding to the erection of a model Hebrew city. There are Hebrew colonies in the land, and now the time has come to begin building cities.'[15]

Given such opinions, it is only natural that the founders expected their neighbourhood to develop along Western, rationalist and modern lines, in contrast to the narrow lanes and continuous rows of houses that were characteristic of the Middle Eastern city. The establishment of a housing development that was the exact opposite of Jaffa also contributed to the creation of the self-image of the renewing Jewish national entity. Not only did the founders want to differentiate themselves from Arab Jaffa, they also intended to create something different from the Jewish neighbourhoods of the 'Old Yishuv', the traditional Jewish *shtetl* in Europe and the industrial cities of Europe.[16] Thus, when referring to their project, they often used terminology such as 'a unique quarter' and 'a modern suburb'.

The establishment of Ahuzat Bayit (1906–09): land acquisition, planning and by-laws

Acquisition of land

The area chosen for the new neighbourhood was known as the 'Jibali Vineyard'. Its advantages were that it was within ten minutes' walking distance from existing Jewish quarters near Jaffa; it was close to the Jaffa–Jerusalem railway line and the road leading from Jaffa to the Jewish agricultural settlement of Petah Tikvah; and there were opportunities for future development. Another reason why the buyers preferred the acquisition of this plot was that the sellers were Jewish land merchants. Though this contradicted the Zionist aspiration to 'redeem' land held by Arabs, it made the transaction simpler and more secure.

The empty belt of land between the new neighbourhood and Jaffa and its Jewish suburbs was compatible with Ebenezer Howard's ideal of separating the new city from its neighbouring settlements through a belt of agricultural land, thus indicating a relationship between Ahuzat Bayit and the garden city idea. However, it should be borne in mind that its physical isolation did not necessarily stem from Howard's theory since, as noted earlier, there were many other considerations that could lead to the same result. Actually, the empty space was much smaller than the belt of agricultural land recommended by Howard to separate the garden city from the 'central city'. This land remained the property of its original owners and therefore, in contrast to Howard's scheme, it was *not* an integral part of Ahuzat Bayit. In other words, the new garden city had no means of influencing the future of this belt of land and ensuring that it would continue to be used for agriculture in the future. As is well known, within two decades all the empty land around Ahuzat Bayit had become the site of construction, and the new neighbourhood had been 'swallowed up' into the built-up area of Tel Aviv.

In March 1908 the Ahuzat Bayit Society bought 85,000 sq m of the Jibali Vineyard, and an additional 43,000 sq m in 1909.[17] The area acquired was larger than the 50,000 sq m needed by the society's members. However, even at this early stage arguments were raised in favour of buying reserve land that would enable future development; moreover, this would benefit the society as a result of the expected rise in the price of land (the price they paid per sq m was already ten times the cost of the land purchased to establish the Neveh Tzedek quarter about two decades earlier). Thus were planted the seeds for the speculative expansion of Ahuzat Bayit, one of the reasons for the wider area over which the unique by-laws of the society were later enforced.

Though some of the members agreed with the traditional opposition of the Zionist Organisation to speculation in land, the majority believed that opposition should be made to speculation by the individual, but not by the community, since speculation by the individual was forbidden but that of the community was acceptable.

Planning

There is no consensus about the identity of the planner of Ahuzat Bayit. Among the names mentioned in the literature are the architect Wilhelm Stiassny of Vienna; Professor Boris Schatz, the director of the Bezalel Art School in Jerusalem; the engineer Joseph Barsky (who planned the water tower, and later also the Herzliyah High School); and the engineer Abraham Goldman. What is certain is that towards the end of 1908 the Ahuzat Bayit Society approached the surveyor Joseph Treidel, requesting that he draw up a plan for the neighbourhood.[18] It is possible that Treidel joined forces with engineer Joseph Levy, who at that time directed the Technical Department of the Palestine Office of the Zionist Organisation. Treidel presented his plan to the committee of Ahuzat Bayit in January 1909.

Treidel's plan proposed locating the houses in the higher sections of the estate, while the lower area would be set aside for a public garden. It allotted 41 per cent of the area for public use. His plan concentrated on parcelling out the plots, and did not contain any actual town planning. The committee decided that the plots would be equal in size, each measuring about 560 sq m, considerably larger than those in other Jewish urban neighbourhoods in Palestine (150–200 sq m) but much smaller than what was customary in middle-class suburbs in Europe. Each plot was a rectangle, with a ratio of 3:2, the shorter side bordering on to the street. The streets were wider than was customary (16 m for main streets and 12 m for the others), though there were already a few precedents for this width in Palestine. On the whole, the plan was spacious, but was not a real breakthrough. The garden city character of Ahuzat Bayit stemmed from its by-laws no less than from Treidel's plan.

By-laws

The first by-laws of Ahuzat Bayit, signed by members of its committee together with Ruppin, were approved at a general meeting of the society around February 1909, before the building of the first houses in August 1909. The following are some of its clauses:

> Clause 1: The objective of the society is to acquire a modern Jewish quarter in Jaffa ... Clause 3: Every member can begin building his house only if the committee agreed to the plan of the house that was drawn up by a construction expert and included details of the building materials

... Clause 5: The buildings must not occupy more than three-tenths of the lot that belongs to each member. Note: The terrace is not included in the area of the building ... Clause 7: Every lot must face the street with a small garden no less than two metres [wide] and fenced in.[19]

Gideon Biger, Ruth Kark and Zvi Shilony ascribe the drafting of the first by-laws to Arthur Ruppin.[20] Ruppin was advised in this matter by two Zionist architects living in Vienna, Wilhelm Stiassny and Oskar Marmorek.

In late 1910 Mordechai Ben Hillel Hacohen presented the committee with new by-laws which he had drawn up at its request, and these were adopted in December 1910. The major emendations were that the building could cover slightly more of the plot (up to one-third) and that a one-metre-wide empty belt must be left at the two sides and the back of the house, in addition to the stipulation for the front of the plot. Furthermore, the establishment of shops, saloons, hotels and other enterprises of this kind was strictly forbidden.

The prohibition of any commercial enterprises, which was common to Ahuzat Bayit and similar housing projects (such as Hadar HaCarmel in Haifa, for example), reflects vacillation between declarations (at times post factum) about creating an independent city and those calling for the establishment of a 'bedroom suburb' economically dependent upon the 'mother city' – in this case, Jaffa. Many, including Ruppin, were unaware that the garden city ideal explicitly called for the establishment of commercial and industrial enterprises as contributing to the communal life and economic independence of garden cities. In this matter, Ahuzat Bayit behaved like a middle-class suburb that aspired to a peaceful atmosphere, outside the large city, by keeping at bay the unpleasantness of economic activity – completely counter to the spirit of the original garden city ideal.

The most important new provision of the by-laws was that the houses would be detached, it being absolutely prohibited to have one building built against another (fig. 7.1). This was a precedent in Jewish urban construction in Palestine, though it was found, of course, in Jewish agricultural colonies, and even earlier in the urban and rural colonies established by the German Templers. Detached houses were also prevalent among upper-class Arabs who built their new estates outside walled cities. It would seem that, in addition to local models, the founders of Ahuzat Bayit were aware of developments in town planning abroad. They probably received the inspiration for a neighbourhood of detached houses from the middle-class suburbs of Europe, and this stemmed from the class consciousness of the members of Ahuzat Bayit. As members of the middle class, they opted for free-standing homes because they could afford them, but probably also because they

Figure 7.1 'Ahuzat Bayit' by Nahum Gutman (courtesy of Gutman Museum, Tel Aviv, and Gutman family).

wanted something that would be a symbol of their independence and status as property owners, just like the middle class in Europe.

It may also be that the choice on the part of the founders of Ahuzat Bayit of a housing pattern which the Zionist Organisation had introduced into its agricultural colonies was related to the fact that they considered themselves to be the urban version of the Zionist agricultural pioneers. As noted, the choice of a type of construction that was based (at least to some degree) on a modern European model suited their desire to create a 'model neighbourhood'. The very fact that their houses were the exact opposite of what was customary in Jaffa enabled them to point to a break with the past that symbolised a 'new start'. Ahuzat Bayit negated not only the disorderly cluttered building by Arabs in Jaffa but also the terrace houses of the 'Old Yishuv'.

In the new by-laws, as in the original ones, there was a clause that limited the percentage of the plot upon which the house could be built (curtilage). The idea behind this was to create a minimal area that would remain as a garden, thus ensuring the pastoral nature of the neighbourhood. This regulation did not limit the floor area of the house, which depended on the number of storeys, multiplied by the area of the ground floor. The fact that there was no limitation to the number of storeys, only of the curtilage, indicates that what lay behind the regulation were concerns relating to landscape, ventilation and so forth, having nothing to do with taxation or the value of the house and the property. While in the first by-laws the built-up area was limited to 30 per cent of the plot (soon – as noted – changed to 33.3 per cent), there was later provision to build a 'covered porch' on another 6.6 per cent, increasing the permitted area to 40 per cent. In any case, this is a clear stand in favour of open spaces over built-up areas. Not that the founders deprived themselves: even one-third of a 560 sq m lot enabled them to build spacious homes. It is noteworthy that a similar ratio of built-up area to open space was also the rule in Jewish neighbourhoods that preceded Ahuzat Bayit, such as Me'ah She'arim in Jerusalem and Neveh Tzedek near Jaffa, at least when they were founded, before various extensions were added to the houses.

An additional unprecedented regulation dealt with leaving room between houses by determining that there would be empty belts (setbacks) along all sides of the plot. The front setback was quite wide – three metres from the street, reflecting the settlers' desire to display a garden visible from the street. A later description reported: 'The house must be distanced from the street, into the yard, three metres, and on these three metres trees and flowers should be planted.'[21] Apparently, as the neighbourhood developed, this well-intentioned regulation was reduced to two metres. Until then, in other residential neighbour-hoods, it was not customary to have side and rear setbacks. In fact, there was no need of them. Since houses were run together in rows, there was no side setback. The greater depth of the plots in compar-ison to their width, together with the need to ensure a supply of light and air for the house from the back of the building (as there were no windows in the sides), dictated leaving an empty space between the back wall and the edge of the plot.

This was not the situation in Ahuzat Bayit, since from the very outset it was decided that the side walls of one house would not touch those of another. The fact that the dimensions of the plots were smaller than those in the Jewish agricultural colonies or in English suburbs, and also not much deeper than their width, mandated having side and rear setbacks. These, as we have seen, were at first set at one metre, but it soon became obvious that this was not enough to ensure privacy, ventilation, gardens and so on. More than likely, establishing the setbacks at one metre resulted from the settlers' inexperience and fear of a too serious infraction on their property rights. In 1925 the 'Proposed Construction Bylaws of Tel Aviv' increased the width of the side and rear setbacks to two metres.[22]

Finally, one would have expected the by-laws to limit the height of the houses, but there was no mention of this specific aspect. Perhaps the committee assumed that since all the buildings in Ahuzat Bayit would be private dwellings, none of them would be more than one- or two-storey buildings. Another possibility was that they assigned little importance to the height of the buildings because it had little influence on the quality of the ventilation. Finally, they may have believed that the building techniques customary in the country in 1909 – before the introduction of concrete to Palestine – made tall buildings economically unfeasible. Within a short time, however, Tel Aviv's committee members found it necessary to regulate the height of the houses as well: 'At a general meeting convened on 23 Nisan 5673 [30 April 1913] ... it was decided: A. To forbid constructing a third storey in Tel Aviv.'[23]

Application of the physical patterns of Ahuzat Bayit to all of early Tel Aviv

There were two major reasons for the expansion of the new neighbour-hood. First of all, as the founders considered their enterprise to be the beginning of the entire Zionist urban undertaking in Palestine, the committee adopted a policy of expansion. Secondly, the original area acquired was twice that needed for Ahuzat Bayit's 60 members. The superfluous land was soon sold to private individuals, to the Jewish National Fund (12,000 sq m for the Herzliyah High School), and to additional settlement societies, such as Nahalat Binyamin. These sales were highly profitable, creating a tradition of 'institutional specula-tion' on the part of Ahuzat Bayit's committee.

To further the policy of expansion, in 1911 23,000 sq m of the land owned by the German Templer settler Georg Kapus were bought near the railway on the south-eastern boundary, as well as 34,000 sq m from David Moyal along the northern perimeter of Tel Aviv, the name given to the union of all the neighbourhoods in 1910. These were divided into building plots of 560 sq m – exactly the size of the original plots of Ahuzat Bayit – and sold to private individuals. Additional areas were not bought by the Tel Aviv committee, but were placed under its management, the committee assuming responsibility for the division into plots and their sale. In these cases, too, the size of the plots was 560 sq m.[24]

Another method of expansion was by incorporating other neighbour-hoods in the vicinity into Tel Aviv. One of the factors that attracted these neighbourhoods was the discovery of a well with an abundant supply of water on its territory. In 1920 the Tel Aviv committee reported that 'Tel Aviv is the only neighbourhood in Jaffa with sanitary plumbing, and many of the neighbours, both Jewish and non-Jewish, would like the piping extended to their homes so that they can also enjoy the pure water of Tel Aviv.'[25] If these neighbouring householders would at least pave their streets and maintain some degree of cleanli-ness, Tel Aviv was willing to sell them water.

Yossi Katz, who reconstructed the growth of Ahuzat Bayit/Tel Aviv in its early years, found that by the end of 1909, 50 houses had been completed in which 500 people resided. Three years later the figures were 116 houses and 980 residents, while on the eve of the war there were already 204 houses with about 2,000 residents. At that time the population of the older Jewish neighbourhoods around Jaffa was three times that number. These were united with Tel Aviv only in May 1921 by order of the British Mandate authorities who granted Tel Aviv the status of a 'township' and set its city limits so that they would include all areas with a Jewish majority. From that year on, the Tel Aviv building by-laws were applied to all new areas in which construc-tion was carried out, though not retrospectively in those that were already built up (fig. 7.2). Ahuzat Bayit's success motivated others to establish modern suburbs elsewhere in Palestine where an affluent and 'progressive' Jewish population resided: Haifa, Jerusalem and Tiberias.[26] Zionist officials also intended to develop similar models for Safed and Gaza. The physical layout of Ahuzat Bayit and its by-laws were to become a source of inspiration for revolutionary urban devel-opment throughout Palestine. However, the physical expansion of the city also influenced its image. While the term 'garden city' was never explicitly mentioned by the founders of Tel Aviv, reference to this ideal is often made when noting what vanished as it expanded. Katz quoted from the Hebrew newspaper *Hatzefirah*, which already on 15 September 1912 reported: 'Tel Aviv, which at first was like a garden city, has begun to assume the character of a regular city; people have begun to build in it inferior and cramped houses.'[27]

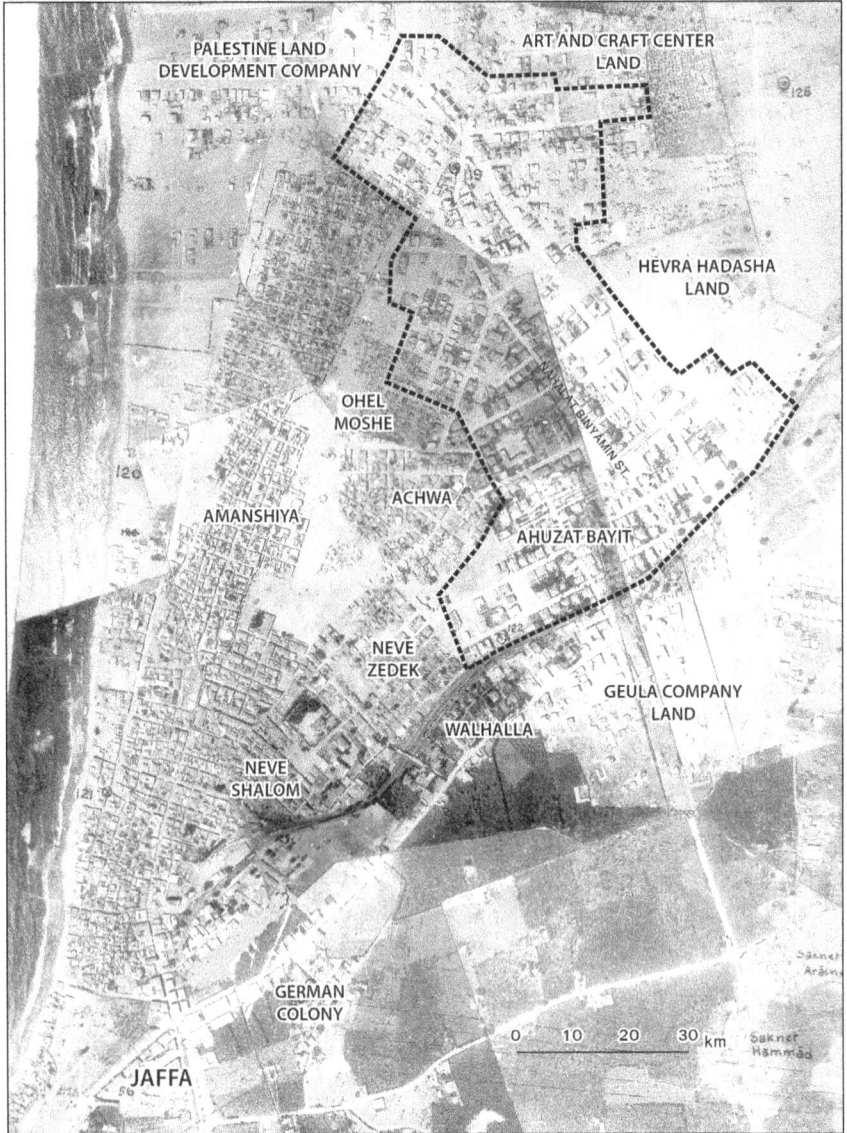

Figure 7.2 Aerial photograph showing the urban pattern of Ahuzat Bayit (within the demarcated area), Jaffa and the old neighbourhoods (courtesy of Dr Dov Gavish, Jerusalem).

Was there a diffusion of concepts?

A reading of the primary sources on the establishment of Ahuzat Bayit does not unequivocally draw a connection between the new neighbourhood and the 'garden city' or 'garden suburb' ideal. Neither of these terms is mentioned in the documentation, even though there are several instances in which the objectives of the founding society are detailed. From the above discussion, it would seem that the founders could have been influenced by many sources which could provide an explanation for the establishment of Ahuzat Bayit, its location and layout, without direct relationship to the garden city idea. It is unclear, therefore, to what extent the society's members were aware of, or actively adopted, the specific concepts of Ebenezer Howard prior to the establishment of the neighbourhood. It is a fact, however, that later many of them accepted and diffused them.

The terms 'garden city' and 'garden suburb' were also not used by the leading candidate for identification as the planner of Ahuzat Bayit, the Haifa surveyor and engineer Joseph Treidel. Even in a 1918 publication, in which he detailed the preferred principles that should govern housing construction in Palestine, Treidel did not refer to these concepts, though by this time the 'garden city' slogan was professed by most of the Zionist planners, including Alexander Baerwald, Alexander Levy, Richard Kauffmann and others.

The planning principles adopted by Ahuzat Bayit's members – detached houses surrounded on all sides by gardens, a plot measuring 560 sq m, wide paved streets lined with trees – all seem to have been the result of the influences discussed above, and did not stem from the garden city ideas. In Letchworth and Hampstead, many of the houses were not detached and their planner, Raymond Unwin, was in favour of different-sized lots and narrower streets with minimal pavement.[28] No trace of Ebenezer Howard's plans for cooperatives or common ownership of the land can be found in the guidelines of Ahuzat Bavit.

Apparently, the person closest to the garden city movement was Arthur Ruppin. Though not a member of Ahuzat Bayit, in his role as intermediary between the society and the Jewish National Fund, which provided loans for the construction of the houses, he greatly influenced the character of the new neighbourhood. His interest in Ahuzat Bayit went far beyond financial matters. He believed that its establishment would be an impetus for an overall transformation of the Jewish community in Palestine; moreover, it was the embodiment of a concept of urban environment which he had already formed for himself.

The only specific mention of garden cities in the early documentation relating to Ahuzat Bayit is connected with Ruppin. This was in the form of a bibliography on town planning which he received in 1908 that included Howard's *Garden Cities of To-Morrow*.[29] Katz maintains that a copy of the list was sent by Professor Otto Warburg, a leader of German Zionism, which would seem to indicate that acceptance of the garden city idea was hierarchically dictated by the Zionist movement. We prefer the claim of Shilony and Emanuel Tal, who believe that the list was sent directly from Vienna by architect Oskar Marmorek.[30] Another fact that argues against seeing this document as the basis for a connection between Ahuzat Bayit and the 'garden city' is that it is a standard bibliography, copied from a book, not a list specifically compiled for Ruppin. Moreover, several items in the list are emphasised (in ink – by the sender?), but Howard's work is not among them.

We believe that Ruppin had been exposed to the garden city concept in Europe, before the establishment of Ahuzat Bayit. In 1904 he joined a group of about ten Zionists who in March 1905 published a pamphlet entitled *Die Stimme der Wahrheit*.[31] Among the members of this group was Davis Trietsch, who did much to further the idea of garden cities in the Zionist movement and published an article about it in 1905.[32] It was Ruppin who accepted responsibility for securing professional information and also took upon himself the task of maintaining construction principles similar to those of garden cities, for example by formulating the building by-laws. In addition, in the letter he wrote from Jaffa on 1 September 1907, he urged the directorate of the Jewish National Fund in Cologne to make receipt of loans conditional upon fulfilment of the dictates concerning construction.[33] It was Ruppin who convinced the general meeting of Ahuzat Bayit that convened in September 1908 to agree that at least 30 per cent of the area acquired should be set aside for public purposes. He apparently made it clear that any plan that allocated a smaller area would not be approved by the directorate of the Jewish National Fund.

Summary: Ahuzat Bayit and the garden city concept

Tel Aviv was not founded as a garden city. The urban models that the founders had in mind were the European middle-class suburb and the urban settlements of European colonists. They also conceived of Ahuzat Bayit as an urban version of the agricultural colonies of the First Aliya, the first wave of Zionist immigration to Palestine (1882–1904), which served as models for them. The desire for social, national and cultural segregation from Jaffa, a 'Middle Eastern' city, together with relatively limited resources, resulted in a scaled down version of a middle-class suburb. Communal solidarity, expressed in joint organisation for land acquisition and planning, together with the national and ideological consciousness of the settlers and the officers of the Zionist Organisation who financed them, led to Ahuzat Bayit being built around a public institution, the Herzliya Gymnasium.[34]

The small plots and the emphasis on being a community enabled Ahuzat Bayit to present itself as a feasible urban model for all Jewish settlers in Palestine, not only for the middle class. The establishment of garden suburbs in England during those same years had a similar objective – to provide the entire population with the living conditions of a middle-class suburb. It seems that Ahuzat Bayit functioned as a garden suburb without its members being conscious of the fact, or even using that terminology.

The connection between Tel Aviv and garden cities was drawn, post factum, on the basis of what was created and their common physical and social characteristics. Like the original garden city, early Tel Aviv was not part of a contiguous metropolitan entity; rather, it was established at some distance from Jaffa with a 'green belt' separating it from that city. All the buildings were detached houses and fulfilled Howard's principle of every house having its own garden, which accounted for 60 to 66 per cent of the plot. As noted, the plots were relatively small (560 sq m), quite like those planned for Letchworth (where they ranged from 300 to 1,000 sq m), but twice the size of those proposed by Howard in his book (280 sq m). With such housing density, significantly greater than customary in the pre-garden-city

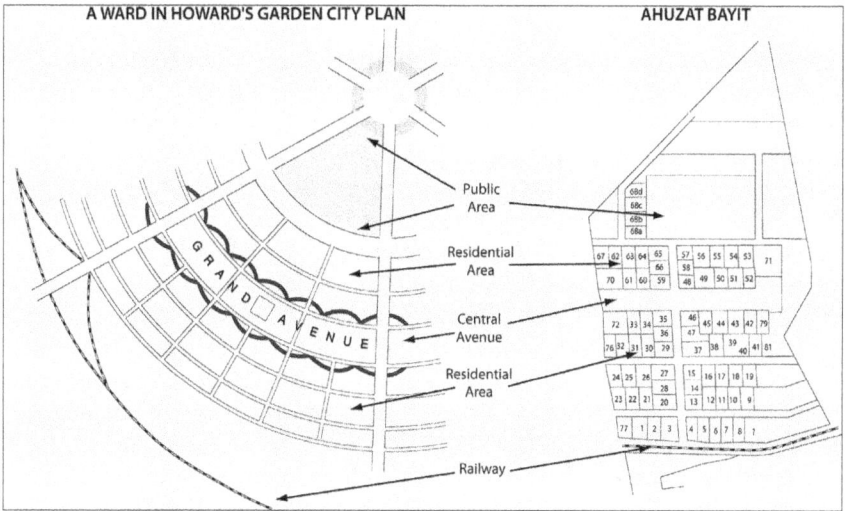

Figure 7.3 Comparison between Howard's planned 'ward' of the garden city and Ahuzat Bayit's plan.

middle-class suburbs, the garden city acquired the nature of an urban community deemed so important by Howard.

Also noteworthy are the relatively wide streets of Ahuzat Bayit. While narrower than the streets in Howard's proposal, they were wider than those laid out by Unwin in Letchworth. The streets seemed even wider due to the gardens in front of each house, which until then were not to be found in cities in Palestine. As in Letchworth, Tel Aviv's gardens conferred upon it a 'green' image that was completely contrary to that of the older cities. Tel Aviv even prided itself on its short boulevard, which may be compared to the circular boulevard transversing Howard's garden city. Setting aside areas for public institutions, a revolutionary concept in England, was taken for granted in Ahuzat Bayit. As in Howard's plan, a public institution – the Herzliya Gymnasium – was located at a spatial, physical and visual focal point of the neighbourhood. At the other end of the main artery, Ahuzat Bayit was bordered by the railway line that connected it to nearby Jaffa, just as circular railway lines demarcated the limits of Howard's garden city. When one views the plan of Ahuzat Bayit in its entirety, it can be seen as one 'ward' of Howard's circular plan (fig. 7.3).

On the organisational level, too, the founders of Tel Aviv had something in common with Howard's vision. Both resulted from the voluntary association of persons who believed that the revolutionary city or neighbourhood they intended to establish would serve as a model for all of society. They hoped to have an entire nation follow in their footsteps, not only in upgrading an inferior type of residential area but also in bringing about overall social reform. In both cases the objective was to create an autonomous settlement based on self-government and equality that would present an alternative to central authorities, whether national-British in the case of Letchworth or imperial-Ottoman in the case of Tel Aviv.

Despite the many similarities, there is no evidence that the founders of Ahuzat Bayit garnered their ideas from Howard's plan for garden cities. We have noted that they could have adopted the idea of segregation from the Levantine city of Jaffa from contemporary colonialist concepts which used arguments of hygiene and culture to justify separate residential areas for European settlers and the indigenous population. Residents of Tel Aviv often expressed their great concern over the state of hygiene in Jaffa and their desire for segregation between Jews and Arabs.

National pride and competition with other ethnic entities in Palestine have been claimed as reasons for Ahuzat Bayit's founders' devotion to innovative forms and aspiration to be a model neighbourhood. Their middle-class aspirations may well explain why they chose the suburban neighbourhood model that, like the European middle-class suburbs with which they were familiar, could best separate them from the residential areas of lower classes. On the one hand, a desire to belong to the propertied class might also explain the economic reasoning that accompanied the establishment of Ahuzat Bayit and the strong desire to own land, the ultimate form of property. On the other hand, limited financial means explain why the plots were much smaller than those customary in European middle-class suburbs. Tel Aviv's 'green' nature and the close ties with landed property can also be ascribed to the precedent of the Zionist agricultural colonies, of which Tel Aviv was intended to be the urban counterpart. It may well be that the colonies were also the source of the idea of establishing a new and separate settlement, and also contributed the similar organisational framework. An indisputable influence on the communal organisation of Ahuzat Bayit, governed by a committee and by-laws, were the Jewish neighbourhoods established outside the walls of Jerusalem and Jaffa in the late nineteenth century and their by-laws.[35]

As for Ahuzat Bayit's planners, here too there is no evidence of their explicit reference to Howard's garden city concept, even though it is quite certain that two of them – Wilhelm Stiassny, who submitted a plan that was rejected, and Arthur Ruppin, who drew up Ahuzat Bayit's building by-laws – were familiar with Howard's text, or at least its principles, as diffused in Germany. There is no evidence of any connection with the garden city movement on the part of the other three planners involved: Joseph Treidel, Abraham Goldman and Joseph Barsky.

While it is impossible to point to an unequivocal relationship between Ahuzat Bayit and the garden city, it should be borne in mind that the latter, too, was not a completely original concept. The garden city idea was inspired by models whose influence was also shared by Ahuzat Bayit. The physical layout of Letchworth was based on nineteenth-century middle-class suburbs that preceded it, while the German garden city movement was inspired by workers' villages established towards the end of the nineteenth century in the Ruhr region. Researchers of town planning in the colonies consider this one of the sources from which Howard drew his ideas.[36] As discussed earlier, these sources may have also influenced the founders of Ahuzat Bayit and its planners, who were of German birth.

While Ahuzat Bayit and garden cities had several things in common, note should also be taken of differences between them. This is a most important point, for Ahuzat Bayit became a model for many later Jewish suburbs established in Palestine. These European-style neighbourhoods to a great degree imitated the physical and organisational features of Ahuzat Bayit, which in several important points differed from the English garden city.

Ahuzat Bayit did not adopt the social structure recommended by Howard, which was grounded in communal ownership of the land, and there were several outstanding differences in the physical aspects. Ahuzat Bayit's size, with a population of no more than a few hundred residents, was much smaller than Howard's vision of a city of 32,000 people. In addition, for ideological reasons, industry, and even commerce, were banned from Ahuzat Bayit, while for Howard they were a vital and central function, an inseparable element of urban life and of the city's ability to function as an independent entity. To its founders, and to Ruppin, early Tel Aviv was a 'bedroom suburb' that left all the 'noisy and contaminating' economic activity to be conducted in Jaffa. In this Tel Aviv resembled middle-class suburbs of European cities which emphasised the separation of the area of residence and 'pure' family life from the difficult masculine environment in which one earned a living.

Ahuzat Bayit's street network was quite simple: a classical grid of straight streets, while Howard's plan was based on a circular scheme. Unwin rejected Howard's scheme and planned Letchworth on the whole as a conglomeration of several networks of grids, whose dispersion emphasised the city centre. He integrated into his plan complex spatial compositions, including cul-de-sacs and curving roads.

As for the plots on which houses were built, what stands out in Tel Aviv is strict adherence to the decision to have detached houses on almost square, equally sized lots. In contrast, in Letchworth and in Hampstead Unwin opted for different-sized lots and for several types of buildings that included detached, semi-detached and terrace houses. As a result of using terraces and an efficient system of streets whose principles were developed by Unwin,[37] the plots were of a more rectangular shape, with a deep back yard. In contrast, the early Tel Aviv model gave preference to a front garden over those at the back and the sides, and in later years houses were built in the centre of the plot with more or less equally wide empty spaces surrounding them.

These physical differences reflect the fact that Ahuzat Bayit was established along lines different from those proposed by Howard. Garden cities were created and planned on the initiative of a group of public-minded persons and wealthy people with a vision. In the case of Tel Aviv, its future residents organised themselves, commissioned the planning and supervised it, so much so that even today the identity of the professional planner who produced the plan of Ahuzat Bayit is uncertain. Detached houses fitted in with the middle-class self-image of its founders. The fact that the organising society was comprised of equals, all partner to the acquisition of the land, its subdivision and planning, dictated the repetitive pattern of the plots which were to be as similar as possible to one another. Even the few slight digressions from equality dictated by the topography were balanced out by means of drawing lots for the plots. In the final tally, such equality contributed to a sense of community, and to some degree played down the individualism reflected in separate houses.

Ahuzat Bayit's pattern of organisation and physical layout were a success, leading to the establishment of other neighbourhoods in the vicinity of Jaffa which imitated Ahuzat Bayit, adopted its building by-laws, and united with it administratively to found the early Tel Aviv. The model for the creation of an urban fabric that differed from that of the 'Middle Eastern city' spread to other cities in Palestine. Though this model was at times referred to as a 'garden city', in fact it was conceptually more akin to the 'garden suburb'. Indeed, there is no clear-cut answer to the question whether Tel Aviv in its early stages was a garden city or not. As of 1910 the spatial-physical pattern of most Jewish construction in Palestine was similar to the garden city model, based on the example of Tel Aviv. Within a short period of time those sectors of the older cities in which construction did not follow this pattern were a negligible minority.

The demographic and economic changes dictated by the 1948 war put an end to the last remains of the traditional urban environment, leaving us with a residential environment that at best can be termed a 'suburban city'. Thus did the wider objective of the garden city movement come to fruition – to create completely new residential surroundings. The physical forms of Ahuzat Bayit, on the one hand, and the 'garden city' concepts, on the other, were the two most influential factors on urban planning in Palestine. So great was their influence that even today, in Israel, planning on various levels employs concepts inspired by the garden city ideal, such as 'diffusion of population', 'neighbourhood units' and 'setback of buildings'.

Notes

1   The leading figures in German Zionism (including Oppenheimer and Trietsch) who contributed to the adoption of the ideals and planning concepts of the garden city movement have been extensively discussed by Ines Sonder, *Gartenstädte für Erez Israel: Zionistische Stadtplannungvisionen von Theodor Herzl bis Richard Kauffmann* (Hildesheim: Georg Olms Verlag, 2005); Miki Zaidman, 'Garden cities – the "Eretz-Israeli" version: Hebrew garden cities and suburbs in Palestine, 1900–1948' (PhD dissertation, the Hebrew University of Jerusalem, 2010) (in Hebrew). Oppenheimer (1864–1943) was Theodor Herzl's adviser on settlement matters and simultaneously served as one of the chief officers of the German branch of the international garden city movement. He wrote the introduction to the first German edition of Ebenezer Howard's classic work: *Gartenstädte in Sicht*, trans.

Maria Wallroth-Unterlip (Jena: Dieterichs, 1907); Davis Trietsch, 'Die Gartenstadt', *Altneuland* 2:11/12 (1905), 349–63.

2 'Eine jüdische Gartenstadt in Palästina', Central Zionist Archives, Jerusalem (hereafter CZA), L1/97; Ruppin to the Central Office of the Jewish National Fund, 21 July 1907, quoted in Arthur Ruppin, *My Life and Work: Autobiography and Diaries* (Tel Aviv: Am Oved, 1968), vol. 2, pp. 9–43 (in Hebrew).

3 Yossi Katz, 'Ideology and urban development: Zionism and the origin of Tel Aviv', *Journal of Historical Geography*, 12 (1986), 402–29; Katz, 'The extension of Ebenezer Howard's ideas on urbanization outside of the British Isles: the example of Palestine', *Geo-Journal*, 34 (1994), 467–73; Katz, 'Garden city in theory and practice: the example of Palestine in the final stages of Ottoman rule', in Zeev Safrai, Yvonne Friedman and Joshua Schwartz (eds), *Studies on the Land: Studies in the History of the Land of Israel Dedicated to Prof. Yehuda Feliks* (Ramat Gan: Bar-Ilan University Press, 1997), pp. 343–53 (in Hebrew); Katz, 'Plans for establishing "garden cities" in Eretz Israel during the second decade of the twentieth century', *Cathedra*, 15 (1980), 198–200 (in Hebrew); Katz, 'Ahuzat Bayit Association 1906–1909: laying the foundations for Tel Aviv', *Cathedra*, 33 (1984), 161–91 (in Hebrew).

4 For the social ideals behind the movement and anarchist influences upon it, see Robert Beevers, *The Garden City Utopia: A Critical Biography of Ebenezer Howard* (New York: St Martins Press, 1988); Stanley Buder, *Visionaries and Planners: The Garden City Movement and the Modern Community* (Oxford: Oxford University Press, 1988); Stephen V. Ward, 'The garden city introduced', in Stephen V. Ward (ed.), *The Garden City: Past, Present and Future* (London: E & FN Spon, 1992), pp. 1–25; Frederick H. Aalen, 'English Origins', in Ward (ed.), *The Garden City*, pp. 26–48.

5 Mervyn Miller, *Letchworth: The First Garden City* (Chichester: Phillimore, 2002).

6 Mervyn Miller and A. Stuart Gray, *Hampstead Garden Suburb* (Chichester: Phillimore, 1992).

7 For urban developments in the Middle East in general, see Charles Issawi, *An Economic History of the Middle East and North Africa* (New York: Columbia University Press, 1982); Roger Owen, *The Middle East in the World Economy, 1800–1914* (London: I.B. Tauris, 1993); for Jaffa, see Ruth Kark, *Jaffa: A City in Evolution 1799–1917* (Jerusalem: Yad Izhak Ben-Zvi, 1990).

8 For the Middle Eastern city, see Ira M. Lapidus, 'Muslim cities and Islamic societies', in Ira M. Lapidus (ed.), *Middle Eastern Cities* (Berkeley: University of California Press, 1969), pp. 47–79; Ruth Kark, 'The traditional Middle Eastern city: the cases of Jerusalem and Jaffa during the nineteenth century', *Zeitschrift des Deutschen Palästina-Vereins*, 97 (1981), 93–108; Vincent F. Costello, *Urbanization in the Middle East* (Cambridge: Cambridge University Press, 1977).

9 Ruppin to the Central Office of the Jewish National Fund, 21 July 1907, quoted in Ruppin, *My Life and Work*, vol. 2, p. 142.

10 For a definition of the middle class in Palestine, see Amir Ben-Porat, *The Bourgeoisie: The History of the Israeli Bourgeoisie* (Jerusalem: Magnes Press, 1999) (in Hebrew).

11 Anthony D. King, *Urbanism, Colonialism, and the World Economy: Cultural and Spatial Foundations of the World Urban System* (London and New York: Routledge, 1990); Robert Home, *Of Planting and Planning: The Making of British Colonial Cities* (London: E & FN Spon, 1997).

12 Edward Said, *Orientalism* (New York: Pantheon Books, 1978).

13 Yossi Katz, *Zionist Private Enterprise in the Building of Eretz-Israel during the Second Aliyah, 1904–1914* (Ramat Gan: Bar-Ilan University Press, 1989), p. 155 (in Hebrew).

14 Ruppin to the Central Office of the Jewish National Fund, 21 July 1907 (note 12 above).

15 Akiva Arieh Weiss, 'How Ahuzat Bayit was founded', in Mordecai Naor (ed.), *The Beginnings of Tel Aviv: Sources, Summaries, Selected Episodes, and Supplemen-*

tary Materials (Jerusalem: Yad Izhak Ben-Zvi, 1984), pp. 2–4 (in Hebrew). The memoir was first published in *Bulletin of the Tel Aviv Municipality*, 1934. The use of 'Hebrew' as an adjective often replaced 'Jewish' in those days.

16 'Old Yishuv', a term for the pre-Zionist, generally ultra-Orthodox Jewish community in Palestine; *shtetl*, a Yiddish diminutive for 'town', denoting a small community in eastern Europe in which Jews were generally a majority.

17 For more details concerning the acquisition of the land for Ahuzat Bayit, see Gideon Biger, 'Development of the built-up area of Tel Aviv, 1909–1934', in Mordecai Naor (ed.), *The Beginnings of Tel Aviv: Sources, Summaries, Selected Episodes, and Supplementary Materials* (Jerusalem: Yad Izhak Ben-Zvi, 1984), pp. 42–61 (in Hebrew); Yossi Katz, 'Land acquisition in Tel Aviv up to World War I', in Ruth Kark (ed.), *Redemption of the Land of Eretz Israel: Ideology and Practice* (Jerusalem: Yad Izhak Ben-Zvi, 1990), p. 168 (in Hebrew).

18 Tel Aviv Municipal Archives, RG1, File 40, correspondence between Weiss and Treidel, January 1909.

19 The regulations are in CZA L2/71. See also Ruppin, *My Life and Work*, vol. 2, pp. 140–4.

20 Biger, 'Development of the built-up area', p. 50; Zvi Shilony, *Ideology and Settlement: The Jewish National Fund, 1897–1914* (Jerusalem: Magnes Press, 1998), pp. 320–3; Kark, *Jaffa*, p. 118.

21 *Bulletin of the Tel Aviv Municipality*, 2 (1925), p. 26 (in Hebrew).

22 *Bulletin of the Tel Aviv Municipality* 2 (1925), p. 26 (in Hebrew).

23 CZA L2/578, 'Notes by Rabbi Binyamin [pseud. of Yehoshua Radler-Feldman] on the history of Tel Aviv', 1919? (in Hebrew).

24 Katz, 'Land acquisition in Tel Aviv', pp. 170–1.

25 Kark, *Jaffa*, p. 122.

26 Yossi Katz, 'Diffusion of the urban idea: "Tel Aviv" as a model for plans to establish modern suburbs in Eretz Israel from the end of the first decade of the [twentieth] century until WWI', *Ofakim Be-Geografiya* [*Horizons – Studies in Geography*], 11/12 (1984), 108–27 (in Hebrew).

27 Katz, 'Land acquisition in Tel Aviv', p. 181.

28 Raymond Unwin, *Town Planning in Practice: An Introduction to the Art of Designing Cities and Suburbs* (London: Fisher & Unwin, 1920 [1909]).

29 The list is in CZA L2/71.

30 Yossi Katz, 'Ahuzat Bayit association 1906–1909: laying the foundations for Tel Aviv', *Cathedra*, 33 (1984), 187–8 (in Hebrew); Shilony, *Ideology and Settlement*, pp. 320–3; Emanuel Tal, 'The structural image of the early kibbutz: from the first living complex proposals to the formulation of design convention' (PhD dissertation, Tel Aviv University, 1991), p. 223 (in Hebrew).

31 Margalit Shilo, *Experiments in Settlement: The Palestine Office of the Zionist Movement 1908–1914* (Jerusalem: Yad Izhak Ben-Zvi, 1988), p. 37 (in Hebrew).

32 Trietsch, 'Die Gartenstadt'.

33 Ruppin to the directorate of the Jewish National Fund, 1 September 1907, quoted in Ruppin, *My Life and Work*, vol. 2, p. 146.

34 Yossi Klein and Ruth Kark, 'La démolition de la *gymnasiya* Herzliya et la construction de la tour Shalom Meir: debut de l'américanisation de Tel-Aviv', *Tsafon: Revue d'études juives du Nord*, 55 (2008), 61–84.

35 For Jerusalem, see Ruth Kark, *Jerusalem Neighborhoods: Planning and By-laws, 1855–1930* (Jerusalem: Magnes Press, 1991).

36 Anthony King, 'Exporting "planning": the colonial and neo-colonial experience', *Urbanism, Past & Present*, 5 (1977/8), 12–22; Robert Home, 'Town planning and garden cities in the British colonial empire', *Planning Perspectives*, 5 (1990), 23–37.

37 Raymond Unwin, *Nothing Gained by Overcrowding: How the Garden City Type of Development May Benefit Both Owner and Occupier* (London: Garden Cities and Town Planning Association Press, 1912).

Multilateral channels, garden cities and colonial planning

Liora Bigon and Yossi Katz

What can be learned from this unprecedented collection of case studies on garden city expressions in colonial Africa and Palestine during the first half of the twentieth century? The two most prominent issues that come into mind are, of course, the rich variety of conceptual and actual garden city translations to our selected colonial sites, and the issue of transnationality in terms of tracing the multilateral channels through which garden city ideas were conveyed to these sites.

As to the variety of garden city models and other related elements in situ, our group of contributors shared a flexible approach regarding defining and capturing this variety. This enabled us not to crystallise an exact list of 'pure' Howardian features and then mark any colonial 'abnormalities' in relation to it, but rather to acknowledge the richness inherent in this model from the start. While from the viewpoint of historiography, varieties of garden city expressions in western Europe and North America, and also in Russia and Japan, are relatively well recognised, this is not the case with their counterparts in the southern hemisphere. Here Palestine and Africa were certainly not considered together in order to provoke, that is to merge the history of a territory which is torn by the complexities of an ongoing vertical conflict and intensely covered by the world press (Israel–Palestine) with the history of another territory (Africa) which, as a name, an idea and an object of academic discourse, has been and remains fraught. In the words of Achille Mbembe and Sarah Nuttal, 'the sign is fraught because Africa so often ends up epitomizing the intractable, the mute, the abject, or the other-wordly ... a failed and incomplete example of something else'.[1]

These territories were put together because of their geographic continuity as well as their historical continuity in terms of colonialism and related colonial imageries (oriental, tropical, experimental terrains), stressing British and French rules – the dominant imperial powers in the modern period. In these colonial contexts, it did not matter how selectively garden city features were applied, which interests they came to serve and which power they normally sought to foster. Even though these features, both physically and perceptually, promoted direct and indirect residential segregation, it might be illuminating to regard them as an integral part of, and as an important development in, the history of the garden city, inherently variegated. This conclusion brings to the fore the transnational issue, because each of our cases – distinctively territorial, regional, local, site-related – is embedded in multiple elsewheres through which the garden city concepts were actually speaking.

Indeed, garden city implementation in Europe before the Second World War usually meant suburban self-contained developments and a community or cooperative developer – under private or public–private partnership. In colonial Africa, on the contrary, most of the implementations until the 1930s simply involved a low-density residential form under government control, with parks or other kinds of greenery. Under indirect or direct rule, these 'garden city' neighbourhoods were the preferred form of residence offered by the colonial authorities to their employees and other white expatriates. Though there were some exceptions, normally in the form of layout or model housing intended for the African (Zanzibar) or the Indian (South Africa) urban population, these also celebrated the colonial power. In the context of colonial Palestine during the second half of the twentieth century, one of the central questions that our collection tries to handle is what caused the seemingly sweeping adoption there of garden city concepts and how these were transformed to fit the local national, social and planning contexts.

It was clear to us from the start that addressing such questions would involve an international group of specialists, and global comparisons and connections would be made, tracing the processes and channels through which the planning ideas were circulated. We adopted the umbrella notion of 'transnationality' to capture these multilateral channels of diffusion and our intellectual interests, as explained in the Introduction. Thus a spectrum of similar notions exists, such as 'world history', 'connected histories', 'entangled history', *'histoire croisée'*, 'new global history', 'shared histories', etc.[2] Another key question that should be raised against the background of the transnational issue is to what extent modern planning was constituted within colonialism itself. As recent analysis reveals and as our collection well exemplifies, modern planning is not at all a simple radiant or a unidirectional 'export' from a European 'heart' to overseas 'peripheries', but rather a product of colonial relations and situations.[3]

This collection appears at a time of growing scholarly interest in international approaches to urban studies and circulation of urban policies and practices. In this respect we see our collection as complementary to several recently published works and edited collections in the field, though it is distinctive both in its historical approach to urban studies and planning literature and in the geographical spheres under discussion. Authors such as Saskia Sassen, for instance, overemphasise the whole new phase of creating a world scale after the Second World War and especially since the 1980s as 'a starkly different project' than the previous nationalistic phase centred on imperial geographies.[4] Arguing that international competition today functions primarily as a mechanism for denationalising capital, the neoliberal economy is portrayed as a unifying and homogenising global project, leading among other things to conceptions of post-national citizenship.[5] In this view, cultural variations among nation states are not an important issue.

Yet, as the urbanist John Friedman, among others, has commented,

> [t]he mantra of globalization poses two problems for students of cities. The first is its obsession with economic relations to the exclusion of other possible perspectives, for example, social, cultural, political; and the second is that it tends to render invisible the impact of economic relations on the everyday life of a city, that is, overshadowing the 'space of places' with the 'space of flows'.[6]

Similarly, the urbanist Bish Sanyal argues in his edited collection entitled *Comparative Planning Cultures* and in response to Friedman's studies of planning culture, 'I am intuitively aware that "culture matters".'[7] Lacking a rigorous methodology for comparison, Sanyal sought to provide a common conceptual framework for discussing the role of culture in planning practice. While this conceptual framework is somewhat innovative in the field, of the eleven case studies selected, in both industrialised and industrialising nations, none deals with Africa. Indeed urban developments in Africa were mentioned in one of the two additional theoretical papers in his collection (Friedman's), yet almost in passing with a focus on Johannesburg, and through only a few secondary sources.[8] As the goal was an intellectual encounter between professionals with very different planning experiences to create a global conversation about the role of planning at a time of rapid and uncertain change, it did not generate a precise formulation of how planning cultures affect planning practices.[9]

Our present volume is focused on urban, planning and cultural histories rather than on understanding contemporary social change and planning culture. It might be judged by Sanyal as 'parochial',[10] yet we certainly intend to compare planning cultures in the light of a particular variable: garden city expressions. In this way our collection breaks away from other recently published collections, and it also gets closer to, and sympathises with, others. Of the eighteen urban cases discussed in the collection titled *Urban Theory beyond the West*, for instance, the chapter on Kinshasa was the sole representative from the African continent.[11] Moreover, it seems that this collection represents a celebration of a variety of non-Western cities. Yet this fact in and of itself constitutes the lowest common denominator, which is also quite vague, considering the fact that except for pointing to some current trends in urban studies (in which Western cities could be included too), thoughts about unifying conclusions or a more inclusive theory that covers the variety of cases are certainly left to the reader.

Another collection that crosses our minds and is closer in spirit to our own aims and intentions is *Spatial Planning Systems of Britain and France: A Comparative Analysis*, especially against the background of the writing of the urbanist Philip Booth, one of its editors.[12] Struck by the limited quality and quantity of truly comparative studies, the editors attempted to explain by reference to historical origins why Britain and France use such different sets of tools and modus operandi to pursue the same set of objectives, namely the public interest in the context of private property rights. In exploring the two radically different town planning systems, the contributors – and here each chapter was written by at least two professionals from both sides of the English Channel – dug down into the histories and tried to trace the institutional, legal, economic and formal paths of urban development.[13]

Beyond being a theoretical and intellectual tool, comparisons between the two systems are also useful for the development of common approaches to planning problems which touch both countries. But there is another issue that arises in the context of *Spatial Planning Systems* and the present volume, which is the availability of books and articles in English regarding certain planning features or case studies in France or French-speaking areas, and vice versa. In fact we are not aware of any similar treatment in English of topics such as that of Alain Sinou here on French Sudan (Mali) (chapter 3), nor of any equivalent in French to Myers and Muhajir's chapter 4 on British colonial Zanzibar – to take almost rudimentary examples.

In addition, as argued by Booth, 'those differences can be understood only if the instruments and processes are recognized as a product of cultural forces, not as independent phenomena whose existence somehow transcends the particular and the local',[14] adapting therefore a historical approach. By this Booth challenges neoliberal perceptions that planning is a single process with universally accepted outcomes, and fosters the growing understanding that planning (virtually rational, technical) is an activity that cannot be distinguished from the general cultural traditions that inform it.[15] This throws some light on the importance of local histories in illuminating our general understanding of planning as a global social practice, and transforms the discussion of planning expressions – what is explicitly shown in our collection – into an almost ethnographic exercise.

Notes

1 Achille Mbembe and Sarah Nutall, 'Writing the world from an African metropolis', *Public Culture*, 16:3 (2004), 347–72 (p. 348). See also Achille Mbembe, *On the Postcolony* (Berkeley: University of California Press, 2001), pp. 1–4.
2 Akira Iriye and Pierre-Yves Saunier, 'Introduction: the professor and the madman', in Iriye and Saunier (eds), *The Palgrave Dictionary of Transnational History from the Mid-19th Century to the Present Day* (Basingstoke: Macmillan, 2009), pp. xvii–x (p. xviii).
3 See, for instance, Libby Porter, *Unlearning the Colonial Cultures of Planning* (Farnham: Ashgate, 2010), p. 3.
4 Saskia Sassen, *Territory, Authority, Rights: From Medieval to Global Assemblages* (Princeton, NJ: Princeton University Press, 2006), p. 140.
5 Sassen, *Territory, Authority, Rights*, p. 147.
6 John Friedmann, 'Globalization and the emerging culture of planning', *Progress in Planning*, 64 (2005), 183–234 (p. 183).
7 Bishwapriya Sanyal, 'Preface', in Sanyal (ed.), *Comparative Planning Cultures* (New York and London: Routledge, 2005), pp. xix–xiv (p. xix).
8 John Friedmann, 'Planning cultures in transition', in Sanyal (ed.), *Comparative Planning Cultures*, pp. 29–44.
9 Bishwapriya Sanyal, 'Hybrid planning cultures: the search for the global cultural commons', in Sanyal (ed.), *Comparative Planning Cultures*, pp. 3–25 (pp. 22–4).
10 'There was never an intention on our part in launching this study to compare planning cultures by some well-calibrated criteria. In the past, efforts to make such comparisons have contributed not to better understanding but to cultural arrogance and parochialism.' Sanyal, 'Hybrid planning cultures', p. 24.
11 Tim Edensor and Mark Jayne (eds), *Urban Theory beyond the West: A World of Cities* (London and New York: Routledge, 2012).
12 Philip Booth, Michèle Breuillard, Charles Fraser and Didier Paris (eds), *Spatial Planning Systems of Britain and France: A Comparative Analysis* (London and New York: Routledge, 2007).
13 For a similar comparative approach, as rare as Booth's but regarding the urban colonial sphere, see Liora Bigon, *A History of Urban Planning in Two West African Colonial Capitals: Residential Segregation in British Lagos and French Dakar (1850–1930)* (Lewiston, NY: Edwin Mellen Press, 2009).
14 Philip Booth, 'The nature of difference: traditions of law and government and their effects on planning in Britain and France', in Sanyal (ed.), *Comparative Planning Cultures*, pp. 259–83 (p. 259).
15 See also Vanessa Watson, *Change and Continuity in Spatial Planning: Metropolitan Planning in Cape Town under Political Transition* (London: Routledge, 2002); Philip Harrison, Alison Todes and Vanessa Watson, *Planning and Transformation: Learning from the Post-Apartheid Experience* (Abingdon: Routledge, 2008).

INDEX

EU authorised representative for GPSR:
Easy Access System Europe, Mustamäe tee 50,
10621 Tallinn, Estonia
gpsr.requests@easproject.com

www.ingramcontent.com/pod-product-compliance
Lightning Source LLC
Chambersburg PA
CBHW022313280326
41932CB00010B/1090